T0358700

The Invention of Science

CULTURAL PERSPECTIVES IN SCIENCE EDUCATION:
RESEARCH DIALOGS

Volume 4

Series editor
Kenneth Tobin, *The Graduate Center, City University of New York, USA*
Catherine Milne, *Steinhardt School o Culture, Education, and Human
Development, New York University*

Scope
Research dialogs consists of books written for undergraduate and graduate students
of science education, teachers, parents, policy makers, and the public at large.
Research dialogs bridge theory, research, and the practice of science education.
Books in the series focus on what we know about key topics in science education –
including, teaching, connecting the learning of science to the culture of students,
emotions and the learning of science, labs, field trips, involving parents, science
and everyday life, scientific literacy, including the latest technologies to facilitate
science learning, expanding the roles of students, after school programs, museums
and science, doing dissections, etc.

The Invention of Science

Why History of Science Matters for the Classroom

Catherine Milne
New York University

SENSE PUBLISHERS
ROTTERDAM/BOSTON/TAIPEI

A C.I.P. record for this book is available from the Library of Congress.

ISBN: 978-94-6091-523-9 (paperback)
ISBN: 978-94-6091-524-6 (hardback)
ISBN: 978-94-6091-525-3 (e-book)

Published by: Sense Publishers,
P.O. Box 21858,
3001 AW Rotterdam,
The Netherlands
www.sensepublishers.com

Printed on acid-free paper

TABLE OF CONTENTS

PREFACE

In this book I seek to introduce people to a history of Eurocentric science: the discipline that today is typically called *science*. Like all authors, in this book I am making an argument, and/or writing a narrative, about how or why something happened. In some cases, I will try to make connections to contemporary issues. The argument about *why* things happen is open to a multitude of explanations but the question of *how* things happened is also open to interpretation as authors use history to try to understand our present. So my version is just that, my take on a history of Eurocentric science. I have reconstructed and recorded events to that make up a particular historical phenomenon, the emergence of Eurocentric science, using specific historical examples to discuss some aspects of knowing that I think are in some way relevant to practice and thought associated with Eurocentric science. For me, an idea attributed to the ancient Greek historian, Thucydides (about 460–395 BCE) is one that has framed this book "that history is philosophy learned from examples".

HISTORIOGRAPHY

Of course, I acknowledge that other authors would most likely produce a different narrative based on their different methods, beliefs, and goals. The study of the ways different historians apply different methods, values, and goals to make different histories is called *historiography*.

Theoretical Lens

Different methods that an author uses to tell her history constitute the *theoretical lens* or *warrant* that the author uses to support the claim she is making. Some of these warrants include:

Great men change history. For example, an author might make the claim that William Gilbert's study of magnetism, which he presented in his book *On Magnetism*, led people to understand how models could be used to understand phenomenon and changed the course of history.

Historical forces. Other authors might claim that ideas or movements become irresistible forces that always win out, usually because they are ethically or cogni-tively superior. Examples could include authors who argue that although the Catholic Church persecuted Galileo Galilei for his support of the theory that the sun was the center of the universe rather than the earth, this theory was ultimately shown to be correct and Galileo was recognized as a hero of science while the Church was seen as out of step with 'true' knowledge. These authors argue that this example shows the march of science over theology or the limitations of the worldview of medieval scholasticism and the strength of the scientific revolution and the mechanistic worldview.

How societies/civilizations respond to a crisis of ideas or technology determines whether they will survive.   In this case, an author might make the claim that Euro-centric science stopped developing and growing in Italy because Italian science remained in the thrall of absolute rulers rather than in a community of practitioners. On the other hand, in a country like England where experimental philosophy was organized and controlled by a community of practitioners, Eurocentric science continued to develop.

Dialectical argument.   We will look at this form of reasoning in a little more detail in Chapter 2 where you will have the chance to explore a range of different forms of reasoning associated with Eurocentric science. Dialectical argument is also a strategy authors use to present their history. Since people began to ask questions about what is real and how we come to know, this form of argument has been central and remains central to contemporary philosophies and religions. The goal of dialectical argument is achieving truth through rational discussion. Generally a dialectical argu-ment is a dialogue in which one participant makes a statement or claim. The other participant seeks internal contradictions and consistencies in the claim and associated justification, which through dialogue initiate modifications to the initial statement, so that a new claim is made. In this way, new knowledge is constructed. One example of this in Eurocentric science is the historic conflict between the biological theories of natural economy and natural selection with natural selection winning out but perhaps including some elements of natural economy.

Geography determines the character of people and gives them advantages and disadvantages.   An example of this is historian Fredrick Jackson Turner's theory that the Frontier shaped the American mind to be open to new ideas and new possibilities. An example from Eurocentric science could be the argument that the names scientists give to their discoveries, such as the whimsical names like *quark* and *charm* developed by US physicists to name fundamental particles and forces, is an outcome of their national character.

The outcome of ideas and practices coming together and their effect cannot be predicted.   Daniel Boorstin[1] sought to differentiate between people who actually did stuff and those who were famous for being famous. He said, "time makes heroes but dissolves celebrities". Boorstin argued that great creators and discoverers put together ideas and practices in new innovative ways. For example, a thesis based on this method might be that a nameless Dutch optician invented the telescope (see Chapter 5 for more), but when it found its way to Italy Galileo Galilei, the famous Italian natural philosopher, refined it and looked up into the Heavens. The rest, they say, is history.

The relationship between history and the writing of history is ambiguous.   This thesis could be called a critical theory approach to history. It encourages researchers and readers to ask what events were available for the telling, which events did an author include or leave out, and what that suggests about the author's values and beliefs. It is in the selection of events for the telling that we can have a sense of the values an author holds with respect to the context about which she is writing.

Of course, my introduction to historical methods, which can be used to understand the emergence of aspects of Eurocentric science, is by no means exhaustive. There are a number of important approaches that I have not mentioned, such as a Marxist approach (although that does share some similarities with the critical approach). Since this book is about science, another theme that I could have mentioned is a rationalist thesis about the role of theory and experimentation in the progress of science, which gives precedence to theory or an inductivist thesis that in turn gives precedence to experiment. These are themes we will explore a little more in the following chapters. Another method is one that sees the history of Eurocentric science as a direct march of progress with no side streets or diversions. This method is characteristic of scientism (see Chapter 5), a simplistic representation of scientific endeavor. A current method or thesis is based around neoliberalism; the idea that through hard work you and everyone else can be successful and if you are not successful, you must not have tried hard enough.

THE NEED FOR A HISTORY OF SCIENCE

Eurocentric science is a cultural-historical phenomenon that emerged over time beginning with practices and theorizing associated with diverse cultures from China, India, Africa, Middle East and Europe. As a form of systematic knowledge it has become a global behemoth, isolated from the sites of local knowledge from which it emerged. As the field of natural philosophy emerged in Europe, some practices or activities became specialized and reified to the extent that by the late seventeenth century natural philosopher Isaac Newton could dismiss critics of his research on optics[2] for not following his methods correctly. In the present, science has emerged as a bounded field that is supported by hundreds of different publications across many sub-fields. Today the boundaries of science are reinforced by the existence of accepted strategies for discovery, validation, and evaluation in science. However, we are left with the question of what constitutes the practices of science and how knowing these practices can make one more knowledgeable about science and a better educator of science. Much of the science students complete in schools is associated with understanding the validation practices of science so there is less attention given to understanding discovery and evaluation practices and the learning of practices such as understanding the development and use of models for investigating questions and peer review of knowledge claims; practices associated with discovery and evaluation, respectively.

I believe that if a goal for science education is that students develop a richer understanding of science, all educators need to have a more robust understanding of the nature of science and, in particular, scientific inquiry. By nature of science I do not mean a single prescription for what science is and how it should be conducted. I do mean developing students' capacities to experience phenomena more deeply, to assist them to understand whether a question in its current form can be examined using scientific practices, what constitutes an explanation or an argument, and how models assist the scientific investigation of phenomena. I also mean valuing discourses including narrative, explanation, and argumentation as communication forms that serve important functions in coming to know science.

Drawing from both historical examples and vignettes of classroom practice, I seek to assist you to feel more comfortable about your use of specific inquiry strategies. I cringe every time I hear someone use the term "canonical" because such a term implies that science as it is represented in schools is so monolithic it should be accepted as a given. In this context, it is not examined critically and students are not supported to be more questioning about the representation of science in the resources that they use. So a further goal of this book is to encourage readers to be more critical of the ways in which science is represented in a range of resources.

An examination of the National Science Education Standards[3] reveals eight practices that are associated with inquiry: making observations, posing questions, examining books and other sources of information to see what is known, planning investigations, reviewing what is already known in light of experimental evidence, using tools to gather and analyze data, proposing explanations/ predictions, and communicating results. In order to be able to perform these practices, students also need to be able to identify assumptions, use critical thinking, and develop experiments that can differentiate between different explanations. However, at a more basic level these practices require each teacher and student to understand more fundamental ideas such as what do we need to accept in order to be able to ask questions science can answer, in other words we need to know about worldview. We need to know how reasoning uses experimental evidence and the nature of facts as tools in this process. We need to understand the nature of a scientific explanation, and the tools that are used to communicate and argue in science. In this book, my goal is to provide an integrated perspective of how a study of the history of Eurocentric science can help you to have a richer understanding of all these terms and ideas that are central to the Eurocentric science that is the basis of most school science.

NOTES

1 Author of The Discoverers and other books. Boorstin, Daniel. (1983). *The Discoverers*. New York: Random House.
2 Philosophical Transactions. (1667). Published by the Royal Society of London and one of the early journals that supported an inductive approach to inquiry promoted by Francis Bacon.
3 National Research Council. (1996). *National Science Education Standards*. Washington, DC: National Academies Press.

WHAT IS SCIENCE?

What is science? One of my goals for this chapter is to help you to understand what a serious and complex question this is and how history can help us to better understand the nature of the science that is taught in schools. I would like you to answer some questions first to get you thinking about the nature of science and what you think is science.

Activity: What is science?[1]

What are your thoughts about the following statements? Write them down.

1. In the past scientists were very often wrong in their knowledge and reasoning. Today scientists understand science correctly.

2. In the past scientists understood science differently because they could not conduct the complex experiments that are performed today.

3. The problem of scientists in the past, which made them often wrong in their views, is the lack of precise and sophisticated instruments and advanced laboratories.

4. Science is a special form of knowledge different from all other forms.

5. Scientific progress can be achieved without advanced technology.

6. Results of scientific research are based on the application of a specific method.

7. Scientists, as well as students, should not study former theories, refuted as incorrect, but focus on the correct scientific knowledge of today

8. Products of scientific research, and scientists' activities, are not affected by factors external to science.

9. Rival scientific theories never co-exist, since scientists decide which of them is correct to hold.

Answering these questions will provide you with a reminder of the beliefs you hold about science. Check your responses once you have worked your way through this book to see if your ideas have changed in any way.

If we look at specific documents, such as the National Science Education Standards (NSES) published in the United States in 1996[2] we can get a sense of how groups that are trying to influence how policy and lawmakers think of science education. The NSES lays out standards of what children and youth need to know about science if they are to be scientifically literate. These requirements include: being familiar with basic scientific ideas and practices, using these ideas and practices to make personal decisions, participating in societal decisions about scientific issues, and using those skills so that people have choices with respect to employment and entrepreneurship. The NSES lays these requirements out as standards of what children need to be able to do at each grade to fulfill these requirements. If you look closely at these Standards, you will note that the question of what is science is a question central to this document. The NSES were published under the auspices of the National Research Council, an umbrella organization for the National Academy of Sciences, the National Academy of Engineering and the Institute of Medicine in the United States of America and developed in response to societal and political pressures demanding more structure in science education at all levels of education. The authors of the Standards answer the question of what is science with the following statement, "Science is a way of knowing that is characterized by empirical criteria, logical argument, and skeptical review"[3], which they follow up with, "The goal of science is to understand the natural world"[4]

What does this statement mean? Four components seem important; *empirical criteria*, *logical argument*, *skeptical review* and the *natural world*. One way to begin to make sense of this statement and perhaps to firm up our own understanding of science is to look at these components in turn. What does the word *empirical* mean in this context? In contemporary usage, the word *empirical* is typically associated with observation both direct, which requires the use of human senses, and indirect, which requires the use of instruments that detect objects and changes that are not available to our senses. This use of the term is associated with *empiricism* a theory of knowledge, made famous by John Locke (1632–1704) that associates true knowledge with sense experiences. According to empiricism, our observations provide us with knowledge about something. For example, you walk outside on a winter's day. Applying your sense of touch, you feel cold. You can claim to know that it is cold. An empiricist would accept your observation as truthful. Empiricism offers one take on how humans know stuff and values what comes to us from our senses above all other forms knowledge. From your experience of scientific experiments, you might note the relationship between observation through the senses, or through the use of instruments when our senses are not sensitive enough, and evidence obtained from experiments. In later chapters we will explore other perspectives on how truthful our senses can be. But even if we acknowledge the possible limitations of empiricism, at some level, empiricism is very important to science.

As a word and associated meaning, *empirical*, has a much older history than that associated with the use of our senses. It comes from the Latin "empiricus" and Greek "empeirikos" meaning *experienced* or *skilled in trial or experiment*. It is a term associated with an ancient school of physicians in Greek medicine called empiricists. Empiricism became one of the dominant medical ideologies in the School of Alexandria established by Alexander the Great at the mouth of the Nile River in Egypt in 331 BCE[5]. The practices of Greek medical empiricists share some similarities with the way we might think of empirical practice today. Empiricists believed that knowledge was accumulated by the remembrance of previous cases. They argued that if the causes of diseases were the same in all places the same remedies ought to be used everywhere also. However, empiricists dismissed inquiry because they viewed Nature as incomprehensible. They argued that relief from sickness was to be sought from the tried and true, that is, from experience. Our actions or practices, not our opinions, were the most important. Valuing what we do above what we say, can be understood as a practice having some connection to the practice aspect of how we understand 'empirical' today even if the connection of 'empirical' to the senses was not as highly emphasized then as it is now. According to the Oxford English Dictionary[6], *criteria*, the plural of criterion, comes to us from Greek where it meant a means for judging, a test. So taken together empirical criteria could be understood as using features of experience to make a judgment about knowledge claims. This examination of the sources of meaning for *empirical criteria* would suggest greater affinity between John Locke's empiricism and that presented in the US National Standards than between the National Standards and that associated with Greek medical empiricists. This example also illustrates how human understanding and use of terms is interrelated with people's understanding of what is important to know.

An image of Aristotle.

For the National Science Education Standards, *logical argument* refers to the following as described in the Standards, "In communicating and defending the results of scientific inquiry, arguments must be logical and demonstrate connections between natural phenomena, investigations, and the historical body of scientific knowledge"[7]. I wonder if this description is all that helpful in supporting our understanding the nature of logical argument. Although we will be examining the nature of argument in more detail in later chapters, we could start here by considering logical argument briefly. Perhaps we could begin by assuming that a logical argument is one that follows the rules of logic and is an argument. This form is often associated with Aristotle (384–322 BCE) who introduced syllogistic reasoning, a form of *deductive argument*. Deductive argument is based on assertions or premises from which a conclusion can logically be drawn. Deductive argument begins with general assertions and assumes that if the assertions are true the conclusions must be true, that is the truth of the conclusion is a logical consequence of the premises.

However, long before Aristotle laid out a structure for deductive reasoning, a form of reasoning based on dialogue called *dialectical reasoning* provided a method for argumentation. In dialectical reasoning, two or more people engaged in a dialogue try to convince each other of the correctness of their point of view by rejecting or modifying hypotheses that contain contradictions and, in the end, coming to a decision about the final argument. World religions such as Buddhism, Hinduism, and Judaism make extensive use of dialectical reasoning. Dialectical reasoning requires all participants to respect the existence of a variety of perspectives. Dialectical reasoning can be noted in the writings of renowned 17th century experimental philosopher, Galileo Galilei, and continues its importance today. One feature of dialectical reasoning that makes it different from the other forms of reasoning, which you will examine in this book, is its requirement that consideration be given to the broader problem as well as its parts (the parts typically are the focus of much science) and, because dialectical argument is a dialogue, participants can be involved in anticipating objections to their claim from other participants.

An image of Francis Bacon.

Another form of argument that has a long history and is associated with the study of science is inductive reasoning, which is associated with the writings of Francis Bacon (1561–1626), a philosopher who promoted *inductive argument* as the basis of formulating true knowledge. Inductive arguments rely on making a generalization from a specific set of observations or facts. In both forms of arguing, drawing a conclusion from premises or facts is called *inferring*, a term typically associated with observation in science texts. Two other forms of reasoning, transduction and abduction, less well known but important to science, will also be examined later. So even the use of the term *logical argument* raises the question of what is the argument to which we are referring and whether *logical* is the best word to use when describing the form of argument that is presented as providing the basis for knowing science.

What is *skeptical review*? Reading beyond the definition of *science as a way of knowing* characterized by three criteria that we are examining here, the NSES present the claim that students should be able to identify what science is and what it is not. This suggests that the authors of the Standards understand that to conduct skeptical review is to be able to identify science from non-science through such a review. But what might that review be? Skeptical is a word that comes to English from the Greek *to look out* or *consider* and is associated with the disciples of Pyrrho (360–270 BCE) who doubted the possibility of certainty about the truth of any knowledge claim or proposition. We really only know about his arguments through the writings of his student, Timon, and through the writings of later authors because, as far as we know, none of his original writings have been preserved. Pyrrho is said to have argued that humans cannot know the inner substance of things only how they appear. A claim that would suggest we could only base our assessment of a person or an object or a process on what we can observe. This position sounds similar to Bacon's inductivism. *Review* comes from the Latin: re – back and view – to see: in other words, to look back over any claims being made.

An image of Pyrrho.

TAKING A DIFFERENT VIEW

By examining the standards used by the National Research Council to describe science, we can begin to have a sense of what the authors of the NSES consider to be important features of science. But is this the only way we can think about science and what it means to know science? In these Standards, science is presented as a singular universal form of knowledge that all students should learn. The Standards represent a *universalist* vision of science. But according to some authors, the nature of science has changed so much over human history that it cannot be made to fit one definition.[8] The Oxford English Dictionary identifies the first English use of the word *science* in a 14th century text when its use was associated with "the state of knowing". Such use is generally more encompassing than many contemporary perspectives especially those associated with *universalists* that understand science as universal knowledge of the natural world which transcends local contexts. During the 14th century and later, authors often contrasted science with the term, conscience, so that they could differentiate the notion of knowledge from that of moral conviction. The word, science, comes originally from Latin *scientia*, which meant knowledge.

In the European Middle Ages, the idea of seven liberal sciences was used inter-changeably with the seven liberal arts and consisted of grammar, logic, rhetoric, arithmetic, music, geometry, and astronomy. The more restricted sense of science that might be more familiar to you did not come into common usage until the 18th century. In 1725, Isaac Watts, a bit of a free thinker and famous hymn composer, published *Logic, or the Right Use of Reason, in the Inquiry After Truth with a Variety of Rules to Guard Against Error in the Affairs of Religion and Human Life, as Well as in the Sciences*[9]. Written as a treatise for the instruction of students to open their way to the sciences and to support young scholars to understand principles of right judgment, it was used as a logic text at Oxford, Cambridge, Yale and Harvard Universities for up to 100 years following its initial publication. In it Watts argues for logic as a practical art (versus a science) useful for inquiries in arts, sciences, and ethics. Watts writes:

> [F]ollowers of *Aristotle*, made *Fire, Air, Earth*, and *Water*, to be four elements of which all earthly things were compounded; and they supposed the heavens to be a *quintessence*, or *fifth* sort of body, distinct from all, these: But, since experimental philosophy and mathematics have been better understood, this doctrine has been abundantly refuted[10].

Watts' comment about *experimental philosophy* introduces a way of making know-ledge that has been constructed into what today is called science. Watts uses the term science in the following way:

> "Yet let it be noted, that the word science is usually applied to a whole body of regular and methodical observations or propositions, which learned men have formed concerning any subject of speculation, deriving one truth from another by a train of arguments"[11].

Question. Does this comment sound like a description of dialectical reasoning?

An image of Isaac Watts.

It was not until the second half of the 19th century that the term *science* became restricted to what had previously been known as experimental or natural philosophy, physical and experimental science, or the systematized knowledge of matter and its properties. John Bernal[12], scientist and historian, associates this restriction of the term with the professionalization of scientific endeavor as *science*, based on values of planning, rationality, and order, came to be the responsibility of specially trained people called scientists, an era and way of thinking also called *modernity*. In their thorough examination of indigenous knowledge and science, Glen Aikenhead and Masakata Ogawa[13] argue that by the 18th century natural and experimental philosophers had seemed so successful at demonstrating their power over nature that entrepreneurial technologists adopted and adapted the same methods to gain power over human production. However by the 1830s English industry and scholarship seemed to be struggling to recover after war with Napoleon, in which England had been one of the victors in 1815 but which had left England depleted. In 1831, the founders of the British Association for the Advancement of Science (modeled on the Society of German Scientists and Physicians Association (GDNÄ) established in 1822) saw this association as a way to support natural philosophy study and practice in England and selected the term, *science*, to describe the systematic study of nature and the term, *scientist*, to identify professionals studying nature[14]. The British Association (BA) also became a model for American professional scientific organizations. So although the word 'science' had been used in English for some time, its association with the practice of experimental philosophy is relatively recent.

However, the idea that nature could be studied either naturally, as was the case with natural philosophy, or worked on through experiments, as was the case with experimental philosophy, has been part of people's thinking for much longer than the 150 or so years associated with modernism. Natural philosophy is associated with the Greek philosopher Aristotle and his observations of nature, which he published in a series of books, including *History of Animals* and *Generation of Animals*. By the seventeenth century, *experimental* philosophy provided a philosophic justification for exploring questions about nature through the use of experiment. For example Henry Power, an early Fellow of the Royal Society of London, one of the earliest societies set up to follow the principles of experimental philosophy writes:

> These are the days that must lay a new foundation of a more magnificent philosophy, never to be overthrown, that will Empirically and Sensibly canvass the *Phenomena* of Nature, deducing the causes of things from such Originals in Nature as we observe are producible by Art, and the infallible demonstration of Mechanicks: and certainly this is the way, and no other to build a true and permanent Philosophy.... [T]o find the various turnings and mysterious process of this divine Art, in the management of this great Machine of the World, must needs be the proper Office of onely the Experimental and Mechanical Philosopher.[15]

However, there are many forms of knowledge and when one uses the word science to describe practices or knowledge there is no guarantee that everyone involved is thinking about the same thing. In order to understand our knowledge traditions as they can be applied to science, cross-cultural, historic, and comparative exploration is needed and will provide the focus for this book. One of the important questions that I want to examine is how science gets talked into being. History provides us with examples from which to explore how we come to be constituted as knowing subjects through the very processes that we construct. Very often, when disciplines like science get constructed into being, it is helpful for individuals to have some knowledge of the history of how discourses and practices that allow people to be identified as knowledgeable within a discipline have evolved. Within disciplines, being knowledgeable is associated with being powerful and the connections between knowledge and power squeeze out myths about the nature of science.

SCIENCE, EUROCENTRIC SCIENCE (ES), AND INDIGENOUS KNOWLEDGE (IK)

When I initially asked the question about how you understand science I recognized that this was a far more complex question than a few definitions would imply. If science can be described as a form of *systematic knowledge*, how does it compare with other forms of systematic knowledge? By systematic I mean a collection of understandings that is organized in some way. Later in this chapter I present specific examples of systematic knowledge, such as those described by anthropologist Peter Worsley, based on his conversations with aborigines living on Groote Eylandt, a large island in the western reaches of the Gulf of Carpentaria in northern Australia. Should there be more recognition given in science classrooms to other forms of systematic knowledge? As Aikenhead and Ogawa note there is an increasing desire for educators "to understand the cultural influence on school science achievement by students whose cultures and languages differ from the predominant Eurocentric culture and language of science"[16] I would like you to consider that the science students learn in school is a form of local knowledge gone viral, or should I say inter-national and which I, following Aikenhead and Ogawa, call Eurocentric science. Some researchers, such as Elizabeth McKinley[17], involved in examining the relation-ship between Indigenous Knowledge and Eurocentric science, argue that language is central to all forms of knowledge. McKinley argues that Indigenous Knowledge is place-based knowledge, which is often dismissed as irrelevant in educational settings as science becomes, if it is not already, increasingly global and universal. With globalization this form of scientific knowledge becomes more and more detached from a local context. Indigenous Knowledge is local and, for people, their knowledge is specific to place. Indigenous Knowledge typically consists of creation stories and cosmologies that explain the origin of the earth and people, codes of ritual/behavior that organize human interactions with the environment, practices and patterns of resource allocation, and a body of factual knowledge[18]. As McKinley notes, with globalization indigenous people become involuntary minorities in their own countries. There is a tendency to present Indigenous Knowledge as static but such a presentation is misleading because, just like Eurocentric science, Indigenous Knowledge is dynamic as practitioners evaluate new knowledge and technologies for inclusion into the corpus of Indigenous Knowledge.[19] Aikenhead and Ogawa also note that other cultures with a written language, which contribute participants to the Eurocentric science enterprise, such as those from Asia and Africa, adopt some ideas from Eurocentric science but mark them as foreign. Thereby accounting for differences in values and ways of knowing nature that can be observed.

Universal and Pluralist Models of Science in Science Education

In science education much of the debate concerning ways of thinking about the relationship between Eurocentric science and Indigenous Knowledge is premised on universal and transnational models. According to the Universal Model, Eurocentric science is universal and more powerful than any Indigenous Knowledge. This is the model presented in the National Science Education Standards. There is a lot of on-going debate about the accuracy and appropriateness of this model but at its most extreme it is associated with a philosophy called *positivism*, which is nested within another philosophy or movement called *modernism*, which I described a little earlier in this chapter.

Question.　What is the universal model trying to communicate about Eurocentric science and Indigenous Knowledge? How successful is it?

For modernism the development of machines and technology, especially in the nineteenth century, ushered in an age where humans could use tools such as science and technology to steadily improve their lot. In this model, science was seen as progressive. In past decades some historians of science have promoted this progressivist view of science presenting science as steadily advancing, never putting a step wrong, a source of solutions for all the world's ills. Mistakes or side-paths were ignored. In many respects, this remains the model of science history that is presented in school science textbooks.

Question.　How widespread is this progressivist model? Read the following section taken from a Press Release on November 23, 2009 from President Obama:

> The key to meeting these challenges – to improving our health and well-being, to harnessing clean energy, to protecting our security, and succeeding in the global economy – will be reaffirming and strengthening America's role as the world's engine of scientific discovery and technological innovation. And that leadership tomorrow depends on how we educate our students today, especially in those fields that hold the promise of producing future innovations and innovators. And that's why education in math and science is so important.
>
> Now the hard truth is that for decades we've been losing ground. One assessment shows American 15-year-olds now rank 21st in science and 25th in math when compared to their peers around the world. And this isn't news. We've seen worrying statistics like this for years. Yet, time and again, we've let partisan and petty bickering stand in the way of progress. And time and again, as a nation, we've let our children down.
>
> So I'm here and you are here because we all believe that we can't allow division and indifference to imperil our position in the world. It's time for all of us – in Washington and across America – to take responsibility for our future.
>
> And that's why I'm committed to moving our country from the middle to the top of the pack in science and math education over the next decade. To meet

this goal, the Recovery Act included the largest investment in education in history while preventing hundreds of thousands of educators from being fired because of state budget shortfalls. Under the outstanding leadership of Arne Duncan, we've launched a $4 billion Race to the Top fund, one of the largest investments in education reform in history.

The context of this statement was a statement on the *Education to Innovate* campaign. What model for science is presented in this statement? Why do you think the President used this model in this case?

Positivism, also called logical empiricism for its valuing of both rational thought and sense-based observations, also celebrated the triumphal march of science helping people find "truth" about Nature. Positivism was based on the belief that if people followed the one true method of Eurocentric science, called "the scientific method," about which you might have heard, they would find and understand real knowledge about Nature. For positivism, truth could only be verified rationally through the use of mathematics or empirically by observations conducted during controlled experiments[20]. Positivism accepted that humans were involved in a struggle for the control of nature and, in order to unlock nature's secrets, use of the scientific method was necessary. According to the universal model, Eurocentric science is a knowledge of power. Maskata Ogawa[21] argues that the science in a slogan like "Science for All" is Eurocentric science. Usually in such science curricula, little space is given to acknowledging that Eurocentric science is an expression of European thought and one way of organizing natural phenomena. Typically, in school science curricula if Indigenous Knowledge or other forms of knowledge are considered, they are diminished or considered of lesser value. Within Eurocentric science, Indigenous Knowledge is considered only to be of value if it is a source of information or data that contributes in some way to Eurocentric science.

Another model, the Pluralist Model, presents all forms of knowledge as equal. The universalist model sets boundaries to what can be called science but with the pluralist model these boundaries are more porous. Pluralist models accept that all forms of knowledge exist in a cultural context so knowledge must be imbued with the values that are espoused by the culture. However, the boundaries are less determinate because people in all cultures adopt practices and tools from other cultural settings if the tools and practices are useful and/or do not contradict existing values and beliefs. Being willing to accept the value-laden nature of knowledge construction is a step towards developing a richer understanding of the nature of a specific discipline, like Eurocentric science. According to McKinley, many of the authors that espouse universalist models seem to have little understanding of the complexities associated with colonization even if some of them are familiar with some aspects of the historical development of Eurocentric science. Indigenous Knowledge exists wherever local cultures are to be found. Some science educators[22] would like to see indigenous knowledge have equal status in a school curriculum with other knowledges such as English, mathematics, science, and social studies but they accept that in an already crowded curriculum, it is not likely. Pluralist perspectives help us to understand why and how youth become alienated from science when, to them, science seems completely disconnected from everyday life and when the knowledge and experiences that youth have in their homes and communities are not valued in science.

Activity

Try your hand at drawing an image of the relationship between Eurocentric science and Indigenous Knowledge for both universalist and pluralist models.

Pluralist Model	Universal Model

The catch-all phrase, *Science for All*, communicates an acceptance of the notion that Eurocentric science is universal and monolithic. McKinley[23] argues that universalist assumptions inform the development of science curriculum. The vision of universal science is associated with the emergence of the industrial revolution and is really a product of that era in which the idea that Eurocentric science was justified true knowledge, which was true throughout time and from one culture to another, predominated thinking about the nature of science. The universal image of science that comes to us from this era is associated with a cannon of scientific method, which celebrates the existence of one correct way to order phenomena and a set of procedures for determining what that ordering is. Look through your school science textbooks and see how the methods of science are represented. Do your textbooks present *one* scientific method as the only method for doing science? What does that suggest to you about how the authors of this textbook understand science?

This understanding of the nature of science is also part of modernism where the story of science was one of unceasing progress ever upwards to a more rational informed view of the world free of emotion, ignorance, and superstition. History allows us to recognize the partial and incomplete nature of such ordering allowing us to examine through time and place multiple examples of attempts at ordering and the variable responses of people involved. History also allows us to examine how representations in a variety of texts supported meaning making for others and in the process became accepted as knowledge. Science as systematic knowledge was never uniquely European as exemplified in the variety of ancient and modern cultures from all corners of the globe associated with the development of systematic knowledge. Some examination of the history of science can help us to be more knowledgeable about the origins of practices and discourses associated with the emergence of Eurocentric science.

Activity

One strategy for examining how people understand science is to ask the overarching question: What is the nature of science? I use the story of umbrellaology, which is a slightly modified version of the letter from an article by John Somerville, which first appeared in *Philosophy of Science*[24]. I ask people to read the letter in which a person is asking whether his (only a male would do this) creation, umbrellaology, was a science. Over the past eighteen years, assisted by a few disciples, he had been collecting materials on the neglected discipline of umbrella study. The findings of these studies are collected in nine volumes. The studies began with an in depth examination of umbrella ownership including number of umbrellas possessed, size, weight and color in the metropolitan area of New York City and surrounding suburbs with plans to extend the study to the "rest of the United States and the whole known world." At this point, the investigator turned to a friend to ask about his right to be recognized as the founder of a new science. The friend who is no longer a friend dismissed the creator's claim as folly because umbrellas were not significant enough, because such a study was of "no use or benefit to mankind," because the findings were too impermanent, and because umbrellaology had entertained no hypotheses and developed no laws or theories. The author of the letter proceeded to refute the arguments of his erstwhile friend.

I then ask them to work in groups to discuss the question of how umbrellaology might or might not represent science. They are asked to compare the letter author's claim about umbrellaology with my stance presented in this chapter. Finally there is a discussion about the question: what is science?

The goal is not to come to one answer about science, deemed correct, but to raise questions for people who often have well-established ideas, based on their previous experiences with Eurocentric science, about the nature of science. This activity also provides a starting point for opening up the conversation to consider the origins of science and Eurocentric science and to introduce questions that will be constantly revisited throughout this book: questions of reality or worldview and position in that world (also called ontology); questions of knowledge (what is) and what it means to know? (also called epistemology); and questions of value (what ought to be) of goals and ethics (also called axiology).

SO WHAT IS SYSTEMATIC KNOWLEDGE AND WHAT ARE THE ORIGINS OF SCIENCE?

David Turnbull who has studied the working of science communities[25] argues that "science in the general sense of systematic knowledge was never uniquely western[26]" because examples of science can be found in all historic and contemporary human societies. As you will have the chance to examine in this book, Eurocentric science is not uniquely western or modern. It has borrowed from knowledge traditions across the world including the Americas, African, Chinese, Indian, Islamic, Arabic, and Pacific. There exist many different knowledge traditions. Knowledge traditions are local, constructing forms of systematic knowledge that can differ in decisions about what counts as knowledge and how different forms of knowledge can be constructed. There exists a recursive relationship between the local construction of systematic knowledge and the community it establishes through its very construction. The community allows the creation of a social space in which knowledge can be constructed.

Turnbull[27] argues that once knowledge is constructed the social labor involved is forgotten and these knowledges take on the air of unchanging "unchallengable naturalness" as the history of their construction is lost and they are communicated and used across generations. Under these conditions, knowledge becomes homogenized and accepted as eternal universal truth rather than a product of local construction. My study of science myths and their role in science education[28] indicated that a loss of memory of the historical construction of science in science education helps to explain why certain practices, such as an emphasis on facts, become the way to do science. However, even though systematic knowledges become homogenized they remain polysemous. In other words, these knowledges can be assembled and used variously, providing space for interpretive and explanatory variability. Such a structure, homogenous but open to multiple uses, also allows any borders to be porous as knowledge construction in all communities, especially at the margins, is dynamic and resistance as well as compliance is always an option.

Sometimes the argument is made that Eurocentric science is different from other forms of systematic knowledge because it is dedicated to theoretical knowledge. One could argue that part of Eurocentric science's attempt to become universal is the focus on theories as the core element of science with Eurocentric science seeking mastery over experience by making experience the handmaiden of unifying theories. Theories allow science to claim a "positionless" vision of nature where laws and theories are universal. However, examination of the role of theories in Eurocentric science suggests a far more nuanced structure. For example, close studies of scientists and their practice, such as those by Susan Leigh Star, has shown that scientists create theories that are both plastic, adaptable to local needs, and coherent, able to incorporate local requirements yet able to retain a recognizable identity[29]. These qualities are necessary if theories are to be robust. For coherence, Star also identified inertia, commitment to specific work practices, and alliances and conflicts that make revision of theories difficult. She identified momentum, social organization of work, and multiple sites as necessary for plasticity. So, while a focus on theory might be central to the practice of Eurocentric science, such a focus does not distinguish Eurocentric science from other forms of systematic knowledge.

Turnbull acknowledges that the debate about what should 'count' as knowledge is one of high stakes, especially when in countries such as the US there continue to be claims for the methods of Eurocentric science to be the epistemological gold standard for constructing new knowledge. I believe that a study of the history of Eurocentric science and of emerging arguments for a nature of science can support us to develop a more nuanced and deeper understanding of science and how school science has turned out the way it has to this time. Turnbull argues that all sciences, including Eurocentric science, should be examined and compared as "forms of local knowledge" so that the emergence of powerful knowledge can be identified in a more nuanced way. Some theorists argue that for knowledge to count as knowledge it must be true through time and across cultures. History provides us with tools that allow us to examine this claim and some of the developments associated with the emergence of what today can be called Eurocentric science.

Emerging Systematic Knowledge

We can never know when people started to create systematized knowledge. Its ubiquity across cultures suggests that constructing such knowledge is not only something that humans feel the need to do but is necessary for survival of humans, which seem to have few natural survival qualities apart from their large brains. Humans are not really big or really fast but they do seem to be able to use their observations of the natural world and experimentation with materials in the natural world to start to create a world that will support their ongoing survival. Turnbull also argues that all forms of knowledge production are localized and an examination of localized knowledge provides the possibility of being able to compare the ways different cultures at different times produced understandings of the natural world. Eurocentric science is a variety of such a knowledge system sharing with other know-ledge systems a localness that has place while also creating a space. Social labor creates the patterns that emerge from this practice. Once the space has been created, the role of humans in this construction is often forgotten so the knowledge takes on a form of timelessness that can be seductive.

Turnbull uses evidence from map production and usage to make the claim for the formation of different knowledge systems in which collective work, social strategies, and tools, support the emergence of different assemblages that are the sources of power differences between knowledge systems.

In his book, Peter Worsley[30], an English anthropologist, writes of specific aboriginal groups living on Groote Eylandt. Worsley ended up conducting fieldwork with Aborigines in Groote Eylandt in the 1950s after being refused permission to do research in Africa and the New Guinea Highlands because of his avowed communist and egalitarian stance to politics. He notes that, when he asked children to draw for him anything of interest to them on an outline of the island he had provided them, many covered the map with criss-crosses, which they told Worsley were roads. He argues that to Whites these roads look like barely discernable tracks across the land. While Whites see a stretch of natural environment or "bush" hostile to human habitation, Aborigines of the region see a land that is culturally dense, full of significant points that can be "read as a Bible" where anyone can see "sacred sites where great Beings passed as they created the world in the Dreamtime"[31] The land can be read like a newspaper but in tracks rather than text. Worsley's work with Aboriginal groups led him to recognize that Aborigines used at least four different forms of thinking: religious, biological, nutritional, and that built into language, depending on context. So perhaps it could be argued that they used at least four different knowledges or sciences to think about living things.

Aborigines of Groote Eylandt were also able to help Worsley understand that, for them, boundaries were identified by reference to the central parts of a territory rather than natural features on the edges that Europeans might give greater significance. They also recognized different ecological zones – eight land and eight sea – which also influenced where they set up camp. As an island culture, the coast held great significance as a rich source of food and personal names. Worsley also identified the use of the nut of the burrawang or zamia palm, a form of cycad (*Cycas angulata*) as a food. These nuts constitute a challenge because the nut inside the fruit contains a neurotoxin. To remove the toxin, Aborigines treated the nuts by heating them on hot stones or in ashes and then pounding or grinding them into flour. Grinding stones used to grind the nuts are often found in groves of cycad palms. The flour is strained using a tool made from fronds to leech out the toxin without losing the flour. From this flour, bread called *damper* can be made.

The fruits of burrawang (Cycas angulata) used to make flour.

John Bradley[32], in his discussion of how the Yanyuwa and Garrwa people of south-west Gulf of Carpentaria in Australia use cycads for food, further supports Worsley's claim of the role of language in establishing forms of systematic knowledge. In the Yanyuwa language the cycad is classified as *wurrana* or 'being of authority' with economic and religious significance to the maritime environment. Bradley reports that the testimonies of local people illustrate its importance as a food source that was filling and healthy unlike the bread of whitemen, which was neither, even as its toxic character was acknowledged. Bradley also reports that old women with lots of experience working with these nuts were able, through feel, to identify nuts that could be eaten and those that needed further treatment to be used as a food source. This use illustrates the role of observation in developing systematic knowledge and how systematic knowledge is communicated across generations becoming part of the cultural historical knowledge of the group much like the domestication and use of cassava and corn in the Americas became distributed[33].

F. Alyward acknowledges the contribution that pre-Columbian (before European arrival to the Americas) cultures from the Americas made to the use and domestication of a multitude of crops including corn (*Zea mays*) and cassava, also called manioc, tapioca, yuka, (*Manihot* genus, a member of the Milkweed family, Euphorbiace). Like burrawang, the tubers of cassava can be toxic, especially the skin, and need to be treated before they can be eaten safely. The roots must be peeled and then leeched to remove hydrogen cyanide (H-C≡N), a poison, which begins to form once tubers have been removed from the plant. Amerindians applied investigative logic to the issue of using cassava tubers as a source of food, specific types of cassava exhibit a range of toxicities, which supported identification of patterns of material relationships they could use to develop more general ideas or theories about food preparation.

Cassava became a significant food crop not only in the Americas but also Africa and Asia through the efforts of Portuguese slavers and traders.

The cassava plant with tubers obtained from:
hekebun.files.wordpress.com/2008/10/cassava.jpg

These examples raise the question of how different cultures came to discover that poisons could be removed. While the answer to this question may never be obtained, there is no doubt that it must have involved both abstract reasoning to work out what was causing the poisoning and use of observation and experimentation to develop strategies for removing the toxin.

Aborigines in Australia also made medicines from living things, such as various plants and parts of plants, beehives and bees, dingo (a type of dog) manure, and powdered cuttlefish bone, and materials, such as seawater and clays. Amerindians also made use of living things and materials. Some of the most famous reported examples include Huron Indians use of spruce to ward off scurvy and their communication of this practice to the 1535 Jacques Cartier expedition in Canada many years before James Lind published his *Treatise of the Scurvy* in 1753[34] and the Peruvian Indians (Quechua) use of quinine to treat fevers, which was recognized as a useful drug for the treatment of malaria.

Other forms of systematic knowledge that have been identified in other cultures include knowledge about landforms and distances. Where would Lewis and Clark be without Sacagawea, the Shoshone Indian, who helped to guide them across North America? The use of fire and tool making and the emergence of pottery and metallurgy provide further evidence of systematized knowledge. Although we might never know when humans first made pottery, the earliest found pottery (about 10,000 years ago) suggest a long prior period of observation and trialing or experimentation associated with chemical and physics knowledge of materials, such as knowing the temperatures at which materials melted or oxides were reduced or further oxidized. Historian Clifford Conner[35] makes the reasonable argument that the development of pottery science was probably an achievement of women around the hearth.

Archeological evidence indicates that the capacity to make metal from ores emerged about 3000 BCE (Before the Common Era), that is about 5000 years ago, in numerous cultural sites across the Earth including Nigeria, Peru, India, China, the Balkans, and South-East Asia. Each site is close to sources of ores for making metals. The Bronze Age, the beginning of which has been associated with the Middle East around 3300 BCE, is named after the alloy of copper and tin that is bronze. Although bronze was more associated with the wealthy, with the poor continuing to use stone, wood, and bone, as source materials for making tools and weapons, the search for copper and tin did encourage trade and interactions between different cultural groups encouraging a sharing of ideas and practices that supported the development of other forms of systematic knowledge.

Unlike bronze, iron was the great leveler. Technology existing at the time did not allow Bronze Age furnaces to melt iron (1537°C) but did allow iron ores to be reduced to an "iron bloom," solid iron mixed with liquid slag, that could be pounded on an anvil to drive out liquid and cinders and drive the metallic particles closer together forming what was called wrought (worked) iron. Oleg Sherby and Jeffrey Wadsworth[36] argue that while there is no direct evidence that Neanderthals made iron, they lived in conditions that included access to iron ore, use of hearths, and high winds, that could have supported the production of temperatures high enough to support the formation of iron bloom. Even if this did not take place, they emphasize the role of careful observation in smithing to make iron. Forging always needed to be carried out in a dark space like a cave. The best iron, called Damascus steel, began to be made about 2000 BCE. It was used to make swords, shields, helmets, and armor. Damascus swords, along with Japanese swords, are considered the most impressive swords ever made because of their cutting edge and beauty. The precise method of manufacture of Damascus swords has been lost but the raw material originally came from India and was traded in the form of cakes. In Persia (now called Iran), black-smiths forged these swords, so their name is misleading. It is thought that the name is due to European traders seeing the swords for sale in Damascus. These swords were so valued it is claimed that when King Puru of India met Alexander the Greek (the Great) about 330 BCE in battle in which he was defeated, he gave Alexander his Damascus sword at the end of the battle. The secrecy associated with the practice of iron making provided impetus for the development of alchemy in many parts of the world.

Some areas of exploration and knowledge development that I have not mentioned so far but are often presented as examples in the development of Eurocentric science include astronomy and calendars, important for navigation and working out the timing of important events, and counting. I do not want to imply that these technologies just happened or were unimportant because, for many groups, the ability to accurately record the passing of time in a calendar was essential for government and religious practices. Also, the capacity for language, which seems to be central to all human groups, involves the regulation of a sequence of sounds, so some form of recognition of time would seem to be central to all groups. Humans' ability to attend and listen to what others are saying probably affects our sense of time. When humans talk there seems to be a propensity towards using the past tense for knowledge, the present tense for feelings and the future tense for desire and obligation[37]. All human groups seem to have developed a strategy for time reckoning based on phases of nature indicated by changes in climate and animal and plant life or by astronomical observations. Permanent solar clocks dating from at least 1500 BCE have been found in Egypt. It makes sense that a country with a lot of sunlight would find the sun a useful resource for keeping time. The Polynesian and Micronesian diasporas involved people using highly developed and complex methods of navigation.

I remember being very surprised when I first learned that initially the Romans did not have the concept of zero, which seems to have developed first in India, where it was in use in some form at least 200 years before the common era, and the Americas, possibly the Olmecs, before the common era. By 400 BCE counting rods used by Chinese mathematicians applied the concept of zero even though at that stage it seems they lacked a symbol for the concept. Babylonians developed place value by 300 BCE. Philosophically, the Greeks had a problem with a number that stood for nothing but Greek astronomers needed at least place value and used it when needed. However, much of the development of the symbol and associated rules of use for zero are associated with Brahmagupta (598–668 CE), a famous Indian mathematician and astronomer. The name we use in English today, zero, comes from the Arabic, *sifr*, possibly because the work of Brahmagupta was interpreted and translated by the Arabic scholars such as al-Khwarizmi (whose name gave English speakers the term, *algorithm*).

An image of al-Khwarizmi on a stamp from the former USSR.
Obtained from: http://www-history.mcs.st-andrews.ac.uk/PictDisplay/Al-Khwarizmi.html

Today the Hindu-Arabic base-10 script for numeric notation is used across the globe. This script reached Europe about the 11th century where Roman numerals were the common script and remained so until well into the 16th century. Conner[38] argues that prior to the introduction to Europe of Hindu-Arabic base-10, with place value and the zero, subtracting, multiplying, and dividing required a high level of expertise which was associated with *Abacists*, people skilled at using numbers. These experts tried to retard the introduction of Hindu-Arabic base-10, which had a democratizing effect on mathematic calculations making them available to skilled workers, such as masons, carpenters, wheelwrights and so forth.

All forms of systematic knowledge provide support for a number of developments beyond careful observation, thoughtful experimentation and abstract reasoning, they also provide support for the emergence of people identified as more or less learned with respect to these knowledges be they religious, biological, food, language, or some other form of knowledge. Forms of knowledge support the need for learning and for specialization. In this chapter, I tried to provide an introduction to some of the big ideas in science education associated with questions about the status and nature of knowledge including Indigenous Knowledges and Eurocentric science. These are complex ideas that would support further exploration in a different context, but my goal in the following chapters is to introduce you to the history of Eurocentric science as a way of understanding both some of its origins, its nature, and its emergence as a powerful form of knowledge.

NOTES

[1] These statements and questions are modified from:
Galili, I., & Hazan, A. (2001). The effect of a history-based course in optics on students' views about science. *Science & Education, 10*, 7–32.
[2] National Research Council. (1996). *National science education standards: Observe, interact, change, learn.* Washington, DC: National Academy.
[3] National Research Council. (1996). p. 21.
[4] National Research Council. (1996). p. 24.
[5] In this book I use the convention of before the common era (BCE) and common era (CE). Like all calendars, it is a cultural/religious convention.
[6] Oxford English Dictionary. (1989). *Oxford English dictionary.* Oxford: Oxford University Press.
[7] National Research Council. (1996). p. 176.
[8] For example, Bernal, J. D. (1971). *Science in history. Vol. 1: The emergence of science.* Cambridge, MA: MIT Press.
[9] Watts, I. (1806). *Logic, or the right use of reason, in the inquiry after truth with a variety of rules to guard against error in the affairs of religion and human life, as well as in the sciences* (3rd American ed.). Boston: Ranlet & Norris.
[10] Watts, I. (1806). p. 17.
[11] Watts, I. (1806). p. 142.
[12] Bernal, J. D. (1971).
[13] Aikenhead, G. S., & Ogawa, M. (2007). Indigenous knowledge and science revisited. *Cultural Studies of Science Education, 2*, 539–620.
[14] See more information at the British Science Association (as it is now called) website http://www.britishscienceassociation.org/web/AboutUs/OurHistory/
[15] Power, H. (1623–1668). 1664, *Experimental philosophy, in three books: Containing new experiments microscopical, mercurial, magnetical : With some deductions, and probable hypotheses, raised from them, in avouchment and illustration of the now famous atomical hypothesis.* London: Printed by T. Roycroft, for John Martin and James Allestry.
[16] Aikenhead, G., & Ogawa, M. (2007). p. 541.
[17] McKinley, E. (2005). Locating the global: Culture, language and science education for indigenous students. *International Journal of Science Education, 27*, 227–241.
[18] Snivley, G., & Corsiglia, J. (2001). Discovering indigenous science: Implications for science education. *Science Education, 85*, 6–34.
[19] Briggs, J. (2005). The use of indigenous knowledge in development: Problems and challenges. *Progress in Development Studies, 5*, 99–114.

[20] See Merchant, C. (2008). "The violence of impediments" Francis Bacon and the origins of experimentation. *Isis, 99,* 731–760.

[21] Ogawa, M. (1995). Science education in a multiscience perspective. *Science Education, 79,* 583–593.

[22] For example, Roberts, M. (1996). Indigenous knowledge and western science: Perspectives from the Pacific. In D. Hodson (Ed.), *Science, technology education, and ethnicity: An Aotearoa/New Zealand perspective* (pp. 59–75). Wellington, NZ: The Royal Society of New Zealand.

[23] McKinley, E. (2005).

[24] Somerville, J. (1941). Umbrellaology, or, methodology in social science. *Philosophy of Science, 8,* 557–566.

[25] Charlesworth, M., Farrall, L., Stokes, T., & Turnbull, D. (1989). *Life among the scientists: An anthropological study of an Australian scientific community.* New York: Oxford University Press.

[26] Turnbull, D. (2000). *Masons, tricksters, and cartographers.* London: Routledge. p. 6.

[27] Turnbull, D. (2000).

[28] Milne, C. (1998). *Science cultural myths and school science: A critical analysis of historical and contemporary discourses.* Unpublished Doctoral Dissertation, Curtin University of Technology, Perth, Western Australia, Australia.

[29] Star, S. L. (1989). *Regions of the mind: Brain research and the quest for scientific certainty.* Stanford, CA: Stanford University Press. p. 21.

[30] Worsley, P. (1997). *Knowledges.* New York: The New Press.

[31] Worsley, P. (1997). p. 17.

[32] Bradley, J. J. (2005). 'Same time poison, same time good tucker': The cycad palm in the south west gulf of Carpentaria. *Journal of Australian Studies, 29,* 119–133.

[33] Alyward, F. (1953). The indigenous foods of Mexico and Central America. *Symposium Proceedings: Unusual foods for human consumption. Proceedings of the Nutrition Society, 12*(1), 48–57.

[34] James Lind, a Scottish naval surgeon, is usually recognized as the discoverer of the value of citrus fruits for curing scurvy, a terrible disease which we now know is a deficiency disease due to a lack of Vitamin C (ascorbic acid) in a person's diet. In his treatise, Lind acknowledges the efficacy of this prior treatment, already used by Indian groups, for scurvy.

[35] Conner, C. D. (2005). *A people's history of science: Miners, midwives, and "low mechanics".* New York: Nation Books. p. 77.

[36] Sherby, O., & Wadsworth, J. (2001). Ancient blacksmiths, the Iron Age, Damascus steels, and modern metallurgy. *Journal of Materials Processing Technology, 117,* 347–353.

[37] Whitrow, G. J. (1988). *Time in history.* Oxford: Oxford University Press.

[38] See Conner, C. D. (2005). p. 73.

MAKING ARGUMENTS

In this chapter we will begin to examine the path that some forms of systematic knowledge took on the way to becoming what we recognize as Eurocentric science. In doing so, we have to acknowledge the influence of some thinkers, and the institutes and movements they inspired, on the practices and policies of hundreds of years of European thought. Communities develop narratives that seek to explain their relationship with the earth and other aspects of the world they observe. Some of the people that we will examine were able to galvanize groups of people in academies and schools to become disciples for their ways of thinking and being. Much of what we know about these movements is tied up with how their ideas continued to be communicated through texts and testimonies, helping us also to acknowledge the importance of a written language for representing ideas. Other aspects worthy of our consideration for understanding the development of Eurocentric science are how these ideas can be preserved through time either through translation or through preservation. For example, as the archeological excavation of Herculaneum proceeds, people hope that more carbonized scrolls will be found that will contain the writings of Greek and Roman philosophers. Destroyed by the eruption of Vesuvius in 79 CE, Herculaneum provides a time capsule of ancient Rome.

When historians began to examine the history of Eurocentric science, especially in the 19th and 20th centuries, they typically elevated the role of Greek thinkers such as Pythagoras, Socrates, Plato, Hippocrates, Democritus, and, of course, Aristotle. Some of these names you might recognize, others might be new, but each of them represents a movement rather than an individual. Emerging Greek cultures have been held up by scholars as unique for their attempts to explain the world without recourse to the occult or supernatural events but, as Worsley demonstrated in his examination of the knowledges of Groote Eylanders, how groups describe and explain what they experience depends very much on context. Aborigines recognize the biological and the mystical as different forms of knowledge but are always willing to use one type of knowledge to inform another.

Sometimes Greek, Roman, and European writers have revered Greek scholars for discoveries that were known previously to other cultures. For example, today Pythagoras (about 570–495 BCE) is remembered by school students for the Pythagorean Theorem, which allows you to calculate the length of any side of a right-angled or right side triangle based on the statement that the area of a square whose side is the hypotenuse of a right-angled triangle is equal to the sum of the squares of the other two sides. The sides of right or right angle triangles are also called Pythagorean triplets. The one most familiar is 3: 4: 5 ($3^2 + 4^2 = 5^2$). Evidence from clay tablets left by Mesopotamians (Sumerian from about 1800–1500 BCE and Babylonian up to about 300 BCE) indicates prior awareness of this theorem and its application.

Other groups including Egyptians and Indians used this theorem empirically in building construction[1]. Although little is known with any certainty about his life, it is possible that Pythagoras also was introduced to the empirical use of Pythagorean triplets on travels to countries such as Babylon, Egypt, or India. Of those named, I have a soft spot for Democritus (about 460–370 BCE) who, along with his mentor Leucippus (early 5th century BCE) and student Epicurus (341–270 BCE), was a proponent of atomism, a theory that proposed everything was composed of small, indivisible, indestructible, eternal atoms. Democritus is presented by his contemporaries as a very engaging person who seems to have traveled far and wide from India to Mesopotamia and Africa, especially Egypt and Ethiopia, in order to learn as much as he could of knowledges, especially mathematical knowledges from scholars in those cultures.

If all these dates are becoming a bit overwhelming, a timeline, like the one provided here, might help you to build some sense of cultural development and people mentioned. This timeline might imply that there are only famous people that you should be concerned about but most of these people, especially in the various iterations of Greek culture, were associated with schools or philosophies that were taken up and promoted by followers and students.

Idiosyncratic timeline of some developments

Time	Place and people	Information
2000 BCE	**Egypt**	Becomes a united kingdom, which it basically remains for 2000 years. Much of what is recorded is directly associated with the ascension of each Pharaoh.
1490–1436 BCE	Tutmose III	12-hour day and development of shadow clocks recorded.
1397–1360 BCE	Amenhotep III	Waterclocks in use.
1027–771 BCE	**China, India, Nigeria**	Emergence of iron working and extensive use of irrigation
560–500 BCE	**Greece** Pythagoras	Geometry. Owed much to the Babylonians. It was understood that vision was caused by something emitted from the eye.
450 BCE	Parmenides	The universe is continuous and unchanging.
492–432 BCE or thereabouts	Empedocles	Proposed combining four elements mentioned by earlier philosophers - earth, water, air and fire – into a coherent system. Elements are not considered identical with the ordinary substances that go by those names but their essential and permanent characteristics. Every material substance is composed of these four elements. For example, wood contains earth (heavy & solid), water (gives off moisture when heated), air (it smokes) and fire (emits flames when heated). Luminous objects emit rays, which meet the rays emitted by the eyes. The universe is a crystal sphere.

Table (Continued)

478 BCE	Leucippus	"Two things exist – atoms and the void" Fire and the human soul were atomic. The atoms of the soul generate warmth in the body: they are a vital force. When there is death the soul disperses. There is no afterlife because there is no soul to experience it. This was a speculative theory.
Birth not known. 460 BCE possible.	Democritus	Pupil of Leucippus. Contemporary of Socrates. Atomist who argued that because everything was composed of atoms it was possible to determine causes associated with matter and emotions.
470–399 BCE	Socrates	Not interested in explaining the natural world
b. 427 BCE	Plato	True reality is permanent and unchanging what we observe is an inadequate imitation of reality because living things will age and die but the essential idea of a living thing will go on forever
about 400 BCE - about 340 BCE	Arete of Cyrene (then part of Greek Empire now Lybia)	Philosopher attended Plato's academy and took over the Cyrenaic School after the death of her father. Promoted hedonism, i.e. seeking a balance between pleasure and pain in everyday life. Egalitarian.
About 460–370 BCE	Hippocrates	Established a school of medicine. The School focused on patient care and prognosis rather than diagnosis, which was difficult considering the Greek ban on dissections, although it might have been acceptable to dissect slaves.
b. 384 BCE	Aristotle	Unlike Plato valued observations of the natural world as the basis for knowledge building.
330 BCE	Pythias of Assos	Biologist. Married Aristotle (denied her the recognition she probably deserved). Thought to have collaborated with him on *Generation of Animals* but involvement unacknowledged.
341–270 BCE	Epicurus	Influenced by Democritus. Gave priority to the use of direct observation (using the senses) for generating new knowledge. Atoms are material. Actually allowed women and slaves to attend his school. Know of his work through Lucretius' (ca. 99–55 BCE) poem, *On the Nature of Things.*
221 BCE	**China** Ch'in (Qin)	Standardization of weights and measures by Ch'in (Qin) establishing "Empire of All Under Heaven" – unification of China. Paper invented.
90–168 CE	**Egypt** Ptolemy	Roman citizen living in Egypt, likely of Greek ancestry, whose synthesis of extant Babylonian and Greek astronomical knowledge within a geocentric model formed the accepted basis of astronomical understanding in Europe until at least the 16th century.

Table (Continued)

Early CE	**China and elsewhere**	Alchemy emerges in many different parts of the world simultaneously and generally independently. Chinese alchemy elixir of life. These elixirs became more and more toxic.
Somewhere in the first to third centuries	Maria of Alexandria (Mary the Jewess)	Invented apparatus for chemical processes such as distillation including the water bath (forms still named after her e.g. bain Marie). First alchemist of note in Afro-European thought?
CE 296	Emperor Diocletian	Claims that he banned alchemy in Roman Empire do not seem to be supported by a range of texts or evidence.
CE 391	**Egypt**	Alexandria library is sacked and burned by Christian mob that destroyed the entire manuscript collection. Hypatia (370–415 CE), Head of Platonist School in Alexandria, is murdered. She promotes a form of *neoplationism* that combines Plato's ideas with other influences, including Mesopotamian, East Asian, African, Christian, and Jewish, but the paganness of the main philosophy upsets some Christians to the extent that a mob murders her.
CE 670	**Syria/ Byzantium** Callinicus of Heliopolis (b. ~673- d. unknown)	Jewish refugee and chemist to Constantinople (Byzantium). Uses "Greek fire" composed of distilled crude oil, potassium nitrate or carbonate (source of oxygen), and quicklime [calcium oxide] (reacts with water to produce heat) to destroy Arab fleet on the Bosphorus.
	Islamic cultures	Scientific development in Arab hands for the next 500 years. Golden age of Islam 8th Century to 11th Century . Islamic cultures flourish in Spain, North Africa, Syria and Iran. In 11th Century revival of Christendom in Spain and move to expel Islamic culture.
		Arab contributions to science included both communication and synthesis of ideas of earlier ages and original work. For these scholars the cosmos was not a physical realm but a domain with a variety of levels of existence illuminated by revelations from Islam.
late 8th and early 9th century	ibn-Hayyan (Jabir)	Accepted Aristotelian doctrine of four elements, four qualities (hot, cold, dry and wet) and proposed two basic principles mercury and sulfur (not the elements but principles of action). It was the 'wedding' of these principles that gave rise to the different metals found in nature and in the right combination to gold. These metals were 'extraterrestrial'. Transmutation of base metals to gold was not just a physical process but also a higher way of operating in the world.
mid-9th Century	al-Battani	Book of Astronomical tables.

Table (Continued)

b. 965 CE	al-Haytham	Proposed that light was a 'ray', proposed the concept of refraction, and other innovations in his book "Optics".
1041–1048	**China** Bi Sheng	Development of movable type (printing). Chinese characters made its use a challenge. Whether this development contributed to the development of moveable type in Europe is a source of scholarly debate.

Activity

Can you identify any other developments that you think should be included in this timeline? Perhaps you can learn more about women associated with the development of science in antiquity and the early Islamic period? Perhaps innovations such as the development of irrigation systems or the making of beer or the development of gunpowder should have been included? You might have thought of other questions such as how do specific people become historically and culturally associated with specific innovations or discoveries? What role does the existence of a written text play in the attribution of discovery to a specific individual or school of thought? How could we find an answer to these questions? What other questions could be asked now?

The person of interest to us now is Aristotle (384–322 BCE) because his ideas had such a significant role in providing justification for a number of developments in questions of which knowledge is of most worth. Aristotle's writings were like a venerated school principal whose rules and practices become sacred to incoming principals, so much so that these rules and practice are not seen as open to change under any circumstances, even if the school is falling apart. His work, as interpreted by Arabic and Christian scholars, became sacred and part of the belief system of a form of philosophy called *medieval scholasticism* or *Aristotleanism*.

WHAT KNOWLEDGE IS OF MOST WORTH: THE PHILOSOPHIES OF PLATO AND ARISTOTLE

Aristotle's philosophy of promoting observation of nature through the senses was very different to that of his first teacher, Plato. Plato's philosophy was based on an anti-empirical coda that reasoned from the abstract or theoretical to the particular. Plato distained arithmetic as something performed by slaves and low workers and promoted geometry. He elevated geometry arguing that it was a form of pure knowledge, a claim followed also by Aristotle. Plato also distained any practical knowledge and promoted a form of systematic knowledge that was not backed by any relationship with practical usefulness. Living in a slave-based society the elite had time to ponder the abstract. A supporter of despotic and misogynistic Sparta, Plato argued that the science of the master was superior to the science of the maker, usually a slave in Greek city-states. You might already be beginning to recognize some aspects of Plato's philosophy in the separation of practical and abstract knowledge in today's schools.

Aristotle maintained Plato's knowledge elitism. He failed to acknowledge any contributions of his wife to his studies. He argued that slaves were necessary to support the work of thinkers but that they should not be part of the state. In *Politics* Aristotle's elitism is captured somewhat when he wrote:

> But with respect to citizens there is a doubt remaining, whether those only are truly so who are allowed to share in the government, or whether the mechanics also are to be considered as such? For if those who are not permitted to rule are to be reckoned among them, it is impossible that the virtue of all the citizens should be the same, for these also are citizens; and if none of them are admitted to be citizens, where shall they be ranked? For they are neither sojourners nor foreigners? Or shall we say that there will no inconvenience arise from their not being citizens, as they are neither slaves nor freedmen: for this is certainly true, that all those are not citizens who are necessary to the existence of a city, as boys are not citizens in the same manner that men are, for those are perfectly so, the others under some conditions; for they are citizens, though imperfect ones: for in former times among some people the mechanics were either slaves or foreigners, for which reason many of them are so now: and indeed the *best regulated states will not permit a mechanic to be a citizen*; but if it be allowed them, we cannot then attribute the virtue we have described to every citizen or freeman, but to those only who are disengaged from servile offices[2].

What is the argument that Aristotle making here about mechanics and citizenship?

This image is taken from the painting by Raffaelo Sanzio (1509) showing Plato on the left and Aristotle on the right. Note Aristotle holds one of his books, Ethics, in his hand. Other observers of this painting have noted that Aristotle is drawn with his hand directed towards the earth while Plato is pointing to the heavens. What could be the significance of such gestures?

Within the soul, Aristotle distinguished between reason and emotion with reason superior. Consistent with the elevation of thinkers as the producers of knowledge, Aristotle distinguished between three types of reasoning/knowledge: *practical*, an example of which was military practice; *theoretical* or speculative; and *productive* reasoning. Aristotle gave highest status to speculative reasoning and the theoretical knowledge that was the outcome of such reasoning, followed by practical reasoning with productive reasoning placing a poor third (see Box). There can be little doubt that Plato and Aristotle's elevation of the role of thinking over the role of doing in the construction of knowledge, contributed to stalling community recognition of the value of mechanical productive knowledge from areas such as metallurgy, smithing, farming, and printing in future European cultures where Platonic and Aristotleian thinking were held in high esteem. Additionally, Plato argued that social hierarchies were framed by God and therefore immutable. This philosophy fitted well with the emerging philosophies of the Christian church.

How Aristotle valued different knowledge fields

Aristotle's classification scheme for knowledge		
Theoretical	*Practical*	*Productive*
Knowledge for its own sake - *Highest Form*	Knowledge about personal and collective (polis) conduct	Knowledge and skills - tools for utility – *Lowest Form*
Examples: metaphysics – nature of reality, physics – natural sciences, mathematics	Examples: Ethics and politics	Examples: dentistry, stonemasonry, home economics, metallurgy, smithing

Aristotle was to have an even greater influence on European human thought than his mentor, perhaps because he was one of the first philosophers to propose a comprehensive system of knowledge including ethics, politics, logic, biological and physical knowledge, and metaphysics. But unlike Plato who accepted women to study at his academy, Aristotle believed women were inferior and he sought to present a scholarly basis for the general Greek acceptance of the inferiority of women[3].

He was born in Macedonia; a member of the aristocracy. At the age of about eighteen he went to study with Plato in his Academy in Athens. He only left the Academy after Plato's death in 347 BCE and traveled to Asia Minor where he conducted observations of the plants and animals of the island of Lesbos. By 343 BCE he was in Macedonia, tutor to Alexander, Prince of Macedonia. Aristotle's elitist philosophy could have been a factor in his encouragement of Alexander to eastern conquests. It does not seem to be known when Pythias of Assos married Aristotle but she predeceased him in 336 BCE. By 335 BCE Aristotle was back in Athens setting up his own school called the *Lyceum*, where he was most philosophically productive until his death in 322 BCE. His last year was quite stressful as first Alexander, and then the Athenian population, threatened his livelihood. Aristotle was a highly prolific author and it is thought that possibly only a third of his writings have been preserved. For the purposes of this examination, areas of significance include his arguments about reasoning, his use of teleology, and his explanatory framework for matter and nature. We will revisit his views on living things and on motion in a later chapter.

Aristotle teaching. An early Islamic portrayal taken from a book in the British library. Note the square portrayed as a tool used by Aristotle. Note also how different cultures are joined by the square. Speculate on some possible messages embedded in this image.

Reasoning and Logic

Reasoning can be described as organizing ideas to reach a conclusion. There are a number of different forms of reasoning that Aristotle and other philosophers examined and for which they worked hard to propose working structures.

Dialectical reasoning. In his texts, *Rhetoric I* and *II*, Aristotle describes the nature of dialectical reasoning. He describes dialectic as the art of using propositions to argue about philosophical problems that can be posed in the form of alternating questions similar to that found in Socratic dialogues. For example, say I asked you a question about sound. My question might be: is sound is caused by objects vibrating? You might say, "Yes, sound is caused that way because when I pluck a guitar string, I can see it vibrating and then I can hear the sound of that movement." To which

I might reply, "But if I hit the air, which is also an object, with my arm I can feel the vibration of the air but I cannot hear it." To which you might respond, "Perhaps sound depends on the type of vibration and our ability to hear different vibrations?" Note that my colleague and I are engaged in a dialogue with a specific structure associated with question posing and responding. In this example, we are also approaching the structure of a scientific argument and if we persisted we would likely be able to propose a conclusion upon which we could both agree. We are using dialectical reasoning as Aristotle proposed it.

Humans come to the study of science with many experiences and ideas already developed but not well organized or integrated for the discipline of science. As this example also illustrates, dialectical reasoning helps us to identify the important ideas and how they might be linked. What a pity that today it is a form of reasoning which seems to have so little traction in most science curricula.

There are some other forms of reasoning that can be assigned logical rules and which might be more familiar to you. Many logicians and philosophers interested in the logic of argument recognize four main types argument or reasoning: analogical, deductive, inductive, and abductive. It is likely that in your everyday life you have used these forms of argument without giving much thought to the fact.

Analogical reasoning. It seems to me that analogical reasoning is the type of reasoning familiar to most because we tend to use observations of our experiences, what statisticians call anecdotal evidence, to make a claim about a relationship between objects or processes when we say one thing is like another in some way. Analogical reasoning is also associated with inductive reasoning, as we will examine later.

Some people have used analogical reasoning to make an argument for a universe created by a supreme being. For example William Paley, an 18–19th century English cleric, argued that because the universe was like a clock there must have been a clockmaker. He began his argument by saying that humans, the collective "we," are not surprised when we experience a stone on the ground, perhaps by kicking it, but if we find a watch in the ground we would be surprised and not accept its presence. Paley asked why we should be so accepting of the stone and not of the watch. Paley described the complexity of the structures in living organisms arguing that such complexity suggested the grand design of a Creator, "The eye would be alone sufficient to support the conclusion which we draw from it as to the necessity of an intelligent Creator[4]." This argument is also a teleological one because Paley was arguing for a purpose or design for specific structures. Paley's ideas found new life in the early 21st century as arguments for *intelligent design* gained traction in educational contexts.

Of course, one of the problems with analogical reasoning is that people can argue your analogy is not very good or that alternative objects can equally map on to the target of your analogy. This is the strategy philosopher David Hume used to critique Paley's claim that the cosmos was like a machine. Hume asked why use a machine as your analogy and why not a living thing, which perhaps looks less well designed?

Deductive reasoning. It is possible to escape this conundrum if, instead of relying on evidence or personal experience, you make an argument for design based on premises. You could frame your argument in the following way:

> *Some things in nature are design-like.*
> *Design-like elements cannot be produced by unguided natural means.*
> *Therefore some things in nature are products of intentional design.*

This type of reasoning is called *deductive reasoning*. It consists of a specific structure also called *syllogism* (This specific syllogism is an example of *dialectic syllogism* because of the probability in the premises and the conclusion.). Its origin as a form of logic is associated with Aristotle and acolytes of his school. Aristotle's development of deductive reasoning was his strategy for addressing a paradox. Originally posed by Plato, the paradox is captured as a discussion between Socrates and Meno about the nature of virtue, which Plato uses to examine the nature of knowledge more generally. Plato argues that a learner cannot search for what he knows because there is no need to search. Nor for what he does not know because how does one know what to look for if one does not know? For example, if a learner already knows what virtue is, then there no need to learn it because it is known. But if the learner does not know what virtue is if she/he is given a definition of virtue he/she would not recognize it. Therefore, it is impossible to learn what virtue is. Plato solved this paradox by claiming that our souls existed in another realm where they knew everything but this knowing was forgotten during birth and learning was a process of recollecting or remembering.

Aristotle objected to this argument on the following grounds: asking how souls could exist before the body, the idea of hidden knowledge, which he said made no sense. He argued that the conundrum of learning could be resolved without Plato's strategy of souls and forgetting and suggested syllogism as a strategy for learning. Syllogistic reasoning consists of: a major premise, which includes a predicate term of the conclusion; a minor premise, the subject term; and a conclusion. According to Aristotle if the premises are true the conclusion must be true and recognizing the truth of the conclusion was learning!

An example of a syllogism is the following:

Major premise: All men are mortal.

This major premise consists of a subject, men, and a predicate, are mortal. From the Latin to proclaim or make known, the predicate is a comment or assertion about the subject and typically consists of a verb and objects or phrases governed by the verb.

Minor premise: Socrates is a man.

The minor premise contains the subject term of the Conclusion, in this case Socrates.

Conclusion: Therefore, Socrates is mortal.

The premises are *categorical propositions* and I have chosen a specific example for the minor premise but this does not need to be the case. The major premise is in the form of a general principle or theory that does not require facts or experience as a basis. It is said to be *a priori*, i.e., before the facts. From Rome onwards, this form of reasoning became the generally accepted strategy for presenting knowledge in Muslim (Arab) and Christian (Eastern and Western) cultures.

Question. Give yourself a minute or two to see if you identify possible limitations of this form of reasoning?

We can also break down the intelligent design syllogism shown previously:

Some things in nature are design-like. Major premise. Subject: some things in nature. Predicate: are design-like.
Design-like elements cannot be produced by unguided natural means. What is the subject term of the Conclusion here?
Therefore some things in nature are products of intentional design.

Note how this syllogism does not exactly follow the rules I laid out previously for syllogisms. Note also that we can also challenge the truth of the premises as they are presented, particularly the minor premise presented here that design-like elements cannot be produced by unguided nature. For example, sometimes creationists use the eye as an example of a complex structure that could not have developed without intelligent design. However, Richard Dawkins, a trenchant critic of intelligent design, in his book, *Climbing Mount Improbable*, takes the reader step by step through the evolution of the eye arguing for its evolution without an intelligent designer[5].

In some respects I have been less than fair to the complexity and depth of Aristotle's thinking because he recognized some of the limitations of deductive reasoning, which he worked to address in his numerous publications. However, in general this form of reasoning remained the keystone of his philosophy. So what were some of these limitations? You might have noted that the argument is somewhat circular because although the premises, especially the major premise, are presented often as universal statements, they are justified by the very conclusions that are drawn from their presentation. Also, the final statement is based on experience even though the original premise was a universal statement.

Inductive reasoning. The aim of Aristotelian science was to understand knowledge that was already known, addressing the question of "How do we understand things?" Part of Aristotle's genius was to develop a philosophy that linked together a way of constructing learning through deduction and recognizing and celebrating the explanations that can be sensed directly and inferred from experience. In his philosophy, he also described *induction*, a form of reasoning that takes us from the particular to the general rather than the general to the particular, which was the focus of deduction. But for Aristotle deduction was key to his philosophy and induction a minor sideshow.

However for completeness and because induction becomes important later in the history of Eurocentric science, here is a short introduction. Inductive reasoning works something like this:

I observe that Renee has a schedule and Barry plays the violin. These observations do not yield any commonalities, so I am unable to induce any general relationship between these two events or observations. For induction I need a common nature that can be related to a common predicate. But if I observe that Renee has a schedule and Barry has a schedule I note that I do have a common predicate. Can you identify what that is from my description? Then I note that DeShawn has a schedule also. All three have a common predicate: <u>they each have a schedule</u>. This seems a common predicate that is linked to a common nature of all these people: <u>they are students</u>. Thus I induce from a common characteristic, studentness, and a common behavior, the having of a schedule, a general statement about students: all students have a schedule.

Of course, from a philosophical perspective, and from an everyday perspective also, induction has its limitations. My most beloved example of the limitations of induction involves swans. Over hundreds of years people living in Europe had observed swans. All the swans they observed had white feathers. From this Europeans induced that all swans are white and that whiteness is a characteristic of all swans. This constitutes a generalization: all swans are white. However, when Europeans visited Australia for the first time they observed a bird that looked very like a swan but this bird had black feathers! Was it a swan? Perhaps you might have heard this problem framed slightly differently in science classrooms when students are reporting an experiment they were asked to conduct. A student writes, "My experiment *proved* that all matter in a chemical reactions is conserved." To which a teacher replies, "Your experiment cannot prove the Law of Conservation but it can *support* this Law." The teacher, whether they understand it or not, is making the claim that philosophers also recognized: inductive reasoning is based on probabilities not the certainties scholars associated with deductive reasoning.

As you become more familiar with inductive reasoning, you might note a relationship between inductive reasoning and some forms of investigation associated with scientific reasoning just as you might have noted such a relationship with deductive reasoning. Both forms of reasoning are considered central to reasoning and experimentation in Eurocentric science. The most famous example of induction from a more recent era with which I am familiar is the case of lung cancer. In 1950 the *British Medical Journal*[6] commented that the steady increase in recorded deaths from lung cancer was startling, rising in a fifteen-fold increase from 1922 to 1947 across England and Wales, a trend that had been observed in most Western countries. The question that was being asked was what could be causing this increase? Medical researchers began to look for an explanation. When researchers began to look closely at the available data from information obtained from patients, they identified what seemed to be two significant pieces of data: the persistence of cigarette smoking amongst patients and the increasing likelihood of lung cancer occurring as the level of cigarette smoking increased. These findings supported the proposal of a generalization that "cigarette smoking causes lung cancer." The generalization was induced creatively from recorded deaths due to cancer of the lung and from information about the level of cigarette smoking for specific individuals.

This example illustrates the other feature of inductive reasoning that I think is important but which is often ignored, which is that *induction is a creative act*. To induce a general relationship between specific instances requires creative thinking. The generalization does not logically flow from the specific instances and yet in representations of "the scientific method" in textbooks the generalization in the form of a hypothesis is often shown as logically emerging from observations. We are selling our students short if we persist in promoting this fabrication. We should be extolling the creativity of our students if they make that creative leap from observations to a generalization. Of course, the generalization that cigarette smoking causes lung cancer, was only the beginning of many, many studies using deductive and inductive reasoning that sought to investigate further the relationship between cigarette smoking and lung cancer first articulated in that generalization. Inductive reasoning was also the form of reasoning of interest to 16th century English philosopher and politician, Francis Bacon who has a major role in the version of Eurocentric science I am presenting to you.

Abductive reasoning. So far I have mentioned dialectical, analogical, deductive and inductive reasoning. Another form of reasoning called abductive reasoning, which some scholars argue was also implicit in Aristotle's writings and historically was subsumed under induction, was developed further by Charles Sanders Pierce in the 19th and early 20th centuries. Pierce was an astronomer, philosopher, and the founder of semiotics or the study of signs and their interpretation. He is associated with the philosophy of pragmatism and it is surprising, considering his scholarship, that today he is less well remembered than John Dewey, one of his students. Pierce claimed that abduction was the only way that new knowledge was constructed. He claimed:

> Abduction is the process of forming an explanatory hypothesis. It is the only logical operation which introduces any new idea; for induction does nothing but determine a value, and deduction merely evolves the necessary consequences of a pure hypothesis.[7]

Pierce argued that deduction was reasoning that started with a hypothesis, the falsity or truth of which had nothing to do with reasoning, that induction was the experimental testing of a theory. Therefore abduction with its process of proposing hypothesis that was the best explanation for the available data was the only form of reasoning that produced new knowledge. Abduction also takes into account what we already know about the world. We can think of abduction in the following way. We experience an event that may be a pleasant or disagreeable surprise and we try to identify what caused it. We can think of this as an anomaly, something that is unexpected. In order to explain the anomaly, we propose (abduce) a hypothesis.

Pierce's model for abduction. The difference between these forms of reasoning can be illustrated with our student example using the convention that Pierce proposed.

An Example to Illustrate the Difference Between Deduction, Induction, and Abduction

Deduction	Induction	Abduction
Rule: All students have a schedule *Case:* Renee is a student *Result:* Therefore, Renee has a schedule	*Case:* Renee is a student Barry is a student DeShawn is a student *Result:* Renee, Barry and DeShawn have schedules *Rule:* All students have a schedule	*Rule:* All students have a schedule *Result:* Renee, Barry, and DeShawn have schedules *Result* (*Hypothesis*): Renee, Barry, and DeShawn are students

These forms of reasoning or argument are often used in stories told about the development of ideas and theories in science. Abduction allows us to make claims for unexpected connections that can then be investigated further through the use of observation and experimentation associated with deduction and induction and that can be challenged through the application of dialectical reasoning. The example of induction that I presented to you, of the generalization about cigarette smoking causing lung cancer, could perhaps be presented as an example of abductive reasoning. What do you think?

Activity

What form of reasoning: dialectical, analogical, deductive, inductive, or abductive, is described in the following narratives? There might be more than one.

Story 1. Tycho Brahe, Danish imperial mathematician to the court of the Holy Roman Emperor, invested enormous amounts of time and energy compiling a remarkably

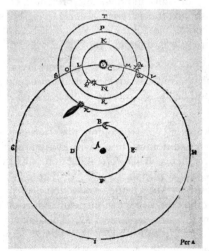

This is a representation of Tycho Brahe's universe. Can you identify the Sun? Can you identify the Earth? What about the moon or comets? Note that this model contains elements of a model of the universe where the Earth is the center of the universe (geocentric model) and a model where the Sun is the center (heliocentric model).

complete database of astronomical observations. On the island of Hveen he constructed a sumptuous observatory, Uraniborg, over which he ruled for many years. Along the wall of the observatory he constructed great quadrants for measuring celestial altitudes that brought the art of astronomical observation to the highest accuracy possible (all without the aid of a telescope). Brahe proposed a cosmology that consisted of the planets orbiting the sun and the whole system orbiting a centrally located Earth (See Figure).

Story 2. In the 1850s it was discovered that within a certain range of temperatures some gaseous chemical substances are only partially dissociated (eg. ammonium chloride [NH_4Cl] to ammonia [NH_3] and hydrogen chloride [HCl]) [The standard model at that time was that reactions went to completion so finding both ammonium chloride and ammonia was contrary to expectations.]. What does this paragraph mean? How do you understand the phrase, "reactions went to completion"?

Leopold Pfundler proposed two explanations for this phenomenon in 1857: either all molecules have undergone the same change or a fraction of all molecules have dissociated and the rest are completely bound. The first explanation did not account for experimental data but the second explanation was at odds with the idea that molecules of the same species were considered the same in every way.

Pfundler found it hard to explain how, at the same temperature, in a collection of apparently identical molecules there could be molecules that dissociated while others were unchanged. He adopted the theory of Rudolf Clausius (1857) that identical molecules can be in a different state of motion. He reasoned that when particles are moving and colliding and their kinetic energy is spread around a mean value related to temperature. So at any given moment at constant temperature and pressure some molecules are decomposing while others are formed by collisions. In a state of equilibrium within a certain period of time the same number of molecules are decomposing as are forming (Pfundler, 1867).

Story 3. Louis Pasteur (1822–1895), French biochemist, proposed a close relation between optical activity and life based on his discovery that one of two amyl alcohols (these are isomeric alcohols that share the formula $C_5H_{11}OH$) formed by the fermentation of sugar was optically active (rotated light) just like the sugar that was the starting material for the formation of amyl alcohol (See Dorothy Sayers "The Documents in the Case" for a story about the role of optical activity). This observation was unexpected because within the scientific community prior to Pasteur's observations the breakdown of sugar was thought to be a simple catalytic reaction yielding carbon dioxide (CO_2) and ethanol (C_2H_5OH). Pasteur argued that because optical activity was due to an unsymmetric arrangement of atoms the fundamental molecular arrangement of atoms must remain intact, for example, whatever made sugar optically active must remain intact in the amyl alcohol formed from fermentation of sugar.

Story 4. As a graduate student at Harvard in 1925, Cecilia Payne-Gaposchkin used M. N. Saha's theory, which combined quantum theory and statistical mechanics with a thermal equilibrium mixture of atoms, ions, and electrons, to propose that stellar atmospheres were composed primarily of hydrogen and helium. This was contrary to the accepted scientific wisdom of the time, which assumed that stars such as the sun were composed of the same elements as the earth, and in similar proportions. According to Peggy Kidwell[8] at that time the leading scientist in this field, Henry Norris Russell, on reading an advance version of Payne's thesis about the abundance of hydrogen and helium in stars responded that it was "clearly impossible that hydrogen should be a million times more abundant than the metals". Kidwell notes that although neither Payne's original draft nor any account of her reaction to Russell's comments have survived, when she submitted a paper on solar abundance of hydrogen and helium she commented that her calculated abundance for helium was "improbably high" and "almost certainly not real"[9]. Even though she was convinced by her supervisor, Harlow Shapely, to moderate her claims in subsequent iterations of her thesis, her work formed the basis of the modern theory that heavier elements are synthesized from hydrogen and helium in stars.

Teleology and the Idea of Causes

I suppose most of you would have heard the joke:

> *Question: Why did the chicken cross the road?*
> *Answer: To get to the other side!*

This 'joke' is a simple example of teleology where the nature of an object is related to its purpose or final goal. Remember that Paley's analogical argument for God, the Creator and Designer, is also an example of teleology because he was arguing that specific structures were designed for a specific purpose. Teleology comes from the Greek *teleos* meaning purpose or end and *–ology*, an area of learning.

Teleology is one of the other areas of thought associated with Aristotle that continues to be an area of debate in science education and biology. Aristotle was a biologist. He made careful observations of many environments and these observations really encouraged him to try and identify functions that were unique to living things. This led him to develop further the idea of causes and to propose final purpose-driven causes along with material, formal, and efficient causes that were already familiar to scholars of his era. For example, Aristotle argued that all seeds use water and soil for growth but it was the teleos of a specific type of seed, like an apple seed, that caused it to grow into an apple tree rather than a yew or a pine or a cycad. Associated with his teleology, Aristotle's four causes for which purpose was the final cause can be described in the following way:

Material Cause - What something is made of, that is, material offering possibilities for making an object, for example, a lump of bronze for making a sword.

Formal Cause - An idea or image (the form) according to which it would be fashioned, for example, the shape of the sword.

Efficient Cause - The primary source of change or rest, agent of change for which the bronze undergoes, the artistry required or the agent that makes it.

Final Cause - The purpose (teleos). A sword is made to be a weapon.

For Aristotle the final cause was the most important because he argued that all things try to move from potentiality to actuality to perfection, which is achieved by motion and change towards the final cause or purpose. Stones fall to earth when dropped because they are material things of the earth and strive for the earth, the lowest and resting point. Flames are of fire and air and strive upwards for the heavens. Objects seek their position according to their nature. Natural objects possess their own teleos. Aristotle's ideas and philosophy was based on his observations of nature where he noted that the natural world seemed organized in a purposeful and complex way. As I mentioned previously, unlike his mentor Plato, Aristotle valued the role observations and from his many observations he developed explanations for these observations and more broadly for why things exist or cease to exist. Such questions are not restricted to Aristotle and have been the focus of humans' thinking probably since humans began taking note of their environment. Aristotle is recognized as having formalized his thinking into these four causes, of which the final cause, the purpose, provided the purpose for structure.

Generally, teleology is considered a "bad thing" in science education because most accepted scientific explanations require mechanistic thinking. We will examine why mechanistic thinking is associated with Eurocentric science, the form of knowledge we think of as science, in more detail in a later chapter. Because of its association with *intelligent design* and *creationism* scholars and educators place great emphasis on identifying "misconceptions" associated with teleological analogical reasoning. In evolutionary biology, there is a tendency to argue the need to explain or answer the "why" question mechanistically or functionally but not teleologically as a final or purposeful cause. Teleological explanations are typically applied to individual organisms removing any need for the explainers to deal with variation within a population, which is a central element of evolutionary theory, while they assign control of change to an outside agent that could be nature, a creator, or something else. From a teleological perspective in evolution, nature selects individuals that are in need of change. However, this is not how evolution is explained in evolutionary biology where natural selection provides a *mechanism* to explain the evolutionary process. First articulated by Charles Darwin (1809–1882), natural selection is based on two assumptions: 1) variation amongst individuals within a population and 2) for survival and reproductive vigor some variations are more advantageous than others. Sandwiched between the mechanistic explanation of natural selection and the teleology of purpose-driven individual survival, we find Lamarckian[10] species-specific adaptation through acquired characteristics over time, which was an early attempt to explain changes in organisms through evolution. Many studies have been conducted in education to examine how children and adults develop and apply teleological explanations.

Activity

Can you identify which of the following are examples of teleology, mechanistic natural selection, Lamarckian explanations, or creationism[11].

1. How do you explain the fact that some bacterial infections are now resistant to the antibiotics that were developed to treat them?

a. As a result of mutation, there is a great deal of variation within a bacterial population. Those strong enough to survive the initial antibiotic treatment will reproduce more, and resistance will become more prominent in the population.

b. Initially, bacterial strains were caught off-guard by antibiotics. Then, they began using more of their natural defences to resist antibiotic treatments. Now, as a result, current generations of bacteria have acquired resistance to antibiotics.

c. The bacteria's goal is survival. To ensure survival of the species, resistance to antibiotics was needed. Consequently, bacterial populations have mutated to obtain more and more resistance over the years.

d. Bacteria were created to be antibiotic-resistant.

2. If their distant ancestors could only achieve speeds between 20 and 30 miles per hour, how do you explain the ability of modern cheetahs to run at speeds in excess of 60 miles per hour for short periods of time?

a. As the cheetahs used their legs more and more to chase prey, they developed strong sprinting muscles. As a result, their offspring inherited the ability to run at high speeds.

b. The cheetahs had to adapt to capture fast-moving prey. Because speed was needed for survival, later generations developed streamlined, muscular bodies.

c. There were a variety of body types in the original cheetah population. Individuals possessing the musculature necessary for short bursts of speed may have been better equipped to survive and reproduce.

d. Cheetahs and their prey were created to run at high speeds.

3. When it was first developed to treat HIV infection, the drug AZT was very effective at decreasing viral levels in the blood. However, the effect was only temporary, and HIV levels eventually became elevated again. How do you explain this?

a. The virus was created with a mechanism to resist pharmacological treatment.

b. The virus gains resistance as it is continuously exposed to AZT. During the asymptomatic phase of infection, the virus will reproduce, and subsequent generations of viruses will inherit the resistance.

c. As the virus mutates during the asymptomatic phase of the infection, a variety of viral antigens are produced. Viruses bearing antigens unrecognizable by the host's immune system will propagate rapidly.

d. To survive, the virus needs to resist the effects of the drug. During the prolonged, asymptomatic phase of infection, the virus mutates to meet its needs.

This activity might leave you with the idea that it is pretty easy to differentiate between these different forms of explanations for various characteristics however, the picture is more complex than most educators will admit and these examples suggest. For example Ernst Mayr, probably one of the most thoughtful and best-known biologists of the 20th century, acknowledged that, from Aristotle onwards, thinkers "have been challenged by the apparent contradiction between a mechanistic interpretation of natural processes and the seemingly purposive sequence of events in organic growth, in reproduction and in animal behavior.[12]" How are the essentials of what it means to be living explained by physiochemical manifestations? In the field of agent-based models in biology, outcomes cannot be precisely predicted. On the other side of the coin, there are fields of biology where the outcomes can be predicted for a population but not for an individual organism (predicting the sex of a prospective new-born comes to mind). The agency of animals and plants continues to be a focus of study.

Aristotle's Universe

Apart from his arguments about reasoning and causes, Aristotle was a deep observer of the universe arguing that it should be observed in its natural state. According to Aristotle, an external observer would note that things on the Earth behaved differently from things in the Heavens [a word that has its origins in Northern European languages but works for this sentence]. For example, the heavens did not fall down or rise but things on the Earth did. Aristotle built on the work of previous philosophers and on observations he made to develop a well-integrated set of knowledges about the Earth and the Heavens.

Activity

Look back over the timeline from earlier in the chapter and see if you can identify the philosopher associated with pulling together the four elements of the earth into a coherent system. Have you found who it is? He lived before Aristotle.

The earth. Aristotle accepted the argument of earlier philosophers that four elements were found on the Earth: fire, earth, air, and water. However, Aristotle's take on these elements was somewhat different because, rather than incorporating emotions into this elemental classification, he used phenomena that could be experienced: wet and dry. Each element had its natural place: earth at the center of the universe, then water, air and fire. When elements were not in their natural place, they had a natural motion towards their rightful place that required no external cause. Since the Earth was the natural place in the center of the Universe where all heavy things accumulated, heavy bodies fell to their natural place, the center of the Earth. The Earth was surrounded by water providing a justification for the oceans around the earth. Water and earth, heavy elements, possessed "gravity" and fell to the center of the Earth. Observations of air bubbles in water and flames rising supported Aristotle's argument that light elements, air and fire, possessed "levity" and their nature position was to rise up to either the air layer which surrounded water or the fire layer which surrounded the air layer.

The heavens. A fifth element, *aether*, made up the Heavens. The Heavens were a vast region outside earth, water, air and fire, moving circularly. It was this circular motion that indicated to Aristotle the Heavens were composed of different material from the terrestrial elements and this is what Aristotle called aether. The natural motion of aether was circular. The visible heavenly bodies such as the moon, sun and five planets (those visible to the naked eye) were carried round the earth in invisible transparent spheres (helped to explain the movement of celestial bodies)[13]. It is important to realize that according to Aristotle, the difference in the elements between the Earth and the Heavens meant that these two parts of the universe were completely different. What implications might this have for people thinking about how the Earth and the Heavens worked?

How we understand things.   According to Aristotle the nature of a thing is dependent on its essence. The fundamental category is *substance* which, if applied to a species or universal form rather than an individual, can be recognized as the essence of that form. Matter and form must be consistent to make a substance. For example, a cup (form = drinking) could not be composed of sand (matter). Matter and form established substance (the essence of universals).

Motion.   Motion was a characteristic of being on Earth because of the elements - earth, water, air and fire – possessed by substances that caused them to move up and down and be changed from one form to the other (that was experienced). The Heavens were immune from such change because they were composed of one substance – aether.

On Earth, motion consisted of two types: *natural*, drawn from the nature of the body, and *violent*, motion from outside the body. These motions could be observed when an object was pushed or thrown. Natural motion could be divided into a further two forms: *up/down* and *circular*. For example, light objects rose because of their air-like essence and heavy objects fell because they had earth-like essence. All objects undergoing violent motion were moved by something other than themselves. If something was moving and the source of the motion was not part of the essence or structure of the object then there must be something else that moved it. Other philosophers immediately identified a problem. What about projectile motion? For example, when a stone is thrown, what mover is responsible for an object's motion after the stone has left the thrower's hand? Aristotle replied something like this. "The original mover gives the power of being the mover to the air or water or something else of the kind naturally adapted for imparting and undergoing motion." In simple terms, the thrower moves the air, which then continues to move the object.

Activity

Draw an image of a projectile moving through the air according to Aristotle's theory.

Causation.   We have already looked at cause as much as we need to for now but it is useful to recognize that Aristotle's causes were fundamental theoretical components of his thinking. The causes are presented here again. Material, because of what it is made of. For example, why does a chair float? Because it is made of wood, which contains elements of air as well as earth. Efficient, because something is done to it. For example, why does an object move? Because something else (an agent) collided with it causing it to move. Formal, because of its nature. For example, how does one know that an ash is a tree? We know that it is a tree from its general form. Aristotle used this concept of general form to propose a classification system. Final, properties or behavior of something because of its purpose. Why does a sapling become a tree? Because its purpose is to be a tree.

Activity

Consistent with his focus on using observation to develop his theory of everything, Aristotle's writings such as those associated with the book, *The History of Animals*, indicate that he or his disciples also conducted experiments[14]. Read the following text taken from this book. Note how much Aristotle is able to tell us about the physiology of embryonic development from these observations, especially with respect to the role of the white and the yolk in that development. Use this description to develop a timeline for the embryonic development of a chick.

Generation from the egg proceeds in an identical manner with all birds, but the full periods from conception to birth differ, *as has been said*. With the common hen after three days and three nights there is the first indication of the embryo; with larger birds the interval being longer, with smaller birds shorter. Meanwhile the yolk comes into being, rising towards the sharp end, where the primal element of the egg is situated, and where the egg gets hatched; and the heart appears, like a speck of blood, in the white of the egg. This point beats and moves as though endowed with life, and from it two vein-ducts with blood in them trend in a convoluted course (as the egg substance goes on growing, towards each of the two circumjacent integuments); and a membrane carrying bloody fibres now envelops the yolk, leading off from the vein-ducts. A little afterwards the body is differentiated, at first very small and white. The head is clearly distinguished, and in it the eyes, swollen out to a great extent. This condition of the eyes late on for a good while, as it is only by degrees that they diminish in size and collapse. At the outset the under portion of the body appears insignificant in comparison with the upper portion. Of the two ducts that lead from the heart, the one proceeds towards the circumjacent integument, and the other, like a navel-string, towards the yolk. The life-element of the chick is in the white of the egg, and the nutriment comes through the navel-string out of the yolk.

When the egg is now **ten days** old the chick and all its parts are distinctly visible. The head is still larger than the rest of its body, and the eyes larger than the head, but still devoid of vision. The eyes, if removed about this time, are found to be larger than beans, and black; if the cuticle be peeled off them there is a white and cold liquid inside, quite glittering in the sunlight, but there is no hard substance whatsoever. Such is the condition of the head and eyes. At this time also the larger internal organs are visible, as also the stomach and the arrangement of the viscera; and veins that seem to proceed from the heart are now close to the navel. From the navel there stretch a pair of veins; one towards the membrane that envelops the yolk (and, by the way, the yolk is now liquid, or more so than is normal), and the other towards that membrane which envelops collectively the membrane wherein the chick lies, the membrane of the yolk, and the intervening liquid. (For, as the chick grows, little by little one part of the yolk goes upward, and another part downward, and the white liquid is between them; and the white of the egg is underneath the lower part of the yolk, as

---

it was at the outset.) On the tenth day the white is at the extreme outer surface, reduced in amount, glutinous, firm in substance, and sallow in colour. The disposition of the several constituent parts is as follows. First and outermost comes the membrane of the egg, not that of the shell, but underneath it. Inside this membrane is a white liquid; then comes the chick, and a membrane round about it, separating it off so as to keep the chick free from the liquid; next after the chick comes the yolk, into which one of the two veins was described as leading, the other one leading into the enveloping white substance. (A membrane with a liquid resembling serum envelops the entire structure. Then comes another membrane right round the embryo, as has been described, separating it off against the liquid. Underneath this comes the yolk, enveloped in another membrane (into which yolk proceeds the navel-string that leads from the heart and the big vein), so as to keep the embryo free of both liquids.) About the twentieth day, if you open the egg and touch the chick, it moves inside and chirps; and it is already coming to be covered with down, when, after the twentieth day is past, the chick begins to break the shell.

Think about whether this is an account of an experiment? Reflect on how you understand the structure of an experiment. I think it is helpful at this point to think of an experiment as an intervention into nature. What do you think? Did Aristotle wait for things to happen or initiate changes so that he was able to make very specific observations? Would this example fit your definition of an experiment? Why or why not?

Activity

The primacy Aristotle claimed for observations also came through in his discussion of bees and the challenges they presented him for explaining their reproductive strategies. In *Generation of Animals* (Book 3) he (or his followers) wrote:

Such appears to be the truth about the generation of bees, judging from theory and from what are believed to be the facts about them; the facts, however, have not yet been sufficiently grasped; if ever they are, then credit must be given rather to observation than to theories, and to theories only if what they affirm agrees with the observed facts.

What is the argument he is trying to make here?

Living things. According to Aristotle, there were fundamental differences between objects and living things based on the souls that each possessed. These souls existed in a hierarchy from vegetable to animal to human. As I have mentioned previously, for Aristotle it was reason that separated humans from all other living things on earth. All living things had a proper place in the universe that was set and unchanging so these positions were eternal and existed because of the different essences each possessed.

Some of Aristotle's writings suggest that he placed great value on the use of observation to make new knowledge. However, his emphasis also on the importance of reasoning, especially deductive reasoning, suggests a tension that his followers resolved in later generations by focusing on the reasoning component of his philosophy and ignoring the role he attributed to observation. The focus on reasoning ushered in a philosophy and worldview based on the works of Aristotle as interpreted by Arab and Roman scholars called *Aristotelianism*, which became a major philosophy of thought and way of life for European cultures as they emerged after the demise of the Roman Empire but that is for the next chapter.

NOTES

[1] Teresi, D. (2002). *Lost discoveries: The ancient roots of modern science from the Babylonians to the Maya*. New York: Simon & Schuster.

[2] Aristotle. (1943). *Aristotle's politics* (B. Jowett, Trans.). New York: The Modern library.

[3] Whaley, L. A. (2003). *Women's history as scientists: A guide to the debates*. Santa Barbara, CA: ABC-CLIO.

[4] Paley, W. (1850/1802). *Natural theology*. Landisville, PA: Coachwich Publications. p. 44.

[5] Dawkins, R. (1996). *Climbing mount improbable*. New York: Norton (Chap. 5).

[6] BMJ. (1950). Cigarettes and cancer. *British Medical Journal*, 2, 767–768.

[7] Peirce, C. S. (1958). *The collected works of Charles Sanders Peirce* (Vol. 5, p. 171). Harvard, MA: Harvard University Press.

[8] Kidwell, P. (1984). An historical introduction to 'The dyer's hand'. In K. Haramundanis (Ed.), *Cecilia Payne-Gaposchkin: An autobiography and other recollections* (pp. 11–37). Cambridge: Cambridge University Press. p. 19.

[9] Kidwell, P. (1984). p. 20.

[10] Named after Jean-Baptiste Lamarck (1744-1829), French biologist. Although Lamarck's evolutionary theories are the focus of criticism in biology textbooks today, Darwin acknowledged how Lamarck's law-based approach to explaining change over time in the organic and inorganic world acclimated he and his colleagues to the application of law-based rather than miraculous explanations for the diversity observed in living things.

[11] Stover, S. K., & Mabry, M. (2007). Influences of teleological and Lamarckian thinking on student understanding of natural selection. *Journal of College Biology Teaching*, 33(1), 11–18. Examples taken from pages 14–15.

[12] Mayr, E. (1961). Cause and effect in biology. *Science*, 134, 1501–1506. p. 1503.

[13] Tyco Brahe's model of the heavens retains some of the features of Aristotle's heavens (Look back at the diagram).

[14] Aristotle. (1910). *Historia Animalium (The history of animals)*. Book 6 (D'Arcy Wentworth Thompson, Trans.). Oxford: Clarendon Press. Retrieved from June 18, 2009, from http://etext.lib.virginia.edu/ modeng/modengA.browse.html

WARRING COSMOLOGIES AND THE EMERGENCE OF EUROCENTRIC SCIENCE

In the previous chapter I said a lot about the arguments Aristotle made about two issues: first, the construction of new knowledge through reason and second, the nature of reality and the role of our senses in understanding that nature. Aristotle and his followers accepted that there was an external objective world that was separate from our consciousness, that we could perceive reality but not create it and for each of us that perception was unique. They accepted that axioms used in deductive reasoning were self-evident fundamental principles that did not need proof and that knowledge came from experience-based reasoning, which for all living things was unique to humans. Consistent with most Greek philosophers, Aristotle believed and argued that matter was continuous. This put him at odds with philosophers called *atomists*, which included both Democritus (usually the only atomistic philosopher presented in chemistry textbooks with the implication that he came up with the idea of atoms when we know from the previous chapter this is a myth) who Aristotle critiques in his writings, and Epicurus, a follower of Democritus.

Only fragments of Epicurus' writings exist today and much of what we know about his philosophy has come to us through the actions of supporters. Like Aristotle, he established his own school called *The Garden* in his house and garden where he admitted women and slaves as a matter of course. A practice very different from those of Aristotle who, as we discussed previously, believed that slaves and women lacked the inherent characteristics, such as reasoning ability, possessed by Greek citizens. The features of Epicurus' philosophy that are useful in this context include his argument that the only things that exist are matter and the void. Atoms make up everything by falling into space (the void). These atoms are indivisible. They are also eternal and come in different shapes and sizes so the universe also has to be unlimited. Of course, saying that everything was made up of atoms and the void could lead to accusations of atheism, one of the criticisms leveled at Epicurus. He in turn argued that he was not against gods it was just that his gods were happy and not constantly looking for fault. He argued further that we can trust our senses when properly used and we do not need to validate them against reason. He put great store by the use of reflection for self-knowledge and even when he was dying was able to look positively on his life.

Although there was debate between the philosophers that thought matter was continuous, like Aristotle, and those that thought it was discrete (the atomists), philosophers of the continuous persuasion were more acceptable to other emerging movements, such as Christianity. So the writings of Aristotle, as interpreted and expanded by Arabic and Christian scholars, became accepted in many fields of thought as the truth. One other philosopher scientist needs to be mentioned because his writings in medicine also became the accepted dogma of centuries across European, Byzantine, and Islamic cultures. Galen (about 129 – about 200 CE) was born in Pergamon in what is modern day Turkey. He was a Roman physician and surgeon of Greek origin, originally serving as a surgeon to the gladiators in Pergamon, who became physician to Roman Emperor Marcus Aurelius. More than 1800 years ago Galen brought together in his copious writings the medical philosophies of dogmatism and empiricism (mentioned in Chapter 1), accepting the features of both of which he approved and establishing a philosophy and body of medical and anatomical knowledge that would be deified for the next fifteen hundred years.

GALEN'S OBSERVATIONS

Galen conducted experiments including severing the spinal cord of a monkey at various points, showing that powers of motion and sense were destroyed in parts below each successive incision. He also described a series of experiments showing that in a living animal urine is produced in the kidneys and flows in an irreversible stream down to ureters and into the bladder (This was at odds with an accepted fact of the time that urine was formed in the bladder). Galen argued that after digestion in the intestines, liquid food was transferred to the liver where it was imbued with the natural spirits. The resultant compound was the blood that was then distributed to all parts of the body via the ebb and flow of the veins. Galen's model organism of choice was the Barbary monkey. Roman law banned dissections being conducted on human beings although it seems likely that Galen's experience as surgeon to gladiators afforded him some access to human anatomy, which he would not have had otherwise.

Galen's studies obviously contributed to the development of anatomy, physiology, and medicine up to that time and he was concerned that his thoughts be recorded, as he wanted them. So hundreds, possibly thousands, of scribes were employed to turn his thoughts and observations into texts. Such a plethora of texts were established that they served to stifle further development in these disciplines, especially in Europe and Byzantium, well into early modern times, about the time when we might say Eurocentric science began to constitute a recognizable area of study. Also, future religions such as Christianity and Islam either had religious restrictions on dissections or banned them outright making it difficult for atomists to publish their work for the next thousand or more years.

Galen's production was prodigious but his influence on European thought was minor when compared with the influence of Aristotle. I think this can be attributed to the logical consistency of Aristotle's philosophy even though over time the contradictions and limitations of some of his claims became more obvious. Of course, we also should not forget that a rich folk or indigenous tradition existed in European communities and also in those communities it became incorporated into classical natural philosophy which is interesting considering the distain of such philosophy for applied knowledge.

ARISTOTELIANISM AS A WORLDVIEW IN MEDIEVAL EUROPE

I would like to begin this section with a very short summary of the history of part of Asia, Europe, and Africa after the relocation and disintegration of the Roman Empire. In 330 CE, Constantine the Great, the first Christian Emperor of Rome, moved his capital from Rome to the city of Byzantium (then called Byzantion) renaming the city Constantinople. Christianity became the state religion. Over time, sections of the empire came under attack, to the west by tribes from Northern Europe and to the east by Persian and Arabic armies.

As we explore the development of Eurocentric science one person of note to this history is Augustine of Hippo, also called Saint Augustine (354–430 CE). He is counted as one of the most significant figures in the emergence of Latinized Christianity. Born a Berber in what is now Algeria, his father was pagan and his mother Christian. He converted to Christianity in 386 CE and was a teacher of some note. His complaints about students not being focused sound as though they could have been made on the 21st century rather than the 4th! He argued that all humans had the capacity to learn and understand nature, even if they were not Christian. However, it was equally important that Christians be able to hold their own as scholars. Also, he argued that the Bible should not be interpreted literally, if our knowledge from science and our reason contradicted biblical text. He has been identified as one of the major scholars responsible for merging classical Greek philosophical traditions and Judeo-Christian traditions[1].

In the period from 500 CE onwards, the Byzantine Emperors retained control of a vast empire that included North Africa and Egypt. However, by the seventh century these provinces had been annexed by Islamic states as the Islamic empires expanded across Northern Africa into the Iberian Peninsula where the countries of Spain and Portugal are now located. From the 9th to the 13th century the Byzantine Empire was able to wrest back from Islamic forces some of their territories in the Mediterranean. Greek became the language of state and church.

In 1204, armies of the 4th Crusade from Latin Europe invaded Constantinople and, although their occupation was short-lived, it ushered in a period of fragmentation of the Byzantine Empire. Ironically the Crusades, a set of religiously sanctioned military campaigns, began in late 11th century after requests from the Byzantine Empire for help resisting incursions from Muslim Turks into Anatolia, a region of the Empire. Crusades were waged against any group that was not Catholic Christian, but mainly against Muslims. In the 15th century, Ottoman Turks finally invaded and took Constantinople, ending Christian control of the region, as Islam became the major religion.

During the same period, Europe was undergoing a series of upheavals as groups within and outside the former Roman Empire migrated throughout Europe jockeying for power and for land. This period is called the Middle Ages by historians and is divided into early, middle and late periods. The Middle Ages are also known as the Islamic Golden Age as Islam became the dominant religion across Mesopotamia and other parts of the Middle East spreading into Northern Africa and then on into the Iberian Peninsula in Europe. Arabic scholars were engaged in developing systematic knowledge associated with the study of Nature.

One image of North Africa, East Mediterranean, and Europe about 1430.

Arabic scholars also translated into Latin and Arabic the works of Greek philosophers, conducted experiments and observations, and developed commentaries that incorporated both. In cases where their observations were at odds with that found in classic texts, Arabic scholars edited the texts adding the more accurate observations[2]. For much of Europe the Catholic Church, which used Latin as a universal language of communication and instruction, was a major unifying cultural influence. Some of the most famous universities were established in Europe in the 11th and 12th century including the University of Bologna (1088), University of Paris (1150), University of Oxford (1167) and University of Padua (1222). These universities were really guilds, originally established to address the need for professional clergy and, like guilds they were able to decide who could gain admission as a teacher or pupil. Women were one group that was excluded from participation.

For Europe, the 12th and 13th centuries have been called The Age of Invention as tools such as spectacles, cannon, well technology and agricultural practices were developed and tools such as gunpowder, compass, and astrolabe were introduced from China and the Middle East to Europe.

However, the 14th century was a period of strife as countries and regions as widely dispersed as China, Western Europe, and North Africa, succumbed to the Plague or Black Death and many countries at the same time were beset with famine after famine. The plague seems to have emerged from Central Asia, jumping animals to become also a disease of humans by some time in the 13th or early 14th century. People had no idea what caused the plague, which left communities completely overwhelmed by the disaster. In some cities, eighty percent of the population died. Outsider groups, such as Jews, become the focus of community outrage as people with no explanation for this pestilence laid the blame on the Jewish community. In 1215, Pope Innocent III enacted a requirement that all Jews wear a yellow round badge. The following century the requirement was extended to other groups, such as Muslims and prostitutes. Even if members of these groups could not be identified by their behavior, they were readily identifiable in European communities where this practice was supported and terrible atrocities were enacted on them. If there is an upside associated with the Plague, it is that the severe reduction of the population created an environment that placed skilled workers in a strong bargaining position. In some countries, the surviving skilled workers were able to negotiate better conditions for themselves and their families and, in the process become the vanguard of a middle class. Also at this time, strong country identities such as France, England, Portugal, and Aragon and Castile in Spain, began to emerge.

Our main interest is on the emergence of Eurocentric science, so we need now to examine the worldview or cosmology that had taken hold of Europe as these developments were taking place.

WHAT IS A WORLDVIEW?

Activity

Look carefully at the two images on the next page. What do these images suggest to you about how the two scholars that constructed them thought about how the world functioned and the questions they could ask of that world?

This image of the Universe comes from Cosmographia by Petrus Apianus (1539). Where is the Earth? What else can you identify?

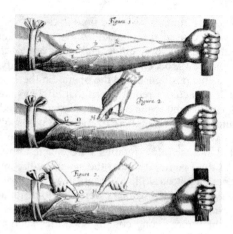

This image comes from the work of William Harvey, a 17ᵗʰ century experimental philosopher.

For me, these images provide insight into two different worldviews. *Worldview* describes our culturally dependent fundamental beliefs about how the world works. Our worldview predisposes us to expect the world and each other to act in specific ways. What does Harvey's image tell us about his expectations about how the world and the living things in it behave? What thinking forms the basis of the assertions he is making? In what type of universe does Petrus Apianus live? How are their visions of the world similar and different? These questions we will explore further in the following sections of this chapter.

Our worldview is our description of the world that shapes and guides our exploration, understanding, and explanations of the world around us including all the stuff. Have you thought of what makes up your worldview? One aspect of worldview is associated with how we understand what is real, with how we understand reality.

Activity

Visit the site: http://about-the-web.com/images/reality_wheel.gif. What vision of reality is implicit in this "reality wheel"? How does this image compare and contrast with your image of what is real and reality?

How each of us understands the nature of what is real is part of our *ontology*, which can be described as our understanding of the nature of being and reality. From the Greek *ontos* understood as *being* and *–logy* for *field of knowledge or discipline*, ontology addresses questions about the nature of reality and existence. The term ontology is associated with post-classical Latin. Its emergence in 17ᵗʰ century England is interesting and I hypothesize it could have been created to communicate to readers a break with terms of the past, such as *metaphysics*, which were associated with Aristotelianism. Students of Aristotle coined the term, *metaphysica* (metaphysics), for his writings that came after physics, which included his attempts to address questions of being, and at a later date became associated with ontology.

As far as I know, the question of what is real with respect to the universe is a question that all humans have asked at some stage. Questions that we answer within our ontology include: What is real? What is the nature of the universe? What metaphors do we use to describe our world and our functioning within it? The debate about the nature of *facts*, so central to the nature of Eurocentric science, is also central to ontology. Aristotle and Plato's attempts to identify essential aspects of all material in the universe and to categorize these aspects were attempts to develop an ontology. The term, ontology, is relatively recent and according to the Oxford English Dictionary was first published in English by Gideon Harvey (1640–1700), no relative of the William Harvey with whom you may be more familiar, in his book, *Archelogia Philosophica Nova*, published in 1663 in which he wrote, "Metaphysics. Is called also the first Philosophy, from its nearest approximation to Philosophy, its most proper Denomination is *Ontology*, or a Discourse of a Being."[3]

Born in Holland, Gideon Harvey practiced medicine in England. He was an interesting character who was reported as having a rather inflated opinion of his own capabilities while being quick to criticize others[4]. He was a physician who wrote a number of books for the public about aspects of medicine. *Archelogia Philosophica Nova* was his first book. He was also critical of atomists like William Harvey who he felt did not follow the first dictate of Hippocrates, "first do no harm."

What about ourselves? Our differentiation between self and non-self is another aspect of ontology because it speaks to the identity that we forge for ourselves, our 'real' self according to each of us, and also how others attempt to impose another vision of identity on each of us and how we respond to that attempted imposition. We also apply separation of self and non-self to other living and inanimate objects. What is the relationship between the knower and the known? You might also think about these questions. How do you think about Nature? Is it something over which you seek mastery? Do you revere it for its beauty? Do you think that humans are inter-connected with Nature? How does what you say you think, affect the way you behave?

As we understand it today in a country like the United States, the concept of the individual and individuality emerged in the 16th century as the work of skeptics, such as Sextus Empiricus (160–210 CE), were translated into Latin. For the first time, such writings became available to philosophers and natural philosophers such as Galileo Galilei (1564–1642), John Locke (1632–1704), René Descartes (1596–1650), and Robert Boyle (1627–1691). These writings influenced scholars' thinking about belief and reason and the role of atoms or corpuscles in the formation of the universe and in human behavior and emotion. Sextus Empiricus also preserved quotes from other classical philosophers in his writings. He argued there was no such thing as true belief and that humans could live without belief and act on habit. He argued also that one could not accept something was true, which is a belief, on the basis of reason. In contrast to Aristotle who argued that matter was continuous, Sextus Empiricus supported the arguments of the atomists such as Democritus who argued that all that was real were atoms and the void so all our understanding should be framed in those terms. One of the famous quotes from Sextus Empiricus evokes Democritus:

Democritus sometimes does away with what appears to the senses, and says that none of these appears according to truth but only according to opinion: the truth in real things is that there are atoms and void. 'By convention sweet', he says, 'by convention bitter, by convention hot, by convention cold, by convention colour: but in reality atoms and void.[5]'

In this quote Democritus seems to be arguing that the only reality consists of atoms and the void. All else is based on societal conventions and opinions. Even our senses, by which Aristotle set so much store, cannot be relied upon to give us truthful information because our observations are always influenced by existing belief.

Question. What role do you think our senses play in supporting us to develop a knowledge of the world? Can our senses be trusted?

Some early experimental philosophers that we will examine in the following chapters answered the question of whether our senses could be trusted with a resounding, "Yes!" Note also how different theories about matter, that is, whether matter is discrete or continuous, have implications for how reality is constructed within that theoretical perspective.

There are two other areas of knowledge that are useful to consider as part of a worldview: epistemology and axiology, both terms came into English use after ontology. *Epistemology* is our understanding of how we come to know and the nature of knowledge. I have mentioned in previous chapters that the early debate between Plato and Aristotle about the role of universal forms in the construction of new knowledge was both ontological and epistemological: as was the debate between Aristotle and the atomists about the essence of objects. The nature of explanations, the form of reasoning that should be valued, and the attribution of causation are claims that hold a central place in theories of how knowledge is constructed. One of the central epistemological debates in the 16th and 17th century associated with the emergence of Eurocentric science was about which form of reasoning, induction or deduction, best supported the emergence of new knowledge.

Axiology is related to the nature of values and the values we each hold and the ethics to which we ascribe. For example, questions such as was Fritz Haber right to develop chemical warfare in World War I or how should scientists make use of animal models in research, ask for an ethical response. Perhaps one of the most complex areas in understanding worldview is associated with ontology and axiology and the interaction between religion and science.

Even today, this interaction is a complex one as indicated by a study from the Pew Research Center[6]. According to the Center, the United States is the most religious industrial democracy in the world and at the same time a leading science power. In a study conducted in 2009, the Center surveyed over 2000 adults. According to the responses, over 80% of the Americans surveyed agreed that science had a mostly positive effect on society and over 60% agreed that science did not conflict with their own religious views. However in general, over half perceived a conflict between science and religion. Those that were most religiously observant were less likely to see a conflict. Almost 90% of the more than 2400 scientists surveyed during an American Association for the Advancement of Science (AAAS) meeting held in 2009 accepted the existence of evolution due to natural processes but just over 30% of the general public surveyed felt the same way. Evangelical Protestants voiced the strongest opposition to any form of evolution with 55% accepting that humans and other living things had existed in their present form since the beginning of time. How might such responses be representative of students in secondary schools? How are these responses representative of the views you hold? These are questions any teacher or prospective teacher needs to ask her/him-self.

THIS IS ALL VERY WELL BUT HOW DOES THIS AFFECT MY SCIENCE TEACHING?

The most important aspects of worldview for teaching are expectations of causality and categorization. Remember Aristotle's final cause explanation, which we call teleology? Although causality and categorization might seem to be rather esoteric ideas, they actually are so pervasive that we tend to be unaware of how much these ideas are used to make sense of the world and to structure language. Ironically, developments in 20th century physics, especially in the field of quantum mechanics, suggest that, at least at the level of fundamental particles, the issue of causation is problematic. Your worldview influences the questions that you ask and the way you understand your way of being in the world. Thus worldview can be very important for inquiry because how you look at the world influences the questions that you ask and your expectations about what would be an acceptable answer to those questions. When people share a worldview they share expectations about what is knowledge and how that knowledge can be built up. Some scholars argue that today there is a scientific worldview. Evidence for this comes from the Pew study, which suggests that scientists share some ideas and values that are less shared by the general population. This observation suggests that, in general in the US, scientists support some features of a worldview that might not be shared by other members of the general population.

Historically in Europe two different worldviews dominated thinking and scholarship in different eras, *Aristotelianism* (*Medieval scholasticism*) and *Mechanism*. Even today mechanism is a powerful worldview (some might argue it is the dominant worldview), which continues to influence the form of reasoning that is valued in forming mechanistic rather than teleological explanations in science. The implications of this domination for students is that they need to be presented with options to understand that within science there are expectations about how questions should be framed within a worldview that continues to be strongly atomistic and mechanistic.

ARISTOTELIANISM AND MECHANISM

The medieval worldview has its antecedents in authoritative texts composed of the works of Aristotle that were supplemented with commentaries from Greek and Arabic scholars, and constituted the accepted "mechanisms of explanation for natural phenomena [and also] served as a gigantic filter through which the world was viewed and pictured"[7]. However, this was not the whole story because by the 13th century much of Aristotle's natural philosophy and metaphysics had been incorporated into Christian theology, so that this worldview, *Aristotelianism* or *medieval scholasticism*, became the dominant intellectual system of Latin Europe. The epistemology of this worldview gave prominence to *dialectic reasoning* and *syllogistic logic* for generating knowledge. As I noted in Chapter 2, dialectic reasoning was aimed at finding arguments for and against particular position statements and syllogisms were based on deductive reasoning where true premises or axioms were used to produce true conclusions that were a direct result of the premises. According to the cosmology of Aristotelianism, there existed fundamental differences between objects and living things that was based on the souls that each possessed. For example, there existed a hierarchy of souls from vegetable soul to animal soul to rational soul (remember Aristotle's claim that only particular humans were rational). All living things had a proper place in the Universe and this place was set and unchanging. Thus these positions were eternal. Some vestiges of Plato's ideas had also been incorporated into this worldview because differences between objects and living things and between living things were believed to occur because of the different essences they possessed.

Aristotelianism became the accepted intellectual system for the curriculum of new universities where Aristotle and Plato's valuing of theoretical knowledge over practical and productive knowledge became entrenched. Look back at the universe shown in Petrus Apianus's *Cosmographia* (1539). This image provides an accurate representation of how the universe was imaged within Aristotelianism. Consistent with Aristotle's writings, the universe was a finite, unique, enormous sphere filled with matter and divided into two parts: the heavens (celestial) and the earth (terrestrial). The heavens were composed of fixed spheres radiating out from the lunar sphere to the fixed stars and beyond to the final sphere of God and the angles also called the empyrean sphere. The heavens were filled with an element called ether that was pure and incorruptible from which all objects in the heavens were formed. All motion in the heavens was circular and uniform. Circular motion was sacred. In contrast, the earth, which lay at the center of the universe, was a place of incessant change as bodies were created and destroyed. All bodies on earth were made up of four elements: fire, air, water, and earth, each of which had its natural place in the earth and natural motion towards that place. Thus, a pebble that was mainly made of earth had a natural motion of falling to the earth. Watery bodies would naturally rise above the earth and fall in the natural place of air. Whatever was the principal element of a body determined the direction of its natural motion.

Activity

Using the Aristotelian model of the cosmos:
— What do you predict would be the natural motion of mainly airy bodies, like a soap bubble, with respect to the other elements?
— How would you explain why a piece of wood floats on water?
    Note that the first question asks for a descriptive response in the form of a prediction that could be tested. The second question asks for a theoretical response. Such questions should help you to recognize that all worldviews allow members to address descriptive and theoretical questions.

Although medieval scholars could accept this cosmology, the devil was in the details. If the cosmos was perfect, what was it like? Was it composed of fluid and fixed spheres? If so, how many spheres? Were the spheres hollow? Were they separated or adjoining?

VIOLENT MOTION

Consistent with Aristotle's philosophy there was another form of motion on earth called *violent motion*, motion from outside the body, such as that observed when an object was pushed or thrown. All objects undergoing violent motion were moved by something other than themselves. According to Aristotelianism, if something was moving and the source of the motion was not part of the essence or structure of the object, then there must be something else that moved it. As I mentioned in the previous chapter, philosophers immediately identified a problem with projectile motion because when a projectile is thrown a question that comes to mind is what mover is responsible for a projectile's motion after it has left the thrower's hand? Why does an object keep on moving? Aristotle's response was that the original mover gave the power of being the mover to the air or water surrounding the projectile.

What caused an element to move to its natural place? Did an element in a compound retain its essence? Was violent motion external or internal? Note how these questions and the ones mentioned previously, provided a basis for exploration and thought associated with the worldview of Aristotelianism.

A Specific Example – On Motion

In *Physics*[8], Aristotle wrote:

Further, in point of fact things that are thrown move though that which gave them their impulse is not touching them, either by reason of mutual replacement, as some maintain, or because the air that has been pushed pushes them with a movement quicker than the natural locomotion of the projectile wherewith it moves to its proper place. But in a void none of these things can take place, nor can anything be moved save as that which is carried is moved.

What is Aristotle saying here? He is trying to explain why a body can move through the air and overcome its purpose, which is to move to its proper place. Is there a place for a void in Aristotle's argument? The material that is being displaced in front of the thrown body, say air, moves behind to maintain the movement of the body.

Further, no one could say why a thing once set in motion should stop anywhere; for why should it stop here rather than here? So that a thing will either be at rest or must be moved ad infinitum, unless something more powerful get in its way…

A body will only stop if something stops it from moving. There must be some sort of resistance.

> Further, the truth of what we assert is plain from the following considerations. We see the same weight or body moving faster than another for two reasons, either because there is a difference in what it moves through, as between water, air, and earth, or because, other things being equal, the moving body differs from the other owing to excess of weight or of lightness.

We observe one body moving faster than another either because it is moving through a different medium or because the bodies are of a different mass.

Aristotle's argument is that both motive force and resistance are necessary for projectile motion. As early as the 6th century, John Philoponos (490–570 CE), a Christian scholar working in Alexandria wrote a comment on Aristotle's Physics[9] in which he argued that the kinetic power must be "impressed on the projectile by the projecting agent"[10]. The kinetic power continues the movement of the object until it is overcome by the projectile's propensity for its natural place. Philoponos' theory was a precursor to the *impetus theory* of Jean Buridan (1295–1358), a French priest and an influential scholar in the Middle Ages, who has been just about forgotten today. However, these ideas did not move directly from Philoponus to Buridan. Arabic scholars such as Avicenna, who also developed commentaries and conducted experiments on the theories, translated Philoponus' writings into Arabic and Latin. These commentaries, indirectly disbursed and collected by travelers, made their way to Latin Europe. Also, Buridan was by no means the only scholar in Europe at that time thinking about this issue. Nor were all scholars convinced that the theory of impetus added anything to knowledge about motion. The impetus theory of scholars who were thinking and writing about motion at this time can be framed in the in the following way:

1. *Initial stage.* Impetus is dominant. Gravity is insignificant. Motion is in a straight line in direction of impetus.
2. *Intermediate stage.* Air resistance slows projectile. Gravity recovers. Path begins to deviate downwards. Path deviates downwards from straight line. This part of the path was conceived as part of a great circle.
3. *Final stage.* Impetus is completely spent. Gravity draws projectile downwards.

Activity

How does impetus theory fit with the worldview of Aristotelianism?

By the 17th century, some scholars in Europe were thinking about motion somewhat differently. Galileo Galilei, one of the leading scholars of the age, had been conducting experiments on specific gravity. Read the following section of text taken from *Dialogues Concerning Two New Sciences* (1638) and identify the argument Galileo is making about motion.

> Salviati: We have already seen that the difference of speed between bodies of different specific gravities is most marked in those media which are the most resistant: thus, in a medium of quicksilver [mercury], gold not merely sinks to the bottom more rapidly than lead but it is the only substance that will descend at all; all other metals and stones rise to the surface and float. On the other hand the variation of speed in air between balls of gold, lead, copper,

porphyry, and other heavy materials is so slight that in a fall of 100 cubits a ball of gold would surely not outstrip one of copper by as much as four fingers. Having observed this I came to the conclusion that in a medium totally devoid of resistance all bodies would fall with the same speed.

Simplico: This is a remarkable statement Salviati. But I shall never believe that even in a vacuum, if motion in such a place were possible, a lock of wool and a bit of lead can fall with the same velocity.

Salv: A little more slowly Simplico. Your difficulty is not so recondite nor am I so imprudent as to warrant you in believing that I have not already considered this matter and found the proper solution. Hence for my justification and your enlightenment hear what I have to say. Our problem is to find out what happens to bodies of different weight moving in a medium devoid of resistance, so that the only difference in speed is that which arises from inequality of weight[11].

Activity

How is Galileo's construction of motion different from that of both Aristotle and Buridan? How is he thinking about motion differently? What does this suggest about his worldview?

What I have tried to present here is an example of one of the features of the Aristotelian worldview, which came under more and more scrutiny as scholars explored the implications of what was the accepted theory of motion. In Latin Europe, this exploration was one of many that began to provide an intellectual and practical environment more consistent with a different worldview, *mechanism.*

Of course, throughout history people have made machines that were designed to perform certain functions. Even if Aristotle did not hold mechanics in high esteem, in many cultures people who developed the skills to make tools and machines were often highly esteemed. For example, Hero of Alexandria who probably lived during the first century of the Common Era was interested in *practical magic* and explored the properties of nature by using air, water, and steam to power various machines. Whether or not he was an atomist is open to debate but he argued that all matter was made up of particles or corpuscles and a vacuum existed between these particles so matter was not continuous. Unlike the atoms of Epicurus, Hero's corpuscles were all alike. He compared them to grains of sand[12]. However, during the Medieval period the arguments of Plato and Aristotle that theoretical knowledge, knowledge for its own sake, was the highest form of knowledge became the accepted view and entrenched in centers of learning, such as universities. It was easy in such an environment to apply less value to mechanical and practical crafts such as smithing, metallurgy, engineering, and cloth making.

Although some of Hero's writings were available in Latin Europe through Arabic translations, more complete translations became available in the 16th century. A number of scholars of the 16th and 17th centuries, including Leonardo da Vinci and Francis Bacon, acknowledged the contribution that Hero's writings made to their thinking. In the 17th century there was increasing interest in the machine as a structuring metaphor of the universe and one of the staunchest proponents of this worldview was Rene Déscartes.

RENE DÉSCARTES AND MECHANISM

This image of Rene Déscartes is from a portrait by Frans Hals.

Rene Déscartes (1596–1650) was probably one of the most influential philosophers in European thought. Although born in France at Le Haye, which in 1802 was renamed Le Haye-Descartes in his honor, he spent most of his adult life in Holland where he studied mathematics after completing a law degree in France. In adulthood, Déscartes sold his inherited feudal titles and invested the proceeds in stocks and shares, which allowed him to live reasonably comfortably for the rest of his life. The period from 1629 to 1649 was his most productive. He rejected (he actually rejected a lot of classical philosophy) teleology as a basis for explaining phenomena. He substantially contributed to the bringing together of geometry and algebra, a useful tool for the development of the scientific reasoning of other experimental philosophers such as Isaac Newton. In 1650, he died in Sweden where he had gone to tutor Queen Christina of Sweden of what seems to have been a serious respiratory infection. In 1663, Pope Alexander VII placed his works on the *Index of Prohibited Books*.

As a rationalist, he argued that true knowledge came from human reason and not from sense experiences because they could mislead.

Activity

Read the following segment from Descartes, *Principles of Philosophy II:*

Let us now accordingly consider the objects that are commonly thought to be [the most easily, and likewise] the most distinctly known, viz., the bodies we touch and see; not, indeed, bodies in general, for these general notions are usually somewhat more confused, but one body in particular. Take, for example, this piece of wax; it is quite fresh, having been but recently taken from the beehive; it has not yet lost the sweetness of the honey it contained; it still retains somewhat of the odor of the flowers from which it was gathered; its color, figure, size, are apparent (to the sight); it is hard, cold, easily handled; and sounds when struck upon with the finger. In fine, all that contributes to make a body as distinctly known as possible is found in the one before us. But, while I am speaking, let it be placed near the fire–what remained of the taste exhales, the smell evaporates, the color changes, its figure is destroyed, its size increases, it becomes liquid, it grows hot, it can hardly be handled, and, although struck upon, it emits no sound. Does the same wax still remain after this change? It must be admitted that it does remain; no one doubts it, or judges otherwise. What, then, was it I knew with so much distinctness in the piece of wax? Assuredly, it could be nothing of all that I observed by means of the senses, since all the things that fell under taste, smell, sight, touch, and hearing are changed, and yet the same wax remains[13].

What do you think is the argument he is making here? Can we rely on our senses? If not, what is real?

Déscartes expressed the question a little differently asking that if he doubted everything, with what was he left that could not be doubted? His answer was that the mind of the self could not be doubted. Although he rejected teleology, Déscartes did not reject all the philosophical arguments of Aristotle and Plato and their supporters (although in his writings he claimed to have rejected the thinking of all others), claiming that of all living things only humans possessed minds and the ability to reason. Unlike Robert Boyle whose writings communicate an empathy with the living things that gave up their lives for the study of matter through the use of his air pump, Déscartes argued that because other living things did not have minds, they could not feel pain. Such an argument provided a rationale for the live vivisections that were the focus of some experimental philosophers and you might even feel there are vestiges of this belief in the way some research is conducted in the 21st century.

Even though Déscartes was critical of the senses, he conducted experiments on light and color amongst other things, arguing in *Principles of Philosophy II:*

We cannot determine by reason alone how big these pieces of matter are, or how fast they move, or what kinds of circle they describe. Since there are countless different configurations which God might have instituted here, experience alone must teach us which configurations he actually selected in preference to the rest. We are thus free to make any assumption on these matters with sole proviso that all the consequences of our assumptions must agree with experience.

What is Déscartes arguing here? There is a place for experiment but one needs always to subject one's interpretation of one's experiences to critical examination. Additionally, if there are a number of possible explanations or hypotheses that are equally valid, our experiences will help us to decide which of these possibilities is likely to be the most valid.

Déscartes proposed a different cosmology from that supported by medieval scholasticism based on his belief that matter was composed of an infinite number of divisible particles. He imagined atoms to be particles that were at least divisible by God. These particles extended beyond space, and therefore, "celestial and terrestrial matter did not differ"[14]. Therefore, the cosmos and the earth were composed of similar material. From there one could argue that if matter behaves in a specific way in one place on the earth, it is likely to behave the same way somewhere else on the earth and even out in the stars. Déscartes argued further that if all objects were made of qualitatively similar objects then any variation in matter was not due to fundamental differences between matter, that is, differences in their essences, but to differing motions of differing parts. According to him, all aspects of the Universe were in motion.

According to scholasticism, however, the cosmic order of objects and living things was based on fundamental differences between objects and living things. These differences were based on the type of soul each object possessed. However, from Déscartes' perspective this cosmology is not appropriate if one accepted his notion of atomism. Déscartes went on to argue that, "the Earth and the whole Universe could be described in the manner of a machine with regard to the shape and movement of parts[15]". He claimed that:

> The only difference I can see between machines and natural objects is that the workings of machines are mostly carried out by apparatus large enough to be readily perceptible by the senses… whereas natural processes almost always depend on parts so small they elude our senses[16].

He argued that not just physical attributes but also emotions such as pain could be described in terms of motion. However, he admonished his readers against confusing his metaphor of the mechanical universe with reality:

> This may give us an idea of the possible constitution of Nature; but we must not conclude that this is the actual constitution[17].

Déscartes' mechanistic description of the world also led him to develop a philosophy of *determinism* which posited that objects and ideas were connected in an orderly way, initially based on God's plan, and that laws of nature existed to explain all the events in the universe. This led him to argue that all aspects of Nature could be explained by the application of scientific laws. This notion was underpinned by two beliefs. Firstly, that objects and ideas were connected in an orderly way and therefore, if we look more and more closely at the fundamental particles that make up the Universe, we would unlock all the secrets of the Universe. Secondly, that because humans were rational beings they could apply scientific laws using mathematics (the one true form of knowledge) to unlock these secrets.

However, once Déscartes had described the body as a machine he was left with the problem of the soul, which lacks material substance and, as such, is absolved of following the laws of physics. Although I will not go into the physiological details that Déscartes used to address this question, he was able to use it to separate the mind from matter (remembering that this meant the human mind from everything else) and we are still trying today to get them back again. This theory called, *Cartesian dualism*, can be detected in a number of different contexts including beliefs that humans have control over nature and can do whatever they like to nature. I also see this theory in contemporary social science research that separates the researcher from the researched. In 17th and 18th century France, this theory influenced garden architecture leading to highly stylized gardens where nature was forced to conform to abstract geometrical shapes.

DÉSCARTES AND THE EXPERIMENTAL PHILOSOPHERS

Déscartes' proposal that the Universe could be described as composed of qualitatively similar particles, together with his determinism, resulted in a cosmology that was vastly different from that of medieval scholasticism. His cosmological theory appealed to those working in the emerging field of experimental philosophy. Consequently, the mechanical universe came to be accepted; not just as a useful explanation, but also as the way the Universe was truly. Déscartes' metaphor of the universe as machine was a powerful 'structuring' metaphor, and provided new insights to the scientists which were Déscartes' contemporaries. However, once this metaphor was posited also as the 'truth' it became an ideology/myth that strongly influenced European conceptions of the nature of the universe. The mechanistic metaphor was no longer accepted as a way of explaining the operation of the Universe but was accepted as the way the Universe really operated. Acceptance of this cosmology, with its mechanistic and deterministic base, led to the belief that if we were to discover the fundamental particles of which the universe and all living things were composed, we could then unlock the secrets of life and the Universe. Concurrent with the development of this mythic belief emerged a further belief, associated with Déscartes' determinism, which proposed that the natural world was underpinned by scientific laws that would be discovered by scientists as they study Nature. Thus, by reducing the universe to its smallest components, an example of *reductionism*, scientists believed they could discover scientific laws that related fundamental particles together. Devotees of mechanism believed that they could describe the Universe mathematically and unlock the secrets of the Universe.

Question. Do you think mechanism continues to be a powerful worldview? Why or why not? What relationships can you draw between these worldviews and the development of theories such as atomic theory, cell theory, the standard theory, and the theory of everything?

Activity

1. *Based on what you have read so far, complete the table below.*

	Aristotelianism (Scholasticism)	Mechanism
Ontology What is reality? What is nature? Metaphor Self-other		
Epistemology Explanations Forms of reasoning		
Axiology Values and ethics	Intrinsic goodness	Goodness can also be understood as a machine

2. *What is the major difference between how Aristotelianism and Mechanism under-stand and value explanations? Consider the following question and explanation:*

> Why did the woman fall off the ladder?
> A1: In order to get a few days off work
> A2: Because the rung broke

Which of these explanations could be Aristotelian and which is more likely Mechanistic? Why?

3. What explanations might an Aristotelianist (A) or a Mechanist (M) give to the following questions?

    a. Why did a man buy his son ice cream?

      (A)

      (M)

    b. Why did the ball fall to the ground?

      (A)

      (M)

Activity

The ubiquity of worldview can also be demonstrated by a simple activity using some sort of black box like the ones with which some of you might be familiar from the FOSS kit on models. I make my own black boxes using plastic digital video cases into which I put numerous items and then cover twice with dense colored paper to make the container impervious to light. I also provide some simple tools that people can use to make observations. I use these boxes for an activity designed to demonstrate aspects of a mechanistic worldview that are common to most beginning and experienced science teachers. For example, if I give you a black box and ask you to work out what is inside, what will you do? I suggest that most of you will make some observations using your senses and will use these observations to propose a model for the internal structure of the box. Even though this is a highly artificial activity, you will be unlikely to suggest some sort of supernatural explanation for what you can hear, feel, and see. For example, what happens if I tip the box to one side? If I hear something that seems to move in easily and in a consistent way, I might surmise there is a solid round body inside the box. If I ask you to record your thought questions, I am confident that most of them will be focused on making sense of the task and on leading you to make specific observations or claims for the internal structure of the box, which in this case is a model. Why not try it yourself?

The Machine Metaphor and Experiments

Contrary to Aristotelianism, the machine rather than the body or organism was the metaphor for mechanism. What implications does the machine metaphor have for how people might think about nature? If bodies are thought of as machines then we can begin to think about how they are made or fabricated rather than generated. We can imagine that they are composed of parts so that if we test one part we can see what effect that test has on anther part of the body and make some assessment of the relationship between these parts. Mechanism supports the attribution of cause and effect in explanations of how things work. According to mechanistic thinking, if we can control one variable, we are then able to make claims about the effect this variable has on a specific feature of nature or organism. Moreover, if certain actions of living things can be reproduced then it makes sense to perform experiments that attempt to recreate and test nature. Can you begin to see evidence of a mechanistic worldview in the way experimentation is used in Eurocentric science? For this mechanistic worldview, the theorizing of bodies as composed of inanimate corpuscles or atoms with space in between provided a model of matter that could used to initiate an explanatory framework.

Worldview and Questions

Have you begun to think about how worldview influences the types of questions we ask? When people ask, "Is this a scientific question?" they are really asking if this question is one that the practices, knowledge, and values of science will foster an answer. I have argued previously that within the set of questions Eurocentric science can be asked to answer, only certain types of questions are amenable to the application of scientifically accepted practices and knowledge. Of course, the asking of questions is a two-edged sword because even if we do not know the answer to a question, the very asking, serves to limit the focus of any associated interaction.

Activity. Either individually, or with a colleague or two, brainstorm some pedagogical activities for creating environments where students can be encouraged to ask questions.

An activity I have used involves people mixing 7 grams of citric acid with 10 grams of sodium bicarbonate in a Ziploc bag containing a thermometer then carefully adding 10 milliliters of water[18]. I ask them to observe what happens and record any questions that come to them as they perform the activity. Once they have finished recording questions we can begin to classify questions as ones that Eurocentric science might be able to answer and questions that Eurocentric science cannot answer. On the simple level we might agree that a question like, "Will I like either of these chemicals?" is a question that is not immediately amenable to Eurocentric-based scientific investigation but questions like, "Is this a chemical reaction?" or "Are the quantities of chemicals important for the reaction to taker place?" are amenable.

Len Fisher[19], physicist and winner of the Ignoble Award, noted that even questions that might seem right for Eurocentric scientific investigation often cannot be answered directly. He explored the question, "How to dunk a cookie?" He and his colleagues recognized that although this could be a question that Eurocentric science could answer, it was not directly amenable to investigation. Their next question was, "What does a cookie look like from a physicist's point of view?" which for them really meant, "How can this question be simplified to the degree that physics can answer it?" In Eurocentric science, one strategy for simplifying a system so that it can be explored is to construct a model of an experienced phenomenon in which the variables are controlled by the application of assumptions or rules. This process is also called *idealization.* Remember the motion example in which Galileo constructed a thought model, which he then applied to experienced phenomenon, in order to be able to focus on specific attributes of the system? When Galileo studied gravity, he idealized motion claiming that if one wanted to understand how objects fall towards the earth one could ignore air resistance and focus on the attributes of objects falling.

One reason for the appeal of mechanism to experimental philosophers was that it provided a way of looking at the world that supported questions such as, "If I focus on a specific variable, what claims can I make about its effect?" I argue that such behaviors indicate human expectations, especially for those with some science in their prior experiences, that the world will behave in predictable and consistent ways. When trying to propose a model for the interior of your black box did you immediately think of supernatural possibilities or did you expect what was inside to behave consistently and predictably even though you could not see inside? To varying degrees, such behavior is consistent with a mechanistic worldview. In the next chapter we will examine how this worldview, with its use of corpuscles or atoms to explain all sorts of behaviors, became a powerful organizing framework for an emerging experimental philosophy, in many ways the precursor philosophy to Eurocentric science and modernism. What is the source of our questions? Responding to this question did you reflect on how our experiences provide the basis for the questions you ask? Although this is a start, I think our responses are a little more complex than that as we filter our experiences through our worldview. Students also filter questions they might have from experiences through their worldview. For teachers, the challenge is to develop pedagogical strategies that support students to develop a sense of the types of questions Eurocentric science might be able to answer and those it cannot.

NOTES

[1]   Lindberg, D. (1995). Medieval science and its religious context. *Osiris, 10*, 60–79.
[2]   Lyons, J. (2009). *The house of wisdom*. New York: Bloomsbury Press.
[3]   Oxford English Dictionary. (1989). *Oxford English dictionary online* (2nd ed.). Oxford: Oxford University Press. Retrieved from http://dictionary.oed.com
[4]   Colwell, H. A., Dr. (1921). Gideon Harvey: On medical life from the restoration to the end of the XVII century. *Annals of Medical History, 3*, 203–237.
[5]   Sextus Empiricus. (1983). Against the Professors, 7, 135. In G. S. Kirk, J. E. Raven & M. Schofield (Eds.), *The presocratic philosophers: A critical history with a selection of texts* (2nd ed., p. 410). Cambridge: Cambridge University Press.
[6]   Pew Research Center study outcomes can be found at http://people-press.org/report/528
[7]   Grant, E. (1978). Aristotelianism and the longevity of the medieval worldview. *History of Science, 16*, 93–106.
[8]   Aristotle. (350 BCE). *Physics*. Book IV (R. P. Hardie & R. K. Gaye, Trans.). Retrieved from http://classics.mit.edu/Aristotle/physics.4.iv.html
[9]   Reported in Clagett, M. (1979). *Studies in medieval physics and mathematics*. London: Valorum Reprints.
[10] Clagett, M. (1979). p. 40.
[11] Galilei, G. (1638/1968). *Dialogues concerning two new sciences* (H. Crew & A. de Salvio (Trans.). Chicago: Northwestern University Press. Original translation 1913.
[12] Boas, M. (1949). Hero's Pneumatica: A study of its transmission and influence. *Isis, 40*, 38–48.
[13] Descartes, R. (1644/1991). *Principles of philosophy II* (V. R. Miller & R. P. Miller, Trans., p. 106). Dordrecht, The Netherlands: Kluwer.
[14] Descartes, R. (1642/1970). Third set of objections and replies containing the controversy between Hobbes and Descartes. In E. Anscombe & P. T. Geach (Eds.), *Descartes philosophical writings* (pp. 127–150). Sunbury-on-Thames, Middlesex: Nelson's University Paperbacks (Based on the original published 1642). p. 208.
[15] Descartes. (1642/1970). p. 225.
[16] Descartes. (1642/1070). p. 236.
[17] Descrates. (1642/1970). p. 237.
[18] This reaction is the basis for how bath bombs work.
[19] Fisher, L. (2004). *How to dunk a doughnut: The science of everyday life*. New York: Penguin.

VALUING PATTERNS AND THE CONTINUING EMERGENCE OF EUROCENTRIC SCIENCE

So far we have examined some of the questions and experimental explorations of classical theoretical claims, such as the nature of motion, and how some notions of atoms or corpuscles and vacuums, provided space for scholars to begin to critically examine the claims embedded in an Aristotelian worldview. At the same time some Europeans, especially Portuguese explorers under the support of Prince Henry the Navigator, had begun a process of discovery that later was to involve other European countries including Spain, France, Holland, and England seeking to expand their spheres of influence across the Earth. The extent of European memory about the structure and extent of the Earth and its continents and oceans can be noted in the image of Ptolemy's map from his book, *Geographia* (First published about 150 CE), which was an attempt to record the extent of Roman knowledge of the world in the second century.

This is a 16th century image of Ptolemy. Note the iconography much of which seems associated with his other famous text, the Almagest (2nd century), his attempt to present a geometrical model of the universe, which Ptolemy claimed was based on astronomical observations spanning over 800 years. The name, Almagest, is the Latinized form of the Arabic translation of the original Greek title, Mathematical Treatise. Consistent with an Aristotelian worldview the Earth was located at the center of the universe. Ptolemy's model was accepted in Arabic and European countries for the next 1300 years or so. Many countries and cultures where timekeeping was important for religious, political, and/or social reasons typically had developed a rich set of astronomical observations.

Ptolemy (90–168 CE), an Egyptian of Roman citizenship, was a scholar of some repute. His *Geographia* included principles known to the classical Greek and Roman world since Eratosthenes (about 276–195 BCE), a Greek scholar from Cyrene (modern day Libya) who developed a system of latitude and longitude. The map shown is a recreation of one of Ptolemy's maps from coordinates he included in *Geographia*. The original maps from the manuscript had been lost over time. Note the area assigned to Africa and Asia. Sri Lanka is depicted much larger and India much smaller than in contemporary depictions that are based on more precise and accurate measurements for length, longitude and latitude.

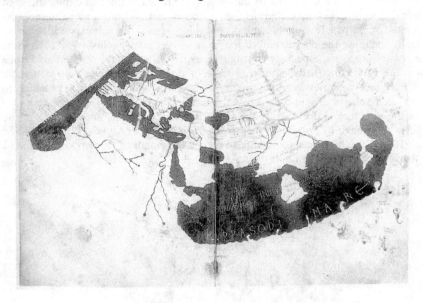

Re-creation of map from Ptolomy's Gerographica

Activity

Look over the map and using your own geographical knowledge identify the parts of the Earth or countries. Are there any aspects of a collective worldview that that is communicated by this map?

EXPLORING THE WORLD: THE RISE OF NATURAL HISTORY

Versions of this map constituted the extent of European geographical knowledge, although in the 13th and 14th centuries, Italian sailors from republics such as Genoa, Venice, and Pisa, in seeking a way round Africa to trade with India had added some-what to this image of Africa making it more of a complete space encircled by water. In 1281 or 1291, explorers from Genoa set sail from North Africa but disappeared soon after. Such disappearances confirmed the challenges of sailing beyond the known world! However, these explorations were by no means the first.

Perhaps the greatest feats of exploration and navigation are associated with Polynesian and Micronesian exploration of the Pacific Ocean. Peter Worsely[1] argues that Pacific Islanders with their vision of the ocean as a highway rather than a barrier had a different worldview to Europeans. With outrigger, ocean going, sailing canoe technology and a developed capacity to navigate by the rising and falling of the stars, Pacific Islanders were able to navigate across the ocean. Beginning about 3500 years ago, ancestors of the Polynesians began to explore and colonize lands in the Pacific Ocean. The final colonizations were associated with outlying lands such as Hawaii and Easter Island made between 200 and 400 and New Zealand some time between 900 and 1200.

In the 15th century, the Ming dynasty of China expanded the ocean exploration that had been supported by previous dynasties, especially the Song (about 960–1270) and Yuan [Mongol Emperors] (about 1271–1368). In particular, this expansion was supported by the warrior prince, Zhu Di who took the throne in 1402 and appointed Muslim eunuch, Zheng He (1371–1433) to command his fleet[2]. Thus began a period of expansion as China, using advanced technologies such as the magnetic compass (developed in the 12th century) and air/water tight chambers, sent huge amardas to explore the Indian Ocean and impress on the nations they visited Chinese power and reach[3]. According to reports, these vessels were huge, much bigger than those available in Europe at the time, and recent archeological evidence has supported these claims. Over a series of voyages, Zheng He explored as far as modern day Somalia in East Africa where he collected amazing beasts such as lions, leopards, ostriches, zebras, and oryxes. However, with the reemergence of Confucian elite in China, ocean exploration abroad was discouraged and money used to finance these explorations was diverted to address other issues such as protecting the empire from the mongols in the west.

Prince Henry the Navigator was born on Porto, Portugal in 1394, a Prince of the Kingdom of Portugal. Along with his brothers and his father he shared a desire to enrich Portugal by opening up Saharan trade routes in the control of Muslim traders. He also wanted to put a stop to Barbary pirates raiding the coast of Portugal for slaves for their markets in North Africa. Along with many in Europe, he shared a desire to discover if Ethiopia, an exotic Christian country isolated from Christian Europe since the rise of Islam, was the site of the lengendary Prester John's Kingdom. Working with his father and brothers, he was able to encourage Portugese exploration not only through financial support but also through the provision of a center for the learning of navigation. Although initially stymied by the challenges of sailing down the western coast of Africa, through persistance these sailors pressed further south discovering lands very different from those indicated in Ptolemy's maps. Their accounts of their explorations also influenced others in Europe to begin to challenege ideas that previously had been thought not to be open to criticism; the possibility that the handed down knowledge from the ancients might not be as reliable as thought. These explorers initiated a new form of writing, the travel and natural history book, in which they described the excitment of discovering, for them and for Latin Europe, new lands, new animals and plants, new peoples, new customs, and new heavens in the form of stars never before seen and not recorded in the authoratative texts.

These explorations indicated that no one was perfect and even the ancients could be wrong. Also, these explorers could claim that because they had observed these phenomena, and even touched them, they must exist[4]. So these explorations gave credence to the reliability of our senses for generating knowledge about the world. Instead of being asked to subject experience to the power of reason, such experiences of new worlds were allowing Europeans to argue that our reason should be subject to the power of our experiences. Also in contrast to Aristotelianism, this movement was being lead by uneducated sailors, not by the theoretically educated elite. These developments began to provide a space for reasoned experience, rather than scholastic discussions, to be accepted as a strategy for generating new knowledge.

The rise of the navigators and sailors and acceptance of their experience as the source of new knowledge was also part of new social development in many parts of Europe as a middle class consisting of skilled workers such as painters, artisans, potters, masons, carpenters, physicians, apothecaries, instrument makers began to emerge. These workers often had intimate knowledge of materials needed to perform their profession and there was emerging respect, even amongst scholars, for the skills developed by these workers.

THEOLOGICAL VOLUNTARISM VERSUS INTELLECTUALISM

By the late Middle Ages the intellectual environment around Aristotelianism had become sterile, even for some Christians. If you pushed Aristotelianism to its rational limits, it decreed a world where there was no change, where no new living things could be created because everything had its place, and where the only allowable motion in the heavens was uniform and circular. Of course, we could argue based on the Pew Study mentioned in the previous chapter that some people continue to support some elements of this worldview. But by the late Middle Ages some Churchmen argued that the Creator was more powerful than reason and humans did not have the right to impose limits on the Creator's power. They argued that one should accept nature as the Creator saw fit to present it, whether or not it conformed to reason. Such a view could allow people to argue that they were justified in exploring nature through observation and experiment because they were seeking to understand the Creator's creation, nature, more fully. This approach was called *theological voluntarism* and was a position that was held to be in opposition with the *intellectualism* of Aristotleianism. Theological voluntarism was endorsed by Pope John XXI in the 13th century and would allow 17th century scholars like Rene Descartes to claim that their experiments and thinking were not designed to support a universe that was not created, but to understand God's creation better. Of course, he could make that argument but that did not stop his writings from being banned by the Catholic Church.

OTHER DEVELOPMENTS

These social developments were some of the more obvious changes occurring over over the late Middle Ages and into the 16th and 17th centuries that supported a weakening of the hold of Aristotleianism on the thinking and worldview of people in countries of Europe previously under the thrall of Aristotelianism. I have not mentioned the emergence of a raft of other developments that also slowly eroded people's reliance on Aristotle and an Aristotlian worldview. These included the development of a mathematical basis for perspective that was informed by the work of scholar, al-Hasan Ibn al-Haytham (965–1039), also named Alhacen (or Alhazen) in Latin[5].

al-Hasan Ibn al-Haytham and perspective. Born in Basra in modern day Iraq, he spent most of his life in Egypt where he died in 1039. We do not really know why Ibn al-Haytham came to Egypt. Apocraphally, it is claimed that he was employed by Al-Hakim bi-Amr Allah, the 6th Fatimid caliph, because al-Haytham claimed that he could develop a method for controlling the seasonal ups and downs of the Nile River[6]. At that time the Fatimid empire was extensive and included all of North Africa including Egypt, the western side of the Arabian peninsula including the cities of Mecca and Medina, and all of the western portions of the Middle East. The Fatimids had also built a House of Wisdom, similar to the House of Wisdom in Baghdad, which might also have been attractive to Ibn al-Haytham as a place of study where he could share elements of his thinking with other scholars.

Anything I say about this scholar will not do him justice. In his book, *Book of Optics*, he developed the first systematic, comprehensive theory of optics to rival Ptolemy's theory proposing a scientifically accurate explanation for the relationship between light, objects, and eyes for sight. He also recognized that vision and visual perception involved the brain, that the eyes were really a conduit between our experiences of the outside and our brains. He has been described as the first experimental psychologist but his exploration of sight and optics extends far beyond perception. One of the statements he makes is the following:

> We find that when the eye looks into exceedingly bright lights, it suffers greatly because of them and is injured. For when an observer looks at the body of the sun, he cannot see it well, since his eye suffers pain because of the light[7].

What is the argument al-Haytham is making here? Unlike Ptolemy who believed that sight required the emission of something from the eye in order for it to work, Ibn al-Haytham was able to build on the arguments of scholars, such as Aristotle, that something had to enter the eye to initiate sight. He also argued that light was reflected in all directions when it struck an object and that a human only captured the reflections that travelled through a transparent medium and hit the human allowing us to see both the object and its color. He used experiments to test his questions showing for example, that if one looks down a tube one is only able to see objects, or parts of objects, directly in front of the tube opening. He also used a tube to show that light radiated equally in all directions from a candle flame.

Activity

Can you follow in the steps of al-Haytham? See if you can describe an experiment that you can perform with a candle and a tube that could test whether light is distributed equally in all directions from a flame. Evaluate your experiment.

With his examination of the structure of the eye and identification of the lens, al-Haytham introduced other scholars and instrument makers to mechanical explanations of biological structures. J. D. Burnal[8] argues that this discovery was to point the way for scholars to think of using glass for making lenses for use in magnification and reading although the invention of spectacles happened later in 14th century Italy.

Other aspects of Arabic science. A feature of Arabic science was that, in contrast with the Greek thinking of Aristotle and Plato, the mechanical arts were held in high esteem partly because time keeping was very important for religious observances. So laboratory practices in fields such as drug making, base and precious metals, and perfume, were developed in Arabic countries supporting further discoveries in these areas. *Chemistry*, the name we give to one of the basic sciences in Eurocentric science, comes from *alchemy* which had its origin in Islamic culture and language. Of course, Arabs were not the first to develop chemical practices. I have already mentioned Babylonian and Egyptian facility with chemical arts in previous chapters. The Arabs also maintained trading links with China supporting an exchange of ideas about chemical knowledge. The Arabs became expert distillers working to purify substances such as perfumes and the production of chemicals such as alum, soda, and nitre. It is possible that the development of chemical ideas in China and Islamic cultures was associated with religious beliefs about chemicals providing insight into life and everlasting life. These ideas were also carried on to Europe in the 15th and 16th centuries.

The emergence of friar organizations. Other developments that might also have influenced the development of Eurocentric science were the establishment of friar organizations including the Franciscans (1223), Dominicans (1216), and Augustinians (1256) (Martin Luther was a member of this order). With goals of living amongst the urban poor as preachers and educators, the friars' mission was supported by the Popes of the Catholic Church who saw them as tools for Papal policy. Under the control of Pope Gregory IX, the Dominicans became entrusted with identifying and punishing heresy during the Inquisition (1233–1478).

Moveable type and the printing press. In the Middle Ages the production of books in Europe was a painstaking task as all texts had to be copied by hand. However, around 1439 the development of moveable type, previously developed in China and Korea[9] and the printing press, often attributed to Johannes Gutenberg, opened up text publication to mass production of inexpensive books. In China, the earliest record is of Bi Sheng (990–1051), a commoner who developed ceramic movable type between 1040 and 1046. According to the Heilbrunn Timeline of Art History produced by the Metropolitian Museum of Art, movable type using more user-friendly wooden blocks, was invented in early to mid-13th century Korea. The type was invented by Choe Yun-ui, an administrator, working under the direction of the Goryeo [Korea, comes from the name of this dynasty] dynasty to print the Buddist canon (*Tripitaka*) which had been destroyed by the Mongols.

We do not know much about the early life of Gutenberg except that he was born in the German city of Mainz around 1398. He learnt the craft of goldsmithing but died in poverty after many of his projects lost money. The development of the press in Europe seems to have been a collaboration between Gutenberg, Andreas Dritzen, a gem cutter, and Adreas Heilmann, a paper mill owner, so it is interesting that Gutenberg is the only person typically remembered. One publication that benefited from the development of moveable type and the printing press was Versalius' opus *On the Workings of the Human Body* [*De Huminus Corpus Fabrica*] (1543). The draughtsmen and engravers who created the justly famous illustrations (not credited or acknowledged) combined perspective with printing to produce fantastic 3D-like illustrations that have remained in print for more than 400 years[10]. However, having a printing press was only part of what was needed to get your book in circulation. Access to white paper for printing was also important. According to James Gleick[11], England lacked any paper mills for producing white paper needed for printing until the middle of the 17th century. Prior to that time, all white paper had to be imported into England making the cost of printing in that country expensive.

The use of vernacular language. In Europe, before the development of the printing press there was a growing interest in the publication of books in the vernacular rather than in Latin, which had been the universal language of scholarship. Dante Alishieri (about 1265–1321), called Dante in English, wrote his most famous work, *Divine Comedy*, in a modified version of the Tuscan language, which Dante called Italian. His use of the vernacular helped to convince people that humanist and complex ideas could be communicated in the vernacular. The use of code switching between Latin and the vernacular was common in some late Middle Ages texts. In Spain during the reign of Alfonso X the Wise (1252–1284), the desire to present new knowledge, including science and medicine, in plain language introduced the Romance vernacular for the first time for this purpose. Consistent with Aristotle's argument that men (not slaves) were the only thinking beings of the universe and the only ones capable of learning theoretical knowledge, the teaching of Latin had tended to be restricted to men. Feminist theory[12] argues that use of the vernacular was democratizing in many ways not the least being that with the vernacular it was easier for women to partici-pate in public discussions about knowledge construction.

Question. Can you think of another reason why countries and individuals might have been interested in promoting the vernacular? Do you think it might also have been associated with the growing desire for countries and people living in those countries to assert a national identity? Remember back to Chapter 1 and McKinley's argument about the role of language in the construction and maintenance of indi-genous knowledges?

In about 1391, Geoffery Chaucer (about 1343–1400), one of the first authors to use English for his writings, composed *Treatise on an Astrolabe* in the vernacular. However, he was forced to use Romance words in translating some actions indicating that English needed some Latin prototypes in order for him to have access to the range of words he wanted and needed for his treatise. His use of English had been preceeded by John Wycliff (mid-1320–1384), an early dissenter, who had published an English version of the Bible in 1382. Also in England, law courts had been required to use English since 1362 because prior to this French had been the language of the courts (a throw back to the Norman invasion of 1066).

As these examples suggest, use of the vernacular alters the community that can engage with the texts being presented. While some scholars might be critical of a 'decline in standards' as more 'common folk' had access to texts, the goal in Spain was for plain language that was appropriate for communicating new knowledge opening up the discourse to a greater range of a nation's population. The willingness of artists such as Dante and Chaucer to write in the vernacular and the need for people to be able to read the Bible for themselves provided further justification for accepting the use of the vernacular. Thomas Glick[13] notes that practical sciences such as medicine and alchemy had an earlier tradition for use of vernacular texts. He argues that within Chaucer's *Treatise*, which could be described as the first 'how to' guide in English, specific discourse types that are now associated with science discourse including: concrete/technical and abstract/scientific nouns, for example "the altitude", the use of extended nominal groups typical of science, such as "proportions" and "celestial body", and clause complexes that carry forward an argument, for example, "And although that a planete have a latitude fro the ecliptik, yit sey somme folk, so that the planete arise in that same signe with eny degre of the forseide face in which his longitude is rekned" [And although that a planet have a latitude from the ecliptic, yet say some folk, so that the planet arise in that same sign with any degree of the foreside face in which his longitude is reckoned]. Spoken gestures, now called *procedures* in science, are also common in this vernacular text. Some examples include, "Tak the altitude of the sonne" [Take the altitude of the sun], "mak a mark" [make a mark], and "lok which degrees" [look which degrees]. While I am not arguing that everybody that read this text in the following years immediately thought about using these grammatical tools, the number and variety of existing original manuscripts of Chaucer's *Treatise* speak to the general popularity of this text and the possibility of its ongoing influence.

Activity

The following text is taken from a recent research article:

Cheng, Hai, Edwards, R. Lawrence, Broecker, Wallace S., Denton, George H., Kong, Xinggong, Wang, Yongjin, Zhang, Rong, & Wang, Xianfeng (2009). Ice age terminations. *Science, 326*, 248–252.

The "sawtooth" character of late Quaternary ice-age cycles, with gradual buildup and rapid collapse of ice sheets, has been known since Emiliani's pioneering oxygen isotope ($\delta^{18}O$) measurements on marine sediments (1). Explanations of the rapid collapses, dubbed "terminations" (2), have long been sought. The ice-age cycles have been linked to changes in Earth's orbital geometry (the Milankovitch or Astronomical theory) through spectral analysis of marine oxygen-isotope records (3), which demonstrate power in the ice-age record at the same three spectral periods as orbitally driven changes in insolation [direct solar radiation at the Earth's surface]. However, explaining the 100 thousand-year (ky)–recurrence period of ice ages has *proved to be problematic because although the 100-ky cycle dominates the ice-volume power spectrum, it is small in the insolation spectrum.* p. 248.

After you have carefully read this paragraph see if you can identify examples of the grammatical structures Chaucer used in his *Treatise on an Astrolabe*. There are other features in this segment that have become common features of science writing which we will examine in a later chapter but can you identify some of these now?

THE EMERGENCE OF EUROCENTRIC SCIENCE

I do not think there was a moment when a specific act can be associated with the emergence of Eurocentric science. However, by the 15th and 16th centuries people had begun to ask questions about a range of practices associated with the tenents Aristotleianism and its cosmology, also tied to beliefs and practices associated with the Catholic Church about the construction of knowledge about the world. These questions suggest a new direction for knowledge making that we can associate with what I have called Eurocentric science, the science that is most familiar to you. New knowledge from outside Europe, the valuing of experiences of new lands, the emergence of a class of skilled workers, the incorporation of ideas that supported people to look at the world in different ways, and the move to the use of national languages all contributed to a rich environment for exploring nature and for thinking about new ways of generating knowledge. Aristotelianism had become bloated and unwieldy as more and more questions had been asked, requiring running repairs to the Aristotelian worldview as Aristotle's integrated theories came to resemble more and more a mismatch of unintegrated topics.

LOOKING FOR PATTERNS: SOME OBSERVATIONS AND DEVELOPMENTS

In this section, I want to introduce you to some of the 16th and 17th century scholars that, according to history of science scholars, contributed in some way to the emergence of Eurocentric science. I think it is useful for you to have a sense our understanding of what these scholars did and what they argued and why that might be important. For example, as people began to make more and more careful observations of the heavens they could identify when there was a change in the night sky. Of course, since the universe was supposed to be unchanging this created a problem, how could you explain these observed changes when the heavens were not supposed to change. Also other scholars began to argue that the models, which supported the existing worldview of Aristotelianism were too complex, and that simpler, more aesthetically pleasing models in which the earth was not the center of the universe would be more consistent with these observations.

It is likely that Nicolaus Copernicus' presentation of a cosmology completely different from the existing cosmology of Latin Europe influenced many people to see the world in a different way. But equally for Copernicus' ideas to spread beyond his local community, he needed outside support. He tested his views with a short summary paper that he sent to scholars he knew. He sent these scholars a commentry on his heliocentric model some time between 1508 and 1514 but his complete vision was not published until he was near death.

The Beginnings of a New Worldview

In 1543, just before his death Nicolaus Copernicus (1473–1543) published *On the Revolutions of Celestial Spheres.* Copernicus was born on Torun, a part of Prussia that had been ceded to Poland after 1466. For most of his life he worked as a church administrator. He began his studies at the University of Cracow and then attended the University of Bologna to study canon law where he had the chance to learn Greek (this might have been important for his further work in astronomy because not all of Ptolemy's available writings had been translated into Latin) and Padua where he studied medicine. The study of medicine required the study of what today we would think of as astronomy and astrology but then was considered one discipline. Copernicus developed a deep interest in astronomy and making astronomical observations. Throughout his professional life as a church administrator, he maintained this interest.

An image of Nicolaus Copernicus from the early 16ᵗʰ century.

This is the title page of the second edition his famous text published in 1566 in Basle, a major city in the protestant Swiss confederation, by Officina Henri Cpetrina.

In his book, *On the Revolutions of Celestial Spheres*, Copernicus argued that the sun and not the Earth existed at the center of the universe. We do not know what led Copernicus to propose a heliocentric (sun-centered) model of the universe although Thomas Kuhn[14] claims his goal was to develop a cosmology that was consistent with Aristotle's original thesis that celestial motion should be uniform and circular. He was not a fan of Ptolemy's attempt to account for observations of backwards motion of some planets and he determined that a heliocentric model was necessary to achieve this. The apparent forwards and backwards motion of the planets that can be observed from the earth could be explained if one accepted the rotation and revolution of the Earth.

Activity

This image comes from *On the Revolution*. Look closely.

Copernicus' model from his book On the Revolutions of Celestial Spheres

What can you identify that supports a new heliocentric model of the universe? What can you identify that remains consistent with an Aristotelian worldview? Can you identify the Earth? What else can you identify even though it is in Latin in Copernicus' hand?

Copernicus also argued that even though it might seem that the skies were revolving it was really the motion of the Earth that made it appear so. The rotation of the earth was responsible for night and day and at the same time the Earth also revolved around the sun. After a run of over sixty years of availability and use, in 1616 *On the Revolution of Celestial Spheres* was placed on the Catholic Church's *Index of Forbidden Books* (established under the control of the Pope in 1559) where it remained until the Index was closed in 1966.

Considering the Theoretical Possibilities

One of the early supporters of Copernicus' heliocentric model was Giodano Bruno (1548–1600), a Dominican priest, philosopher, and astronomer born in the Kingdom of Naples. It is possible that you have never heard of him but it is likely that his thoughts about the nature of the universe and motion influenced natural philosophers, such as Galileo Galilei, who are more familiar to you. Bruno's arrest and execution for heresy in 1600 made people wary of referencing his works and so, in many ways, he disappeared from people's memories, which is ironic because he also became well known for the mnemonic strategies he developed to improve memory. Bruno argued that people should be able to communicate directly with the cosmos and not rely on 'authorities' to do the translations for them. Some scholars have claimed that he was also a follower of Renaissence hermetic philosophy[15] but perhaps he was more of a humanist influenced by hermeticism. Bruno rejected the distiction, argued by Aristotle, of the difference between the heavens and the earth and argued that if we accept that the sun is the center of the universe then the stars we observe are also suns only more distant. The universe was infinite not limited as Aristotle had claimed. Bruno wrote:

> *Filoteo.* I believe and I understand that beyond and further beyond that imagined border of the sky there will always be a cosmic region and physical worlds, stars, earths, suns; and they are all absolutely sensible according to their own [physical] law and with respect to those that are in them or near them, although they are not perceptible to us becasue of their remoteness and distance [from us][16].

What is Bruno arguing here? What is he saying about physical laws? Why is this important in contemporary physics?

Copernicus' sun was stationary and Bruno, as far as can be asertained, was the first person to suggest that the sun also rotated.

USING PHYSICAL MODELS SUPPORTING A DIFFERENT WORLDVIEW

About the same time that Bruno was espousing his cosmology, William Gilbert (1544–1603), a wealthy Englishman of nobility, was conducting experiments on magnetism and electricity, which he published in his book, *De Magnete* [On the

Magnet]. I have chosen to also mention Gilbert because he used physical models to explore questions that he had about the Earth's magnetism. Gilbert's work was informed by the work of Robert Norman, an earlier author, experimental philosopher, and navigator (his day job), who identified magnetic dip (although the first record of the concept of magnetic dip can be attributed to Chiense polymath and administrator, Shen Kuo (1031–1095) who also described the magnetic needle compass in his text, *Dream Pool Essays*[17]). Norman described his experiments in his book, *The Newe Attraction*. Unlike Gilbert who wrote in Latin, Norman wrote in English. In his book, Norman defended the ability of those experienced in mechanical arts to write about their experiences. In the introduction to his book he wrote:

> [T]here are in this land divers [many and varied] Mechanicians, that in their several faculties and professions, have the use of those Artes at the fingers ends, and can apply them to their several purposes, as effectively and more readily, than those that would most condemne them[18].

Gilbert[19] acknowledges that he built on Norman's published work but in his studies he addressed many more questions about electricity as well as magnetism and his was a far more sophisticated analysis. In this analysis, Gilbert proposed new terms such as "electric force" and new ways of using existng terms such as "north pole" and "south pole" which he applied to describe the ends of the lodestone (magnetite, Fe_3O_4 [Can you work out how magnetite can have that empirical formula?]) or any object that had been magnetized by the loadestone. According to tradition, magnetite was named after Magnes, a Greek sheppard, who discovered magnetite on Mt. Ida after noticing that the rock stuck to nails in his shoes. Gilbert also explored electric bodies (what we today would call static electricity) conducting experiments which showed that a range of substances, not just amber or jet, could "attract" other substances. He identified a difference, based on attraction, between magnetism and electricity. He noticed that moisture disrupted static electricity (e.g., from moist breath) but a coating of oil did not, and that electric forces in materials attracted water droplets. He observed that magnetic forces persisted across a flame but that magnetic iron lost its power when raised to red heat. Rod Wilson, in describing Gilbert as the first paleomagnetist, identifies some of Gilbert's claims and theories that suggest how innovative his thinking was[20]:

Phase change

This was one of the gems I missed on first reading. Gilbert was well aware that heating iron could eliminate its magnetic property altogether, but he goes further and guesses the nature of the change:

> "Still, as Cardan [an Italian mathematician, gambler, and physician] not injudiciously remarks, red-hot iron is not iron, but something lying outside its own nature, until it returns to itself. For just as, by the cold of the ambient air, water is changed from its own nature into ice, so iron made white-hot by fire has a confused, disordered form, and therefore is not attracted by a loadstone, and even loses its power of attracting, however acquired," (B2, C4, 108).

This remarkable intuition about a magnetic phase change similar to the water-ice change, even down to the use of the term "disordered", left me astounded that anyone should have grasped it 400 years ago when there was no distinction between heat and temperature, and no temperature scale beyond touch and colour. It was to be more than 300 years before the notions of a magnetic order/disorder transition and associated Curie temperature became clear.

While accepting Wilson's claim that Gilbert was an innovative thinker what strikes me is that Gilbert's statement is suggestive of a different worldview, a mechanical rather than an Aristotelian worldview, in which Gilbert is thinking of materials as being composed of discrete particles rather than of continuous matter.

An image of William Gilbert. Note the iconography?

Your experience with the black box activity should have indicated to you a relationship between the questions you ask, the observations you make that are informed by your expectations and your worldview [that is modern day humans with some science experience]. Gilbert's comments suggest similar set of expectations. If you think about your friends and colleagues and about worldview, you would probably recognize that while your worldview, like those of your friends and colleagues, is unique and idiosyncratic, at the same time you share some understandings and expectations with them. When you work together as a group on a task, such as proposing a model for the interior of a black box, you find that the group is probably able to negotiate a collective model that they would be willing to share publicly.

Consistent with a mechanistic worldview [the expectation that another object will behave in a similar way to the object one wants to study because they share specific characteristics] Gilbert developed a physical model for the Earth which he called a *terella* (meaning *little earth*):

Take then a strong lodestone, solid, of convenient size, uniform, hard, without flaw; on a lathe, such as is used in turning crystals and some precious stones, or on any like instrument ... give the lodestone the form of a ball. This stone thus prepared is a true homogeneous off-spring of the earth and is of the same shape, having got from art the orbicular that nature in the beginning gave to the earth, the common mother[21].

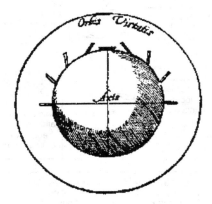

An image of Gilbert's terella from his book, De magnete.

In Gilbert's statement I identify a mix of Aristotleian and mechanistic worldviews: Aristotelian because of the the sense of a shared essesence between the earth and the lodestone that came from the earth. Gilbert's argument also contains mechanistic elements because of his expectation that the tarella and the earth behave in qualitatively similar ways because similar materials behave similarly everywhere on earth. Gilbert argues that this sperical model will allow him, and others who make the same model, to make assertions about aspects of the earth's nature that are not availble to direct observation. Although models were central to classical thinking about the nature of the cosmos, central to Gilbert's use of this model is an acceptance of the similarity between the material of which the model is composed and that of the earth itself and the extectation that, based on the behavior of the terella, assertions can be made about the magnetic nature of the earth. Such a use of models is central to the practice of all disciplines within Eurocentric science. Think of how model organisms as varied as bread molds, roundworms, mice, and chimpanzees have been used by scientists to make assertions about the physiology of living things, especially humans! Note also that assumptions must be made about the variables upon which the experimenter is going to focus. In Gilbert's case, we are being asked to focus on the variable of the magnetism of the lodestone as a corollary of the variable of the magnetism of the earth and ignore other factors in the process.

Similar to how scientists use models today, the terella supported Gilbert to ask specific questions about the magnetism of the earth and to begin a line of inquiry about magnetism. Through inquiry, a question drives the development of a system around a model and observational data and it looks something like this:

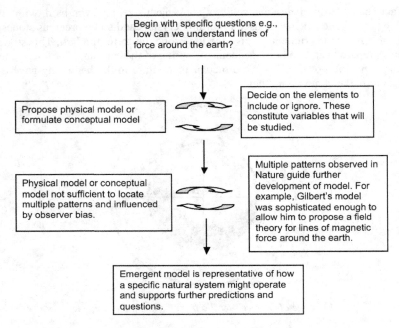

Contemporary representation of modeling phenomena.

This model is my attempt to communicate how Gilbert used the physical model of the terella and how his use was consistent with the way modern-day scientists use models. Note the role of dialectical reasoning as we move between observational data and modeling. For the argument about Gilbert and the concept of a magnetic field see also Rom Harré's book, *Great Scientific Experiments*[22]. In Eurocentric science most (I am tempted to say "all!") complex systems are studied through the use of models and the analogical relationship between models and the focus of empirical study is used by scientists to develop theory. This is just what Gilbert did when he made a connection between the disordered nature of white hot iron and ice show and used that connection to propose theory.

Activity

In *De magnete*, Gilbert confirmed his guess of temporary ("induced") magnetism by an original experiment (see drawing). Using strings, he hung two parallel iron bars above the pole of a terella, and noted that they repelled each other. Under the influence of the terella, each became a temporary magnet with the same polarities, and the temporary poles of each bar repelled those of the other one[23].

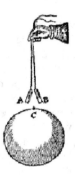

Develop and conduct an experiment of your own making that is based on Gilbert's original test shown here. Collect evidence that you can share with other people.

DISRUPTING PATTERNS IN THE SKY: A FURTHER CHALLENGE TO ARISTOTLEIANISM?

A further challenge to Aristotelianism came from the observations of Tycho Brahe (1546–1601), a wealthy Danish astronomer. His observations stand out for their detail in the time before the invention of the telescope.

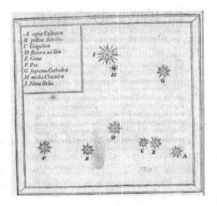

An image from Brahe's "Stella Nova" [New star] (Figure I) Constellation Cassiopeia with a new star, 1572[24].

In *De Stello Nova*, Brahe wrote:

Its First Appearance in 1572. Last year, in the month of November, on the eleventh day of that month, in the evening, after sunset, when, according to my habit, I was contemplating the stars in a clear sky, I noticed that a new and unusual star, surpassing all others in brilliancy, was shining almost directly above my head; and since I had, almost from boyhood, known all the stars of the heavens perfectly (there is no great difficulty in attaining that knowledge), it was quite evident to me that there had never before been any star in that place in the sky, even the smallest, to say nothing of a star so conspicuously bright as this. I was so astonished at this sight that I was not ashamed to doubt the trustworthiness of my own eyes. But when I observed that others, too, on having the place pointed out to them, could see that there was a star there, I had no further doubts. A miracle indeed ... For all philosophers agree, and facts clearly prove it to be the case, that in the ethereal region of the celestial world no change, in the way of either generation or of corruption, takes place; but that the heavens and the celestial bodies in the heavens are without increase or diminution, and that they undergo no alteration, either in number or in size... that they always remain the same[25]

Brahe also conducted a series of calculations, which he describes in *De Stello Nova*, that allow him to argue the new object he observed existed in the sphere of stars and not in the sphere below the moon where comets were found. He concluded it was a new star.

Activity

Do you think Brahe was correct to label the phenomenon a new star? Why or why not? What is the argument that Brahe is making here? How might this observation be of importance as evidence against Aristotelianism? Go back to Chapter 2 and look at Brahe's model of the universe shown there. What can you say about Brahe's model of the universe and the observation and argument he is recording in his quotation above? In Catholic European countries, Brahe's model of the universe had a longer life than it did in Protestant countries such as England, Holland, and Denmark. Speculate on why that might be the case.

In this endeavor, as in all his astronomical endeavors, numerous skilled craftsmen assisted Brahe with the provision of the best instruments that could be made at the time. He could afford to employ them because he was a beneficiary of an award of perpetual control of the island of Hven and all the people living there from King Fredrick II of Denmark[26]. Brahe was driven to learn more about the cosmos and was virtually willing to enslave artisans and workers to achieve this goal. On Hven he had constructed a state of the art observatory, study center called Stjernborg and a palace and zoo that he called Uranienborg. However, in time, Brahe had a falling out with the King of Denmark and in 1597 Brahe accepted the invitation of Rudolph II, the King of Bohemia and Holy Roman Emperor, to be imperial astronomer. He built a new observatory in Prague. There, Johannes Kepler (1571–1630) who later used the observations from Brahe's observatory to propose his Laws of planetary motion, was his assistant.

WHAT IS A LAW, SCIENTIFICALLY?

Brahe was the consummate observer. He believed that if one wanted to make claims about nature, such as ones about the motion of planets and other celestial bodies, it was important to have the best tools available to make the best possible observations of the phenomenon. Unlike Brahe, Kepler accepted the Copernican heliocentric theory and he realized that he could use Brahe's observations to address the question of how planets go round the sun. According to Richard Feynman[27], Kepler proposed the first modern physical mathematical law showing that planetary motion was an elipse and not the theorized circle of the Aristotelian cosmology. He was also able to address the question of whether the motion of planets was faster or slower near the sun by comparing the area transcribed by a planet in a certain time close to the sun and further away. Thirdly, he was also able to show that the square of a planet's time of revolution around the sun is proportional to the cube of the mean between a planet's maximum and minimum distances from the sun, a law that is used these days by scientists making predictions about the possibility of a life supporting planet in another solar system.

As a student of science in some form or other, you have probably used scientific laws and realize that they are different from legal laws or spirtual laws but do you know much about the idea of a scientific law? In Eurocentric science, what is the difference between a law, a fact, and a theory? The English word 'law' has been used since the time of Old English with the word coming originally from Old Norse meaning something laid or fixed[28]. The National Science Education Standards contain the following statement:

Implementing the *National Science Education Standards* implies the acquisition of scientific knowledge and the development of understanding. Scientific knowledge refers to facts, concepts, principles, laws, theories, and models and can be acquired in many ways. Understanding science requires that an individual integrate a complex structure of many types of knowledge, including the ideas of science, relationships between ideas, reasons for these relationships, ways to use the ideas to explain and predict other natural phenomena, and ways to apply them to many events[29].

Indeed in at least five different places in the NSES, reference is made to laws as well as other tools of scientific inquiry but how we might understand the nature of a law is not addressed explicitly. So we are still left with the question of how we understand a scientific law. An early published record of the use of the term, "law", as a law in the Eurocentric science sense, was in Robert Hooke's *Micrographia* [30] published in 1665:

But because we are certain, from the Laws *of refraction (which I have experimentally found to be so, by an Instrument I shall presently describe) that* the lines of the angles of Incidence are proportionate to the lines of the angles of Refraction, *therefore if Glasses could be made of those kind of Figures, or some other, such as the most incomparable* Des Cartes *has invented, and demonstrated in his Philosophical and Mathematical Works, we might hope for a much greater perfection of Opticks then can be rationally expected from spherical ones[.]*

This book was reviewed in the first (1665) volume of *Philosophical Transactions*, the journal of the first scientific organization in England, the Royal Society of London. In a review of Robert Hooke's book, *Micrographia*, the reviewer writes about some new tools that Hooke uses to make claims about new knowledge the following way:

A *New Instrument*, by which the *Refraction* of all kinds of Liquors may be exactly measured, thereby to give the curious an opportunity of making Trials of that kind, to establish the *Laws of Refraction*, to wit, whether the *Sines of the Angles of Refraction are respectively proportionable to the Sines of the Angles of Incedence*: This Instrument being very proper to examine very accurately, and with little trouble, and in small quantities, the *Refraction* of any Liquor, not onely for *one* inclination, but for all whereby he is enabled to make accurate *Tables*[31].

Note that this is not the sort of book review with which you might be more familiar but really a summary of the information that one might find if one decided to purchase a copy of *Micrographia*. Note also that both Hooke's and the reviewer's use of the term, "Law," suggest they expect their readers to be familiar with this use of the term. In other words, such use implies a culturally accepted practice associated with the development of a specific law. The reviewer writes that the measurement of refraction in various media [Liquors] will provide enough data [Trials] that will allow the establishment of a specific example of the Laws of Refraction associated with a ratio between sines of angles of refraction and angles of incidence. What does this tell you about the nature of a law in this context? For me, it indicates that in the 17th century a Law in natural philosophy was very similar to how we understand a scientific law in contemporary science. A scientific law is a representation of a pattern constructed from data that usually can be represented mathematically in a formula but importantly this pattern is not obvious or rational. Instead intitution and creativity are needed for someone to make a claim for a relationship or a pattern in data that framed as a law.

As Feynman said in his lecture on the character of a physical law, "Nature obeys an elegent law. How clever she is to pay attention to it.[32]" However, as even this the brief historical example indicates, laws are human constructions. In order to propose a law, one must have access to data that is meticulously collected using the best instruments available, just like Kepler was able to do using observations collected by Brahe and his workers. But his development of a law from these celestial observations was a creative act. It was only after he had constructed the law that others could 'see' it.

Why do scientific laws persist? It seems to me that they persist not only because of their utility as tools in the field of science but also for their simplicity and elegance. For Feynman, the power of scientific laws is that laws allow you [the scientist] to think beyond the data and context that you experience to make predictions. Feynman also claimed that the best laws are beautiful and simple in pattern but not in action.

By that he means that a 'good' law can often be represented relatively simply mathematically but has implications far beyond the specific context in which it was proposed initially. For example, Kepler's laws were refined by Isaac Newton as part of his Law of Gravitation, which could be applied not only the largest structures that humans could observe but also to the smallest; from the cosmos to the atom[33]. So laws that are designated as fundamental laws in Eurocentric science are also considered to be universal; they 'work' everywhere. Scientific laws also need to be 'worked on' over time. For example, they continue to be refined as instruments for data collection improve and as scientists work to keep them relevant.

Activity – So What is Needed for a Law? Seeing Patterns in the Data

Let us start with a simple activity. If we accept that laws can be represented by mathematical formula, how many laws can you draw using the data points presented on the chart[34]? You can probably draw one without any problems but can you draw four?

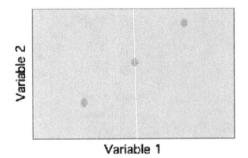

Finding laws in data

Were you able to draw four laws using the data points provided? If you found this activity a challenge try asking someone else to see if they have some ideas? What assumed knowledge do you need to be able to complete this activity? What does this activity tell you about the nature and development of scientific laws?

Activity: Patterns and Laws

Laws are patterns that people construct from the observations they make. Think about weather forcasting. Everyday we are bombarded with information about the weather we can expect that day based on weather patterns. Also, with a collection of patterns, meteorologists are able to make predictions about the weather. Of course, the tools of the meteorologist, such as improvements to satellite imaging, are designed to improve the ability of meteorologists to make predictions upon which humans can rely. How would you go if you were asked if there were patterns in data? In the following dice sides see if you can work out what should/could be on the bottom face, the one with the question mark[35].

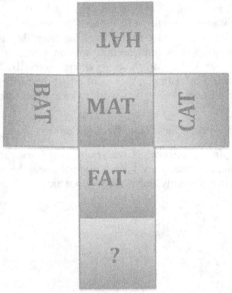

Example A.

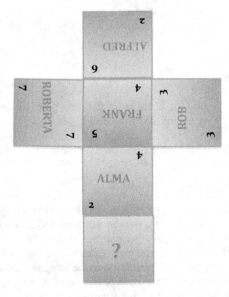

Example B.

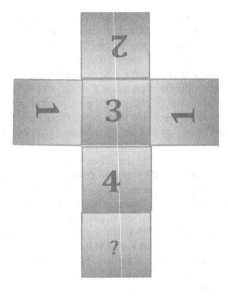

Example C.

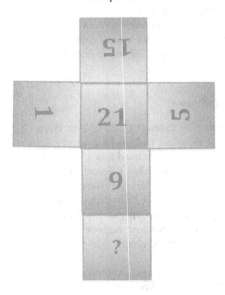

Example D.

Were you able to identify a pattern in the data presented on the five faces of each die and suggest a response for the bottom face? Were you able to propose a law for each example? Could this law be applied in other contexts? If you worked with a couple of other people to develop an answer for each bottom face, how strongly did you all feel about the answer you developed. Were you able to propose a mathematical law for each set of data? How strongly did you feel about the law you proposed? Think about how creative you needed to be to make those laws. What do you think? If you were able develop a law for each example, then you are engaged in a practice that is analogous to the practice of natural philosophers developing laws from observations of nature. Give your law to someone else and see if they can generate the same answer as you did for the bottom face. What does that suggest to you about scientific laws?

In the die activity, the fact that the die faces were provided is not supposed to be analogous to any broader notion of intelligent design but rather an analogy of nature. Interestingly, the designers of the original data had no pattern in mind for the set of data (the numbers or words on the faces of each die) presented in example C[36], so any pattern you developed is based on a pattern you have constructed. For me, this helps us to recognize that laws are subtle and constructed. Psychologial studies of human behavior show that humans have a propensity for finding patterns in information[37]. So you should not be too concerned at the variety of patterns people find. One of the strategies available in the practice of science is that a law should continue to 'work' even as more information is collected in an increasing range of different contexts. However, that is the simple version. Like all humans, scientists have the propensity to find patterns where there are none and to hold on to patterns even if the data is not conclusive. A classic example of this is the study of the honey bee "dance[38]" for which Karl von Frisch shared the Nobel Prize in Medicine and Physiology in 1973. Explore this example yourself. What do you think?

Activity – What is an Inference?

My claim about laws can be extended also to inferences. Some of you might have seen a representation of dinosaur or bird foot impressions sometimes called Tricky Tracks[39]. Perhaps many of you have used this activity? Look at the tracks and record as many observations as you can. What inferences can you make?

Now here is the hard part; is there a difference between inferences and observations? Instead of differentiating between inferences and observations would we be better discussing what we might call low-inference and high-inference observations? How would you differentiate between an observation and an inference? In Chapter 5 you will have more chances to examine the theory-laden nature of observations.

I ask these questions because I want you to think deeply about the nature of a law because of how central scientific laws are to Eurocentric science. The construction of laws is not just about looking at nature and identifying the laws that nature has provided. Feynman's joke, "How clever she is to pay attention to it," acknowledges the tension between the role of scientists in developing laws and the ability of science to see these laws in action in nature.

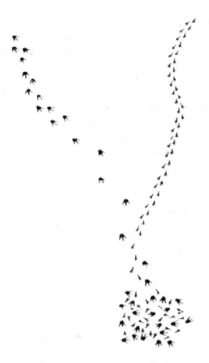

Tricky Tracks. What happened?

SUMMING UP

Within Eurocentric science, the physical sciences are repleat with laws, many of which are required knowledge for disciplines such as physics and chemistry. These laws can also be applied to other fields. For example, capillary action has an important role plant transpiration. There are also principles called laws in fields, such as geology and biology, that although they tend to lack the mathematical component are sometimes called laws, such as the law of superposition in geology. Some laws of science, such as the law of gravitation and the law of conservation of energy, are described by the science community as universal because they seem to work across space and time and can be expressed in a mathematical form that is consistent across space and time. Such laws were developed from observations of the physical universe and are used in Eurocentric science to present the universe as as an ordered system that can be described through the application of specific laws. Such laws have been retained because empirical evidence in the form of precise and accurate mearuements to collect data continues to be consistent with the application of such laws. Of course, one could argue that the presence and acceptance of Laws also influences the way measurements are developed and represented. These laws, once proclaimed continue to be tested by new data.

Unlike models, scientific laws in their current forms are not applied to the agents, like atoms or waves, which are necessary to help address "why" questions used to *explain* the operation of a law (and/or provide a mechanism to explain the observations); explanations require theory. For example, the Law of Gravitation can tell you how something moves but not why. Gas Laws can tell you about a relationship between pressure and volume but not why that relation can be observed. Note these examples come from the fields of physics and chemistry. When one begins to work with living things it seems to be more difficult to develop universal laws. In biology, reasoning tends to be more probabalistic than exact and in any context there are often agents, organisms involved that have the ability to act, their actions tend to be probabalistic rather than certain. Those of you familiar with aspects of quantum mechanics might also note the role of probabalistic models in that context.

The proposal and development of scientific laws constituted a very productive tool for the development of Eurocentric science. Such laws were not just applied locally in the production of local knowledge but also could be applied across the cosmos and everywhere inbetween. As such, experimental and natural philsophy was going global!

NOTES

[1]   Worsley, P. (1997). *Knowledges*. London: The New Press. p. 126.
[2]   Originally from the province of Yunan (north of Vietnam), Zheng He was castrated when captured as a boy by the Chinese army.
[3]   In the words of the Chinese record keepers, "to collect tribute from barbarians across the sea."
[4]   Hooykaas, R. (1987). The rise of modern science: When and why? *British Journal for the History of Science, 20*, 453–473.
[5]   Sabra, A. I. (2003, September and October). Ibn al-Haytham: Brief life of an Arab mathematician: Died circa 1040. *Harvard Magazine*, pp. 54–55.
[6]   Of course, this was beyond even his capabilities, which did not sit well with the Caliph, and he was placed under house arrest or perhaps decided to lie low. Whatever the reason for his enforced solitude, this was the time when he composed his *Book of Optics*.
[7]   Lindberg, D. C. (1967). Alhazen's theory of vision and its reception in the West. *Isis, 58*, 321–341. p. 322.
[8]   Burnal, J. D. (1965). *Science in history Vol. 1: The emergence of science* (3rd ed., p. 287). Cambridge, MA: MIT Press.
[9]   Author. (2001). Korea, 1000–1400 A.D. In *Heilbrunn timeline of art history*. New York: The Metropolitan Museum of Art. Retrieved from http://www.metmuseum.org/toah/ht/07/eak/ht07eak.htm
[10] Meggs, P. B. (1998). *A history of graphic design*. New York: John Wiley.
[11] Gleick, J. (2003). *Isaac Newton*. New York: Vintage Books.
[12] For example, Hekman, S. J. (1990). *Gender and knowledge: Elements of a postmodern feminism*. Boston: Northeastern University Press.
[13] Glick, T. F. (2005). Communication. In T. Glick, S. J. Livesey & F. Wallis (Eds.), *Medieval science, technology, and medicine: An encyclopedia* (pp. 135–139). New York: Routledge.
[14] Kuhn, T. (1957). *The Copernican revolution*. Cambridge, MA: Harvard University Press.
[15] Hermeticism was associated with a god that combined Egyptian and Greek elements. Hermetists, like Bruno, believed that Hermes Trismegistus was a pagan philosopher who foresaw the coming of Christianity. Hermeticists also believed that all religions, Buddhism, Judiaism, Islam, Christianity and even forms of Paganism, shared a core of common beliefs. For hermeticists wisdom of the

universe was associated with three areas of knowledge. Alchemy associated with physical and mystical transmutation, purification, and change, which helps us to understand their interest in attempting to convert base metals like lead to gold, and in distillation and fermentation. Astrology was based on the idea that the movement of celestial bodies held knowledge about our mind and about human existence. Theurgy was associated with the idea of divine magic as a way of perfecting oneself. These three areas were interrelated and dependent on each other all with the goal of attaining perfection.

[16]   Patterson, A. M. (1970). *The infinite worlds of Giodano Bruno* (p. 30). Springfield, IL: Charles C. Thomas.

[17]   Elisseeff, V. (2000). *The silk roads: Highways of culture and commerce*. New York: Berghahn Books.

[18]   Norman, R. (1581). *The newe attractive*. London. pp. i–ii.

[19]   Gilbert, W. (1600/1893). *De magnete* (P. Fleury Mottelay, Trans.). New York: Dover.

[20]   Wilson, R. (2000). William Gilbert: The first paleomagnetist. *Astronomy & Geophysics, 41*, 3.16–3.19. pp. 3.17–3.18.

[21]   Gilbert, W. (1600/1893). p. 23–24.

[22]   Harré, R. (1981/2002). *Great scientific experiments: Twenty experiments that changed our view of the world*. Mineola, NY: Dover.

[23]   Gilbert, W. (1600/1893). p. 203.

[24]   Taken from an online version of Tyco Brahe's publication at: http://www.texts.dnlb.dk/DeNovaStella/Index.html

[25]   Brahe, T. (1573). *De stello. nova* (On the New Star) Reported in H. Shapley & A. E. Howarth (Eds.), *Source book in astronomy* (1929) (pp. 13–14). New York: McGraw-Hill. Retrieved from http://www.ulib.org/cgi-bin/ulibcgi/ulibreader_path/bookReader.cgi

[26]   Conner, C. D. (2005). *A people's history of science*. p. 321.

[27]   Feynman, R. (1964). *The character of physical law*. BBC Video available at: http://research.microsoft.com/apps/tools/tuva/#data=3|||

[28]   Simpson, J. (Ed.). (1989). *Oxford English dictionary* (2nd ed.). Oxford: Clarendon Press.

[29]   National Research Council. (1996). *National science education standards* (p. 29). Washington, DC: National Academies Press.

[30]   Hooke, R. (1665/2003). *Micrographia*. Mineola, NY: Dover.

[31]   Hooke, R. (1665). Account of Micrgraphia, or the physiological descriptions of minute bodies. *Philosophical Transactions, 1*, 27–32.

[32]   Feynman, R. (1964). *The character of a physical law*.

[33]   Henry Cavendish conducted a now famous experiment originally to determine the density of the earth but is now used in educational contexts to show that the force of gravity acted on small objects (see utube) as well as it did on planets and other much more massive objects. The original publication was: Cavendish, H. (1798). Experiments to determine the density of the Earth. *Philosophical Transactions, 88*, 469–526.

[34]   This activity was developed from an example used by Rom Harré. Harré, R. (1981). *Great scientific experiments* (p. 16). London: Phaidon Press.

[35]   These dice are modified from Lederman, N., & Abd-El-Khalick, F. (1998). Avoiding de-natured science: Activities that promote understandings of the nature of science. In W. F. McComas (Ed.), *The nature of science in science education* (pp. 83–126). Dordrecht, The Netherlands: Kluwer. The activity is somewhat different in goal and tasks.

[36]   Lederman & Abd-El-Khalick. (1998). p. 120.

[37]   Whitson, J., A., & Galinsky, A., D. (2008). Lacking control increases illusory pattern perception. *Science, 322*, 115–117.

[38]   See: Wenner, A. M. (2002). The elusive honey bee dance "language" hypothesis. *Journal of Insect Behavior, 15*, 859–878. Wenner is a critic of von Frisch's initial studies. Also, Veldink, C. (1989). The honey-bee language controversy. *Interdisciplinary Science Reviews, 14*, 166–175.

[39]   There are versions of this image published in a selection of activities. Davis, A., & Evans, A. (1993). *Tricky tracks*. South Fremantle, WA, Australia: Sandcastle Books.

5. JUST THE FACTS, PLEASE

Inductivism has its Day

A fact is something that is usually observed and is proven beyond all measure of doubt.

I think it [facts] is a vital part [of learning] because otherwise you just have speculation and no one really knows where things are going. So if you say, 'These are the facts and this is how it is', then people can say, 'Oh, I've learnt something', otherwise it's like, 'What do you think about this?' and it's just everyone's opinion and no one learns anything.

Nicolee, a young woman preparing to become a science teacher and working on a research project with me, made these statements when asked her definition of a fact and the role of facts in learning science. Just from these statements what assessments can you make about how she thinks of facts? Does she think that facts are based on observations or something else? What does she say about the certainty or ambiguity of facts? Why is the certainty or ambiguity of facts important for arguments about learning? What do you understand a fact to be? As I hope to convince you in this chapter, practitioners of Eurocentric science began to associate the idea of a fact with the validity and reliability of using one's senses to identify true realities of nature. According to the Oxford English Dictionary, the term, *fact*, was not used in English until the 16th century where its use was associated with the Latin sense of the word (from factum) meaning something done or performed. This meaning is now obsolete but sometimes the Latin form had been extended to stand for an event (that had been performed) so the contemporary claim for a fact as something that had really occurred, or was actually the case, does have some connection to the original Latin meaning of this word. Experimental philosophers talked of *matters of fact* by which the truth of a fact, as something that actually occurred, was supported by direct observation of the natural world or of an experiment designed to test some aspect of the natural world.

FRANCIS BACON AND A NEW WAY OF MAKING FACTS

Of course, I could have chosen different statements from other current or prospective science teachers who might have responded differently to my question about facts than Nicolee did. But, for me, her comments serve to capture firmly held beliefs of many science teachers about the role of *facts* in learning science. Facts are important and their importance is confirmed, not by their relationship to scientific laws or their role in the development of scientific theory, but because they are easy to assess on an exam or quiz. Facts become incorporated into a metaphor of science as 'the right answer'. This focus on facts as fundamental to knowing science can be linked back to the ideas of a 17th Century philosopher, Francis Bacon, and his experimental proponents including Robert Boyle, Robert Hooke, and Isaac Newton and scientific societies, especially the Royal Society of London.

As I mentioned in Chapter 1, Francis Bacon was a trenchant critic of medieval scholasticism (Aristotelianism) proposing an alternative approach to the conduct of developing new knowledge. He claimed that the work of understanding was clouded by a mind "occupied with unsound doctrines[1]" (medieval scholasticism) and that the only way to rectify this situation was to start afresh with thoughts purged of such doctrine. Bacon maintained that while he revered the writings of the ancients the approach that he proposed would lead practitioners to truth and understanding. He claimed that a discourse based on deductive argument that was popular in ancient texts was not appropriate for inventing new knowledge. Bacon's criticism of the language used in deductive reasoning formed the basis of his proposal that the search for human understanding be based on direct observations rather than theories that had emerged from the studies of the ancients, which should be eliminated:

> The syllogism consists of propositions, propositions consist of words, words are symbols of notions. Therefore if the notions themselves (which is the root of the matter) are confused and over-hastily abstracted from the facts, there can be no firmness in the superstructure. Our only hope therefore lies in true induction[2].

What is the argument Bacon is making here? If notions, what we might call premises, are not thoughtful but confused, then the words used to present these notions to others do not present an accurate picture of the material world. So these notions have only a confused relation to reality. Logic could not be appropriately applied to reality because it was dependent on confused notions. According to Bacon, there were two ways of searching for the truth. One way was from unchanging foundational axioms which are believed to be the truth and which lead to the discovery of particulars. This was deductive reasoning characteristic of Aristotelianism. The other way, which he believed was the untried but true way, was from the senses and particulars to middle axioms, to experimentation, and then to general axioms[3] that is inductivism with a bit of abductive reasoning as well.

Question. Can you identify a place for abductive reasoning in Bacon's scheme described above?

According to Bacon, by using the senses natural philosophers could collect lots of observations from which they could generate a more general statement that could be tested by conducting experiments from which would come a truthful generalization. Bacon believed that nature was more subtle than argument or empty dogma. If observations of nature contradicted aspects of an axiom then the axiom should be changed, but the tendency of Aristotelianism had been to rescue and preserve the axiom by some "frivolous distinction". Bacon argued that experimental philosophers needed to put their faith in observations. It was from making observations that reality would be revealed. Of course, as we know from earlier chapters Aristotle also made an argument for the importance of the senses for making observations of nature, although he made a stronger argument for deduction. Bacon's position can be described as belonging to a philosophy called *realism*, which accepts that the universe and all objects in it are real and will continue to exist even if human beings no longer existed. For Bacon, in order to be able to access this reality, humans needed to clear their minds of thoughts that could mislead and then observe nature truly with an 'open mind' not clouded by ideas of axioms. Bacon's realist ontology ran counter to ontologies, such as *idealism* (Plato was a proponent), which is based on the notion that that human knowledge of the external world comes to us via the mind and not the senses. In philosophic circles, the debate between these ontologies and various iterations of them is ongoing. I suggest that in contemporary Eurocentric science the ontology is more what could be called *scientific realism*, in which science practice is based on an acknowledgment that while we cannot know that what we have observed is 'true' reality what we have seems to work and we will continue to act as though it is reality until we learn it is not. This vision of realism is also consistent with the mechanistic worldview you examined in Chapter 3.

Like all people who believe they have a new way for doing something, Bacon wanted to convince others that his method would support the construction of new knowledge. He wrote:

> The men of experiment are like the ant, they only collect and use; the reasoners resemble spiders, who make cobwebs out of their own substance. But the bee takes the middle course: it gathers its material from the flowers of the garden and field, but transforms and digests it by a power of its own. Not unlike this is the true business of philosophy (science); for it neither relies solely or chiefly on the powers of the mind, nor does it take the matter which it gathers from natural history and mechanical experiments and lay up in the memory whole, as it finds it, but lays it up in the understanding altered and digested. Therefore, from a closer and purer league between these two faculties, the experimental and the rational (such as has never been made), much may be hoped[4].

Activity

What sense can you make of Bacon's metaphor? If you were an ant, how would you use information from an experiment? How do you think Bacon was using the spider's cobweb as a metaphor? What would the 'middle course', the course taken by the bee, be like?

Bacon's was a nuanced argument based on the idea that people who wished to study science using the method that he proposed had to guard against false notions that cloud human understanding. For Bacon, these false notions included: Idols of the Tribe, which undermine the consistency and objectivity of human perception; Idols of the Cave, which afflict the individual spirit or personality; Idols of the Theatre, that are due to the effects of philosophical dogma and received systems that are not real because they are based on insufficient observations and experiments (Aristotle) or are too specialized (empirical); and Idols of the Marketplace, which result from the language used because words can distort understanding by being used to represent something that is non-existent or by confusing the nature of things. Consistent with the value Bacon ascribed to experiment, he also argued for recognizing the value of the mechanical arts, the trades that "exhibit and alter natural bodies" and reveal the nature of these bodies: and the people involved in such activities. How does this compare with Aristotle's arguments about knowledge and the role of the mechanical arts?

MATTERS OF FACT – THE EMERGENCE OF SCIENTIFIC FACTS

As proposed by Bacon, experimental philosophy was based on the acceptance of both the importance of observation and the belief that human observations should be a record of Nature's reality. Acceptance of this philosophy supported the emergence of a new sort of information, fundamental human constructs called *scientific facts* which were taken as representing a record of these observations. Experimental philosophers could then present records of observations obtained during the conduct of experiments as matters of fact, or scientific facts. Bacon's philosophy was based on five principles:

1. Matters of fact are a record of the observations obtained during the conduct of experiments.
2. Matters of fact are records of reality obtained from the conduct of experiments.
3. You convince people that you have observed Nature truly by creating a 'visual source' through descriptions of your experiments[5].
4. Because they are based on observations of nature, facts have greater certainty than scientific theories.
5. Because matters of fact come directly from Nature and are not dependent on an observer's opinion they possess moral and cognitive certainty. (Perhaps in science classrooms they continue to do so?)

These arguments formed the basis of an emerging experimental philosophy and made observing a pre-eminent activity of experimentation. Implicit with this belief was the idea that there existed a direct pathway from the reality of Nature to observation that was not influenced by the observer's beliefs. Simply expressed, Bacon argued for theory-free observations. According to Barbara Shapiro[6], the English legal system at the time had already sensitized people to the role of observation and authentic testimony in matters of fact (Bacon had studied law). So within the community there was a general acceptance of the idea of matters of fact. Also mentioned previously, according to the Oxford English Dictionary[7] early English usage was associated with a fact as an act, with something done, rather than with something said. Both of these cultural developments would seem to place English natural philosophy in an environment that was accepting of using matters of fact as the basis for a 'new' philosophy for constructing knowledge. Within this model, theory would be developed once the facts had been extracted from nature. Bacon's model resurrected an exciting way of looking at nature but experimental philosophers were left with the question just as we are today, of whether it is even possible to make theory-free observations.

Activity – Are Theory-free Observations Possible?

The question of whether observations can be theory-free is definitely open to debate but I would think most scholars accept that observations are theory-laden and not theory-free. I wonder if Bacon ever really believed that observations could be free or if he just wanted people to try and not be quite so influenced by the axioms that had become the basis for medieval scholasticism. So here is something for you to try to see what you think about theory-free observations.

Look at the image. Can you can find the man?

Can you find the man?

If you could find the man, can you find the *cow* in the following image[8]?

Can you find the cow? (Hint: The image is of a field from above)

I think you will agree that the cow is much more difficult to find than the man and, even when I show some people where the cow is located, they remain unconvinced that there is a cow in the image. There are many other examples of this type of challenge often associated with discussions of visual perception. However, for me they provide some of the simplest evidence I can think of for the theory-ladenness of observations. If you know where to look, you can construct the phenomenon you are experiencing into the shape that you have been told. The cow is much more difficult to find because the shapes on the image do not resolve themselves into a well-defined pattern. As you know from the previous chapter, a pattern is what you need if you are going to construct a law based on multiple experiences. Finding patterns in observations and constructing law-like statements is one of the bases of Eurocentric science. Some people can become very frustrated and annoyed with their inability to "see" the pattern.

Another piece of evidence that really influenced my appreciation for the theory-ladenness of observations was an incident from my secondary school teaching practice. I was teaching a four-week unit on cells to a Grade 8 science class. Students had been engaged in making wet mounts and looking at cells under a microscope. I thought the unit had gone very well. The students seemed engaged and seemed to have learned a lot about cells. Towards the end of the unit I asked a young male student who was looking at his cheek cells under the microscope whether or not he could see good cells. To which he replied that his cells were really good, round with round dark round walls! Immediately from his description, I understood he was describing air bubbles that had been trapped under the coverslip of his wet mount and not cheek cells. I understood that even though he had been observing for almost four weeks and had written and drawn things down. He was unable to discern whether or not what he was looking at under the microscope was actually a cell. This experience emphasized for me the role of theory in making observations because if this student had a theoretical sense of what a cell should look like, I believe that he would have had a much better chance of "observing" cells. This experience raised another issue for me, the relationship between theory and phenomenon in science education. Prior to this experience, I would have said students should experience phenomenon first before they learn a theory to explain their observations but now I think such an approach is simplistic and for education you need to integrate phenomena and theory, which is the pedagogical approach I have tried to enact ever since.

Activity – How Reliable is One of Your Other Senses?

Another way to examine the reliability of your senses is to use this historic test. Set up three containers of water – one containing cold water, one hot (but not too hot for your hand) and one at room temperature (about 25 degrees Celsius). Simultaneously put one hand in the cold water and the other in the hot water. Hold them in there for 30 seconds. Once the time has past immediately plunge both hands into the bowl containing water at room temperature. What did you observe? How do you think people who accepted that the world was composed of four elements: earth, water, air, and fire, would have thought about hot and cold? What was their reality? Would they have thought about doing an experiment like this? Why or why not? How might your thinking about these questions influence your thinking about the teaching and learning of youth?

Convincing Others About Matters of Fact

One of the earliest proponents of matters of fact was the experimental philosopher, Robert Boyle (1627–1691). Boyle, like other experimental philosophers, had to give some thought to how he might convince his peers that he, and the assistants he employed who were rarely acknowledged, had observed Nature truly. According to science historian Steven Shapin[9], Boyle achieved this by creating a 'visual source' through the rich descriptions of his experiments in much the same way that contemporary qualitative researchers attempt to create rich descriptions of their research in order to convince their readers that their research has rigor[10]. Using a literary approach, Boyle's goal was to convince his readers that he had conducted experiments that yielded matters of fact. For example, how vivid do you find the following description from Boyle?

> We will add (by way of confirmation) the following experiment: in such a small receiver, as those wherein we killed divers birds, we carefully closed up one, who, though for a quarter of an hour he seemed not much prejudiced by the closeness of his prison, afterwards began to first pant very vehemently, and keep his bill very open, and then to appear very sick; and last of all, after some long and violent strainings, to cast up some little matter out of his stomach; which he did several times, till growing so sick that he staggered and gasped, as being just ready to die. We perceived, that within about three quarters of an hour from the time that he was put in, he had so sickened and tainted the air with the streams of his body, that it was become altogether unfit for the use of respiration[11].

Does this description of the experiment convince you that air quality is important for continued life? Boyle's literary style was designed to convince the reader that an experiment was conducted and it provided an appropriate method for achieving correspondence between observations of Nature and 'true' Nature. Note Boyle's use of "we". What does this suggest to you?

While Bacon argued that matters of fact were obtained by holding a *mirror* to reality, scientific theories were a totally different proposition. Being dependent on human reason and opinion they lacked the 'truth' of scientific facts. Alternatively because facts came from nature, God's creation, they had moral as well as cognitive power making them difficult to argue against. Do you think in contemporary science classrooms there is a resonance of the status assigned to facts? What implications does such a resonance have for the way science is taught in classrooms where this notion of the moral value of facts has a powerful presence? The idea that facts existed in nature to be discovered has further implications for how discovery in science is often represented in both the scientific and broader communities and how concepts are represented in science textbooks.

THE NEED OF A LABORATORY

Of course, if you are going to make observations from experiments, where you bring nature into a space and modify it in some way, you need a space in which this can be done. Matters of fact required the existence of an appropriate physical environment for scientists to demonstrate their experiments to witnesses. Thus, the laboratory was born. Laboratories were to be public areas where like-minded experimental philosophers could work cooperatively and where matters of fact could be demonstrated. These spaces contrasted with existing practical working areas maintained by alchemists that had been secretive and closed to the public. The laboratories of the seventeenth century experimental philosophers formed the precursors of modern laboratories. In his *History of the Royal Society*, Thomas Sprat (1635–1713) relates the use of the laboratory with the establishment of a matter of fact as he describes the value of the types of papers submitted to *Philosophical Transactions*, the journal of the Royal Society of London[12]:

> Those to whom the conduct of the *Experiment* is committed … carry the eyes and the imaginations of the whole company into the *Laboratory* with them. And after they have perform'd the *Trial* they bring all the *History* of its *process* back again to the *test*. Then comes in the second great work of the *Assembly*, which is to *judg[e]* and *resolve* upon the matter of *Fact*.

Boyle was a staunch supporter of Baconian philosophy and believed strongly that knowledge that was generated by conducting experiments in laboratories in front of witnesses should be available to other interested individuals. Presenting knowledge in this way helped to reinforce its matter of fact status. According to sociologist of science Bruno Latour[13], two of the major features that distinguish science from other forms of knowledge are the use of the laboratory and experimental apparatus and the rhetoric of argument in scientific discourse.

SO HOW EXACTLY SHOULD THIS NEW KNOWLEDGE BE PRODUCED? THE NEED OF AN EXPERIMENTAL PROCEDURE

In *Parasceve* (or *Description of a Natural and Experimental History, such as may serve for the Foundation of a True Philosophy*), which was first published in 1620, Bacon prescribed the structure an experiment should have if an experimental philosopher wanted to make claims about making new knowledge:

> I will myself now supply, by diligently and exactly setting forth the method and description of a history of this kind, such as shall satisfy my intention; lest men for wont of warning set to work the wrong way, and guide themselves by the example of the natural histories now in use, and so go far astray from my design[14].

Step 1. According to Bacon, an investigation should start with questions "in order to provoke and stimulate further inquiry[15]" Boyle and Hooke used a statement of purpose or questions at the beginning of their accounts in order to provide a rationale for their studies; as Hooke writes in the Preface of *Micrographia*:

> Toward the prosecution [treat in more detail] of this method in *Physical Inquiries*, I have here and there *gleaned* up an *handful* of Observations, in the collection of most of which I made use of *Microscopes*, ... that improve the sense; which way I have hereintaken ... only to promote the use of Mechanical helps for the Senses, both in the surveying of the already visible world, and for the discovery of many others hitherto unknown ... so many others to be discovered, every considerable improvements of Telescopes or Microscopes producing new worlds and Terra Incognitions to our view[16].

Step 2. Bacon:

> [I]n any new ... experiment the manner in which the experiment was conducted should be added, that men may be free to judge for themselves whether the information obtained from that experiment be trustworthy or fallacious; and also that men's industry may be roused to discover if possible methods are more exact[17].

Both Boyle and Hooke included a detailed description of the new tools, including extensive diagrams, which they used in the experiments. For Boyle, an important new 'big' tool was the air pump and for Hooke, the microscope. These were both examples of new technology that was helping them and their colleagues to put different questions to nature. In their narratives of their experiments, each included thorough accounts of the procedure that they followed for each experiment, at the same time referencing the replicability of the experiments. In accordance with the arguments of Bacon about the structure of these experimental procedures, Boyle writes in the Preface to one of his most famous books of experimentation, *New Experiments Physico-Mechanical*:

> I thought it necessary to deliver things circumstantially, that the person addressed them to might, without mistake, and with as little trouble as possible be able to repeat such unusual experiments; and that after I consented to let my obser-vations be made public, the most ordinary reason for my prolixity was that, foreseeing that such a trouble that I met with making those trials carefully, and the great expense of time that they necessarily require (not to mention the charges of making the engine, and employing a man to manage it) will probably keep most men from trying again these experiments I thought I might do the generality of my readers no unacceptable piece of service by so punctually [carefully] relating what I carefully observed, that they may look upon these narratives as standing records of our new pneumatics[18].

In the account above Boyle's attempt to convince his readers that the experiments were conducted in the manner that he described, was consistent with Bacon's directive. By providing detail of the experiment Boyle presented his readers with the detail necessary to either repeat the experiments or be able to imagine the reality of the experiment and therefore be convinced of the experimental results.

Step 3. Bacon:

> [I]f in any statement there be anything doubtful or questionable, I would by no means have it suppressed or passed in silence, but plainly and perspicuously set down by way of note or admonition[19].

Boyle also fulfilled these requirements by including in his extensive portfolio of experiments on pneumatics, experiments that were not successful:

> But to verify what we say in another discourse [Two essays concerning the unsuccessfulness of experiments included in *Certain physiological essays* (I. Birch Ed., 318–353)] where we show that even true experiments may, by reason of the easy mistake of some unheeded circumstance, be unsuccessfully tried; we will advertise, on this occasion, we did often times in vain try the breaking of the bladders after the manner above mentioned[20].

By doing this, Boyle complied with the recommendations of Bacon in *Parasceve* and supported notions of his reliability and modesty. In *Micrographia*, Hooke also included references to his work that were designed to reinforce his modesty and believability as well as highlight his belief in the value of the new experimental philosophy:

> I here present to the world my imperfect endeavours; which though they shall prove no other way considerable, yet, I hope, they may be in some measure useful to the main Design of a reformation in Philosophy, if it be only by showing, that there is not so much required towards it[21].

Step 4. Bacon:

> Observations be interspersed occasionally as the results of experimentation. [A] brief review ... of the opinions now received, ... that they may touch and arouse the intellect[22].

Both Boyle and Hooke included a presentation of the results of experiments as an account of observations. These results were designed to convince the reader that the experiment had been conducted as described and that the results obtained constituted facts of nature. In *Micrographia,* Hooke also used very detailed diagrams to reinforce his account and to help the reader to visualize his observations under the microscope. For Boyle and Hooke, diagrams were naturalistic representations of apparatus and observations of natural phenomena, another way to establish matters of fact. Both Boyle and Hooke completed accounts of their experiments by discussing the significance and implications of the results for the development of theory or for the setting up of further experimentation. As Boyle writes in Experiment 1 of New experiments physico-mechanical:

> For the more easy understanding of the experiments triable by our engine, I thought it not superfluous or unseasonable in the recital of this first of them to insinuate that notion, by which it seems likely, that most, if not all of them, will prove explicable. Your Lordship will easily suppose that the notion I speak of is, that there is a spring, or elastical power in the air we live in[23].

Step 5. Bacon, "[W]hether it was a thing of which, if it really happened, there must needs have been many witnesses[24]". In his papers on pneumatics, Boyle often referred to the witnesses who were present while he conducted experiments and who, by their own public stature, reinforced his claims about the results of experiments:

> This experiment was a few days after repeated in the presence of those excellent and deservedly famous Mathematic Professors, Dr. *Wallis*, Dr. *Ward*, and Mr. *Wren* who were pleased to honour it with their presence and whom I name, both as justly counting it an honour to be known to them, and as being glad of such judicious and illustrious witnesses of our experiment[.][25]

This particular structure of the conduct of experiments also required a new strategy for representing and communicating these experiments. In England, the report endorsed by the emerging professional organization for experimental philosophers, the Royal Society of London, modeled these steps. It was with the publication of the journal of the Royal Society, *Philosophical Transactions*, that the structure for reports of experimental activity was outlined explicitly. This prestigious journal defined both the language that was appropriate for experimental philosophers to use in their reports and the structure that the reports should have if they were to be published in the journal. *Experimental reports* were constructed within a particular social milieu so legitimation of knowledge was a public endeavor and, consequently, accounts had to be convincing in their accuracy, believability, and veracity. The experimental report, as presented by Boyle, Hooke and by scientists who belong to more recent eras, owes much of its literary structure to the emerging experimental philosophy based on induction, the structure of which was promoted by the writings of Francis Bacon. Experimental philosophers were familiar with the genre of the personal letter and so their reports of their experiments initially tended to follow that form of writing but a historical survey of *Philosophical Transactions*, the Journal of the Royal Society, shows the evolution of such reports to a format more similar to that which you can find in any contemporary science journal.

Do you recognize from the previous account, an emerging cultural structure that could be used by those in power to decide what constituted an experimental report? If you think about the implementation of this structure as the basis for generating new knowledge and as a road map of what this process might look like, then people saw themselves as agents who could use this structure to enact a new form of culture. During the 17th century other tools, including new philosophies and new instruments, became available that further supported these agents' actions. With respect to the experimental report, in order for a report to be an experimental it had to begin with a question or an aim; followed by a detailed description of the method, which contained a list of the apparatus and materials used and possibly a diagram of the apparatus; a results section and a discussion of the implications of the results. For many, this structure became the only acceptable one for an experimental report and so became an ideology of science. As experimental philosophy became accepted by society as a powerful method for generating new knowledge and revealing reality, greater prominence was given to the data as a record of nature, not the observer, providing justification for the removal of the active voice from accounts of method and results in experimental reports.

Researchers such as Steve Woolgar and Bruno Latour[26] in their studies of laboratories have shown that the practice of science is far removed from the published experimental report of science. Contemporary scientific experimental reports tend to have a rhetorical character similar to that of experimental reports of the 17th century. As J. M. Ziman wrote in *Public Knowledge*:

> It is extraordinary to consider that the general form of a scientific paper has changed less in nearly 300 years, than any other class of literature except the bedroom farce[27].

According to linguist Kathryn Riley[28], contemporary experimental reports can be divided into separate sections on the basis of the use of voice. She argues that in the Introduction of an experimental report where the author is chronicling and critiquing previous research, the active voice is the voice of choice of the researcher. In the Methods section, the use of passive voice imputes a global connotation implying any reasonable scientist from the field in any laboratory could conduct the experiment. The use of the passive voice in the Results section helps to "universalise the results[29]" and remove the author. Such an approach to the results section remains consistent with the ideology that observations of nature are observations of reality and exist independently of the observer. Finally in the Discussion section, where the researcher is interpreting the data and advocating new theory, active voice is deemed to be appropriate. Perhaps you could check out a recent experimental report from a science journal to examine the veracity of this claim?

Question. If you ask students to write a report of an investigation that they conducted, how would you expect them to structure such a report? What role would descriptions have? How would you ask students to use voice in their reports and why? What sections would you want them to include and why?

I am wondering if you have begun to make a connection between Bacon's representation of a method for making new knowledge and "the scientific method" presented in many science textbooks? An emphasis on using the correct method as the path to legitimate true knowledge about science is highly valued in science education and is presented by some practitioners, teachers, textbooks, and the media, as the reality of science. However, as you might have noted from this history, "the method" is based on people's ideas of how science should be represented. There is no such thing as a/the method of science. Some science educators[30] have identified this perspective as an ideology and a mythology called *scientism*. This ideology, identified in the teaching of science in high schools, emerges from teacher and school beliefs related to the legitimation of specific practices and knowledge in science and to the moral and socio-political value of contemporary science. R. Nadeau and Jacques Désautels[31] claim that:

> Scientism implies an attitude toward science that sees it not only as an activity involving special knowledge, because of its specific and time tested method of solving problems, but as one with a cognitive basis that is beyond question.

Such a definition sounds so much like Bacon's argument for generating new knowledge that it is uncanny. Consistent with Baconian philosophy, such a definition imputes that scientific knowledge is legitimated by the way scientific endeavor is conducted, and that scientific knowledge can be criticized only by the evolution of disparate knowledge, which is attained by using similar procedures. I think you will agree that this definition conforms very well to the arguments Bacon made about how one should go about constructing of matters of fact and the moral and cognitive power of those constructed facts. Bacon wanted people to break away from the structures of medieval scholasticism, which he thought was strangling the exploration of new knowledge, and so one can understand his passionate espousal of a different method. However, without history one loses sense of the constructed nature of this argument, which is exactly what happens in many science classrooms. Equating science with a particular procedure, a scientific method, is an example of *metonymy* where one feature is taken to represent the totality of a specific process. Scientism also has connections to modernism with its acceptance of science as solely a progressive endeavor based on a succession of great European men who saw further than anyone else.

Although I believe that scientism emerged as Bacon's methodology for generating scientific knowledge became accepted as the *only* acceptable method for generating knowledge, his criticism of false Idols indicates that he may have been equally critical of dogma, such as scientism, where a specific method has become an ideology. Some evidence of this can be discerned in the developments associated with how critique of knowledge claims was to be pursued.

Deciding the Power of Critique

As the experimental report became directly associated with experimental activity there developed an acceptance of the notion that only experimental philosophers who had attempted to replicate an experiment, which had been described in a report, could critique the author's claims. According to this practice, only practitioners from within the culture of science could criticize the generation and legitimation of scientific knowledge. For example, Isaac Newton's perspective is clear in his letter of July 8, 1672 printed in *Philosophical Transactions* after Ignatius Pardies, Professor of Mathematics at Parisian College, had criticized Newton's argument about light. Pardies was a supporter of Descartes' theory of light, which proposed the notion that light was a pure color. This theory had been rebutted by the results of experiments conducted by Newton in which he had demonstrated that white light was a composite of other colors. Newton wrote:

> You know, the proper Method for *inquiring* after the properties of things is, to deduce them from Experiments. And I told you that the Theory, which I propounded, was evinced to me, not by inferring 'tis thus because not otherwise, that is, not by deducing it by confutation of contrary suppositions, but by deriving it from Experiments concluding profitably and directly. The way therefore to examine it is, by considering whether the Experiments which I propound do prove those parts of the Theory, to which they are applied, or by prosecuting other Experiments which the Theory may suggest for its examination. And this I would have done in a due Method; the Laws of *Refraction* being thoroughly

inquired into and determined before the nature of *Colours* be taken into consideration[32].

I interpret Newton's comments as evidence of a discourse repertoire, called *interpretive repertoires*, identified in 1984 by sociologists of science, G. Nigel Gilbert and Michael Mulkay[33]. In their study of scientific discovery and justification in biochemistry, they followed a number of major scientists [one won the Noble Prize] into their lab spaces and other informal environments, interviewing them and observing their behavior and monitoring their use of language at conferences. In this study, Gilbert and Mulkay found competing interpretations for experimental data were variously presented by scientists, depending on each scientist's commitment to one of the competing interpretations. Generally, individual scientists presented themselves as holding the interpretation that was the correct representation of reality. They represented members of the other competing theoretical camp, which failed to acknowledge and accept their view of the physical world, as typically misled by non-cognitive factors beyond the empirical and technical including factors, such as emotional commitment and personal influence. However, they presented themselves as having interpreted the empirical data correctly and rationally.

In the public world, scientists were expected to conform to community-ideology of empirical, rational, polite standards of science where their disagreements about how data could be understood were tempered by these standards. However in informal, non-public settings, scientists were more likely to use contingent repertoires that represented scientists with opposing positions as having dogmatic, non-rational attachment to a specific theory, or being personally stupid, referring to other scientists in a non-complementary fashion, which they never would publically. Gilbert and Mulkay were able to confirm the status of the experimental report or research paper as a public literary genre and a discourse of power, which defined the appropriate form for legitimating scientific knowledge. Newton's comments indicate that, even in the 17th century as societies were still in the process of deciding the form of the experimental report, researchers of his stature were comfortable directing how others should structure the report of their studies if they wished to challenge knowledge claims, especially those he made. The promotion by science societies of the experimental report as a specific genre ensured that power was retained by this genre in the reporting of scientific discoveries. These developments also placed scientific societies in the powerful position of deciding what counted as "true" new knowledge because through peer review they could decide which papers to include in their journals and which to leave out.

Was the Experimental Report the Only Way to Represent New Knowledge?

At the time that Robert Boyle was developing the experimental report and using the genre to describe his experiments, observations, and theoretical musings, another approach for presenting new scientific knowledge, argumentative disputation in the form of dialectical reasoning, was very popular in the Italian courts. Galileo Galilei (1564–1642), the pre-eminent natural philosopher of his day, was the foremost practitioner of this form of reasoning, which he used to support his claims to have discovered new knowledge by experimentation. All of his published books were dedicated to a person in power, including the Grand Duke of Tuscany, *Dialogue Concerning the Two Chief World Systems: Ptolemaic and Copernican*, and a Pope, Urban VIII, *The Assayer*. In his dedication in *Dialogue Concerning Two World Systems* he writes:

> Therefore if any men might claim extreme distinction in intellect above all mankind, Ptolemy and Copernicus were such men, whose gaze was thus raised on high and who philosophized about the constitution of the world. These dialogues of mine revolving principally around these works, it seemed to me that I should not dedicate them to anyone except Your Highness[34].

In the abstract to this book, Galileo explains that he chose to present his explanations in the form of a dialogue because that would allow him to digress from the restrictions adherence to explanations using only mathematical laws would involve.

Question. For an example of this dialogic approach to writing experimental philosophy look back in Chapter 3 and reread the example from Galileo given there. What do you think would be the strengths and limitations of this approach to reporting the outcomes of empirical study compared with that proposed by Bacon and used by experimental philosophers such as Boyle and Hooke?

Although Galileo Galilei came from a Florentine patrician family, after the death of his musician father he was left with the responsibility of looking after his family, including his mother and siblings. He had a mathematics professorship at the University of Pisa that was not well paid and in 1592 accepted a more lucrative position at the University of Padua near Venice where he worked for eighteen years. Needing to be financially secure to support his family, Galileo used his abilities to find the most remunerative patronage available. In Venice, a republic, patronage came from the major families but such patronage was piecemeal and Galileo found he was still forced to take in boarders and teach out of session to make ends meet. However, during this time all was not lost because it was also a period of productivity for him as an experimental philosopher. He was able to conduct studies on projectile and natural motion (gravity) developing some of the theories that would, in the long run, make him famous, and providing the experimental data that he could use to propose his cosmology in his two final and probably best known publications, *Dialogue on the Two Chief World Systems* (1632), and *Dialogues Concerning Two New Sciences* (1638).

In 1609, he learned through a colleague of a new tool, the telescope, likely one developed/invented by Hans Lippershey, a German-Dutch lens maker. Galileo improved the original telescope design, grinding and polishing his own lenses. Very quickly, as the draft letter below suggests, Galileo recognized the military and commercial possibilities the telescope could afford. The publication in 1610 of his book, *Starry Messenger*, dedicated to the Grand Duke of Tuscany, excited much interest amongst the top tiers of European society and he was able to parley this into employment and patronage by the ruling family of the Duchy of Tuscany (which included Florence), the de Medicis.

The image on the following page comes from the University of Michigan's online special collection. The page is in Galileo's hand. The top half the draft of this page contains a note to the Doge of Venice (Elected for life Chief Magistrate) about 1609. It reads[35]:

> Most Serene Prince. Galileo Galilei most humbly prostrates himself before Your Highness, watching carefully, and with all spirit of willingness, not only to satisfy what concerns the reading of mathematics in the study of Padua, but to write of having decided to present to Your Highness a telescope that will be a great help in maritime and land enterprises. I assure you I shall keep this new invention a great secret and show it only to Your Highness. The telescope was made for the most accurate study of distances. This telescope has the advantage of discovering the ships of the enemy two hours before they can be seen with the natural vision and to distinguish the number and quality of the ships and to judge their strength and be ready to chase them, to fight them, or to flee from them; or, in the open country to see all details and to distinguish every movement and preparation.

Question. On the following page, look closely at what Galileo has written. The bottom section of the page contains, in Galileo's hand, some of his observations of Jupiter's moons obtained using his new tool, the telescope. These observations were published in his book, *Starry Messenger.* Can you identify how many moons Galileo observed? This group of moons is now called the Galilean moons. Can you identify his recording of longitude and latitude? What else are you able to observe?

Late in 1615, Galileo went to Rome to seek approval for Copernicus' heliocentric theory from important Church officials. However, his visit possibly contributed to the opposite effect. In 1616, the Congregation of the Index required that Copernicus' book be removed until certain edits were made and Galileo was told not to promote such doctrines. Interestingly, the original publication of Copernicus' text had not affected the leadership of the Catholic Church this way and there is speculation that the concerns of the Church Fathers' about Copernicus' theory only emerged when people began to debate whether the theory was presented as a hypothesis or as a truth. The Church's decision in 1616 made it heresy to endorse heliocentrism. By 1620, Galileo had also antagonized the Jesuits over debates in print concerning the nature of sunspots and comets. *The Assayer*, published in 1623 was designed to challenge the Jesuit Orazio Grassi's geocentric argument for explaining the movement of newly observed comets. In that year with the election of Pope Urban VIII, Galileo assessed that this Pope's previous opposition to the 1616 decree would give Galileo more leeway to advocate for heliocentrism. In 1632, *Dialogue on the Two Chief World Systems* was published in Italian with a dedication to Urban VIII. However, Galileo had misread the situation and was ordered to come to Rome and face the Inquisition even though he was nearing 70 years of age and beginning to show the effects of old age. *Dialogue* was banned less than six months after its publication but by then the genie had been let out of the bottle. Galileo was placed under house arrest in 1633 providing him with quiet time to complete his final major work, *Dialogues Concerning Two New Sciences*, which he had published in Holland in 1638. He died in 1642.

In his own hand: Galileo observes the night sky

In his final two books, Galileo developed a cosmology that supported others to imagine the world differently to that based on an Aristotelian cosmology. *Dialogue on the Two Chief World Systems* addressed the issues of the ubiquity of natural motion, which we came to call gravity, the relativity of observed motion [only motion that is not shared can be observed], heliocentrism, and the tides as evidence for heliocentrism. In *Dialogues Concerning Two New Sciences*, Galileo addressed two fundamental questions: what is matter and what is motion. In both books, Galileo used a dialogic structure to develop his arguments using mathematical laws based on empirical evidence in which he focused on the variables relevant to his investigation. It is interesting to speculate on what Eurocentric science might have looked like today if the dialogic model of discourse used by Galileo had been adopted by experimental philosophers rather than of the structure proposed by Francis Bacon.

The form of scientific discourse beginning to be used in England, represented by Robert Boyle and Robert Hooke, emerged in a socio-political environment where there were no absolute rulers, once they had been removed by the Civil War, and where social conventions and politeness were considered to be important aspects of the presentation of any argument, including scientific arguments. Boyle attempted to convince his gentlemen peers while Galileo's presentations and his writing tended to be adversarial and polemical. However, as we examined in Chapter 2, both forms of presentation were specific examples of argumentation and reasoning, Boyle's was based on observations of nature and inductive reasoning and Galileo's on dialectical reasoning and the status of mathematical relationships. But as Gilbert and Mulkay were able to show in their study, some elements of both approaches prevail in contemporary science where public politeness and social convention remain important to the interpretive repertories of contemporary scientists.

Activity

Galileo made some further suggestions about how one can make a claim from an experiment. Again refer back to Chapter 3 and reread the section of text taken from *Dialogues Concerning Two New Sciences*. Galileo had been conducting experiments on specific gravity. Identify the argument Galileo is making there about experiments, variables, and making an argument.

I think the question of how scientists and experimental philosophers understand which variables need to be the focus of attention has implications for how we understand scientific inquiry and of the role of theory in that inquiry.

Francesco Redi, the Court and Experimental Structure

For court-based natural philosophers like Galileo, the court became the laboratory. A natural philosopher of note that also worked under the patronage of the de Medici's was Francesco Redi (1626–1697) who was in his sixteenth year when Galileo died. Redi studied medicine at the University of Pisa in Tuscany. As a doctor, he tended to the Grand Dukes, being appointed Court Physician under the relatively liberal Ferdinand II and then the more challenging and vain Cosimo III. He is famous for a number of books that he published on his observations of living organisms including vipers (snakes) and insects, which also included spiders. These books were written in Italian. Some time later, like Galileo's books, Redi's books were translated into Latin. Why would there be a need for these books to be translated to Latin when they were already published in Italian? In his book, *On the Generation of Insects*, Redi lays out his experimental philosophy in the dedication, which I think you will agree, is very evocative of Bacon's philosophy:

> Hence, though my philosophical studies have been pursued with more zeal than profundity, I have nevertheless given myself all possible trouble and have taken the greatest care to convince myself of facts with my own eyes by means of accurate and continued experiments before submitting them to my mind as matters for reflection. In this manner, though I may not have arrived at perfect knowledge of anything, I have gone far enough to perceive that I am still entirely ignorant of many things the nature of which I supposed was known to me, and when I discover a palpable falsehood in ancient writings or in modern belief, I feel so irresolute and doubtful of my own knowledge that I scarcely dare attack it without first consulting some learned and prudent friends[36].

In the dedication, in keeping with court patronage, he follows this statement with one extolling the virtues of the Grand Duke to be able to understand and accept the quality of the arguments presented. Redi's approach to presenting his experiments was to begin with an assessment of the accepted knowledge. He is as willing as Galileo to be critical, in a polite way, of previous scholars' claims. He begins *On the Generation of Insects* with an examination of the case of *spontaneous generation*. The accepted theory of the time was that there were three ways that the fetus of an animal was engendered; ova, seminal fluid, and putrefaction. The idea of spontaneous generation was that some animals arose spontaneously from an act of nature associated with purification or decay[37].

According to this theory, a decaying dead body engendered worms. Redi wanted to examine decay to see if evidence from experiments would support this theory. In order to test the theory, he conducted a series of experiments. Using dead snakes/eels, he began by observing that, if he covered up a container once maggots had appeared on decaying meat, different types flies could be identified after they all went through an egg-like stage that we now call the pupa. After confirming that a range of different meats and both raw and cooked meat support fly development, he hypothesized that "all worms found in meat came directly from flies and not from the putrefaction of the meat." In order to test this hypothesis he took eight flasks. Into four, he put a different type of meat in each one and sealed the flasks. Into the other four flasks, he put the same different types of meat but left the flasks unsealed. He reports that over many days the meats in the closed flasks putrefied but did not have worms but worms did appear in the open flasks. He then describes a series of experiments he conducted to further test his initial hypothesis. In other words, I think we can assume that he did not expect his readers to accept his claims on the basis of one set of experiments. Next, he uses his results and the hypothesis supported by these results to explain the erroneous results of other natural philosophers, critically analyzing their practice in light of his practice. Finally, he makes connect-ions back to faith critiquing those who would try to connect human resurrection with spontaneous generation separating the "holy mysteries of our faith" from natural things that can be understood by humans.

Activity

Redi's studies were very popular with English experimental philosophers and *Philo-sophical Transactions* has reviews of Latin editions of his books. Using the des-cription of Redi's experiments presented here, identify some of the similarities and differences between Redi's presentation of experiments and that of Boyle and Hooke. What features of Redi's experiment described here are evidence of a controlled experi-ment. Why do you think Redi chose this method for his experiment? Unfortunately, as much as I admire Redi for the studies he conducted, his experiments contained enough troubling inconsistencies in practice and results for supporters of the theory of spontaneous generation to find fault with his experimental design or find alternative explanations for the observations Redi presented. It was not until the 19th century and the work of Louis Pasteur (1822–1895), Ferdinand Cohn (1828–1898) and Robert Koch (1843–1910) that the theory of spontaneous generation was finally put to rest and cell theory and the germ theory of disease took its place.

HOW TO JUDGE THE QUALITY OF THE NEW KNOWLEDGE?

The experiences of Galileo and Redi illustrate that in the 17th century, acceptance of claims for generating new knowledge were not dependent solely on the primacy of the experimenter and their observations, although reading their accounts I do have a sense that they felt as though they were involved in constructing a new form of knowledge. Accounts of observations and experiments, such as those of Boyle and Hooke, were laden with detail about how experiments were conducted. These details became a tool for readers to visualize the experiments and observations or a tool for readers to replicate the procedure if they so wished. Also, in Northern European countries, there was a definite development towards legitimation of know-ledge by claims of fact via experiments that had been observed by 'gentlemen witnesses.'

The Emergence of Learned Societies

In many European countries at this time, the search for legitimation of scientific knowledge also led to the development of professional organizations, such as the Royal Society of London and the Royal College of Physicians in England, and The Academy of Sciences in France, which were set up to provide a supportive environ-ment for men exploring phenomena using new tools such as the telescope and the microscope. The first societies of this type were established in Italy. Academy of the Investigations was established in Naples out of dispute between the followers of scholasticism and the 'new' sciences, and the Academy of the Experiment [Academia de Cimento], was established in 1657 with the goal of following the experimental philosophies of Galileo.

The Academy of the Experiment met in Florence under the patronage of the Medici family from 1657 but was in decline by 1662 and ceased to meet in 1667. Its most distinguished member was Evangelista Torricelli, a student of Galileo, whose 'apparatus' was discussed across Europe and was the catalyst to new work on pneumatics. It was the first professional organization, which helped to bring together gentlemen of different opinions who could examine the legitimation of factual knowledge obtained by experimentation and observation. The Royal Society of London was established in 1660 under a Royal charter from Charles II, the King of England, but no financial support. Carrying out experiments and exploring ideas was very trendy at the time and King Charles had his own laboratory. Early members included some of the people already mentioned in the chapters of this book, including Hooke, Boyle, and Sprat.

The Royal Society of London began the publication of their professional journal, *Philosophical Transactions*, in 1665 and it continues today but in a much expanded form; can you suggest why that might be the case? Journals constituted a new form of genre for the presentation and evaluation of knowledge claims. In *Philosophical Transactions*, Bacon's recommendations for the method for this 'new' experimental philosophy provided the basis for the discourse of the journal. Today any professional organization 'worth its salt' is expected to publish its own journal, often more than one, and the role of a journal in presenting new knowledge has become not just accepted but accepted as central to the operation of the professional organization.

Associated with the emergence of professional journals was the concept of *peer review* where peers, rather than autocratic rulers, became the group that determined what constituted new knowledge by accepting, or declining to accept for publication, papers submitted for review. In one famous example historian of science, Stephen Brush[38], in his history of kinetic theory recounts the experience of John James Waterston (1811–1883), a Scottish engineer working in India. Waterston sent his paper to *Philosophical Transactions* for review in 1845. One of his reviewers was Baden Powell, Professor of Geometry at Oxford University, who was a liberal theologian and supporter of evolutionary theory (His son, Robert, started the scouting movement). In his review, Baden Powell wrote Waterston's basic principle that the pressure of a gas is due to impacts of molecules against the surface of the container was, "very difficult to admit and by no means a satisfactory basis for mathematical theory."[39] Today we accept that this idea is one of the fundamental principles of kinetic molecular theory. In 1892 Lord Rayleigh, the Secretary of the Royal Society, recognizing the insight of Waterston's paper, which had been rediscovered in the Society's archives, caused the paper finally to be published in *Philosophical Transactions*[40].

As Elizabeth Wagner[41] notes in her examination of peer review in science journals, editors of prestigious journals, such as the *British Medical Journal* and *The Lancet*, are critical of peer review arguing that it is a flawed process with little evidence that it works. Further, the available evidence indicates that this process is unjust, insulting, and ignorant. Its continuing use is based on *belief* rather than evidence and perhaps the onus is on the audience of scientific journals to imagine other ways to evaluate Eurocentric science claims for new knowledge.

Where's the Women?

In examining the role of women in professional societies I would like to examine the experiences of two women of the 17th and early 18th century from somewhat different backgrounds, Margaret Cavendish and Maria Sibylla Merian.

A portrait of Margaret Cavendish.

Theoretician and Actor. Margaret Cavendish, Duchess of Newcastle (1623–1673), was the youngest child of landed gentry. Born about 1623, her father died when she was very young and she was left without a dowry, making it more difficult for her to make a "good match" and marry well. According to Eileen O'Neill in her introduction to an updated edition of Cavendish's *Observations Upon Experimental Philosophy*[42] originally published in 1666, Margaret Cavendish was very shy and slow to communicate with people outside of her immediate family. However, Cavendish acknowledges a desire to be known for her thinking when she writes that she hopes her readers will understand that what she has written in *Observations* was written, "not out of an ambitious humour, to fill the world with useless books, but to explain and illustrate my own opinions"[43]. Her desire for a separate identity perhaps drove her to engage in activities not associated with the nobility at the time and at odds with the cultural norms of the day, including publishing books, poems, and plays under her own name and designing her own wardrobe. Cavendish was also born in England during the era of the Stuart kings. Unlike the preceding period of the Tudor kings when it was considered acceptable for noble women to be highly educated (for example Lady Jane Grey had studied Latin, Greek, and Hebrew as well as contemporary languages), during the period of the Stuarts noble women were expected to learn "domestic skills" and "ladylike accomplishments"[44] but typically did not have access to further education. A counter example to Margaret Cavendish is provided by the philosopher, Anne Conway (1631–1679), also a member of the nobility in England who was first home schooled and then taught through letters by philosopher Henry Moore. Conway's treatise, *The Principles of the Most Ancient and Modern Philosophy*, was published close to the end of her life, anonymously, and overseas. Cavendish wrote under her own name, throughout her life, and contracted an English woman publisher to print her final works. Cavendish wrote:

> But that I am not versed in learning, nobody, I hope, will blame me for it, since it is sufficiently known, that our sex being not suffered to be instructed in schools and universities, cannot be bred up to it. I will not say, but many of our sex may have as much wit, and be capable of learning as well as men; but since they want instructions, it is not possible they attain it: for learning is artificial but wit is natural[45]

Question. What is Cavendish arguing here?

The Lucases, Margaret's family, became associated with the court of Charles I and, in 1642 with the outbreak of the Civil War, allied themselves with the Royalists. In 1643 Margaret left to become maid of honor to Queen Henrietta Maria, wife of Charles I of England. Margaret chaffed at the regulated nature of the Royal Court and she was so quiet that she was described as an "idiot". However, her mother refused to let her leave and she escaped with Henrietta Maria's entourage to France in 1644 after Parliament accused Henrietta Maria of high treason.

While in exile, Margaret met William Cavendish, Marquess of Newcastle, whom she would marry in 1645. They apparently remained devoted to each other until her untimely death in 1673. Following the Royalist cause, the Cavendishs moved to Holland in 1648. In 1651, William was named a traitor and Margaret traveled to England to petition for access to financial support from his properties. In 1653 she published her first book, *Poems and Fancies*, and went on to publish numerous plays, books, a biography of her husband and an autobiography. This is one of the poems Cavendish published in *Poems and Fancies*:

The weight of Atomes

If *Atomes* are as small, as small can bee,
They must in *quantity* of *Matter* all agree:
And if consisting *Matter* of the same (be right,)
Then every *Atome* must weigh just alike.
Thus *Quantity*, *Quality* and *Weight*, all
Together meets in every *Atome* small.

Question. If this poem was your only source of evidence, how would you describe Cavendish's philosophy?

This is the frontispiece of Margaret Cavendish's science fiction narrative published in 1668. Note that the printer is A. Maxwell. This is Anne Maxwell.

By 1666, Cavendish had published *Observations upon Experimental Philosophy* in which she critiqued the work of a number of well-known experimental philosophers and atomists, including Robert Hooke and Robert Boyle. We are so far removed from the 17th century that it is difficult to know whether her criticism came only from her philosophical differences or if she was also somewhat critical of the sudden rise to prominence of experimental philosophers and the Royal Society when some of members belonged to "lower" strata of society. In 1667 after some politicking, after all she had just criticized a number of members of the Royal Society in print, the Royal Society of London agreed to invite her to their meeting after she had expressed to George Berkley, a friend and colleague, a desire to attend. In her autobiography, Cavendish admits she found the visit a strain even though Robert Boyle, the politest and most inclusive of men (for his day), conducted a number of experiments using his expensive tool, the air pump, and she had the opportunity to look through a microscope, an instrument the use of which she had critiqued, along with Robert Hooke's work using the microscope in *Observations*. This visit was the last time a woman was admitted to meetings of the Royal Society until 1945, almost 300 years later.

Cavendish was a theorist. Initially in her writings, such as the one presented above, she espoused the atomist cause but as her writing and thinking evolved, she became more and more critical of the theory that all matter was composed of atoms as she wrote:

> Although I am of the opinion, that nature is a self-moving, and consequently a self-living and self-knowing infinite body, divisible into infinite parts; yet I do not mean, that these parts are atoms; for there can be no atom, that is, an indivisible body in nature; because whatsoever has body, or is material, has quantity; and what has quantity, is divisible[46]

Cavendish argued that internal motion was the major feature that animated objects and motion was needed for change. She was critical of an atomistic theory that presented atoms as indivisible particles. As you might note, this statement represents a different stance on the nature of matter to the one that she espoused in her earlier book. Cavendish writings suggest a dialectic approach to making sense of the world. After her untimely death, Cavendish's writings came under more and more criticism over the centuries but she has found supporters more recently as her contributions to science and feminism are reevaluated. Like most people, Cavendish's stances on various aspects of nature and social organization can seem contradictory. I think there is little doubt that she had a hierarchical view of social order and did not think that the "lower" classes should have the same power and influence as the class to which she belonged. However, she was a first in many ways and perhaps scientific thinking might have taken a slightly different path if she had been able to muster more support for the positions she espoused.

The observer in the field. Those promoting the formation of professional organizations for experimental philosophy had as a model the craft guilds established in Europe from the 11th century onwards. These guilds were formed to advance the professional interests of members and provide mutual aid. One other area of similarity between craft guilds and professional scientific organizations was in the exclusion of women from their membership. For example, in the German states associated with the Holy Roman Empire, the guilds exerted great power making many/all craft professions limited to men. Kim Todd in her biography of Maria Sibylla Merian (1647–1717)[47], one of the earliest natural philosophers and illustrators to focus on context for representing insects, describes how powerful craft guilds throughout Germany excluded women from the process of professionalization within the guild from apprentice, to journeyman, to master. Merian was born in Frankfurt, so access to the skills she would use for her illustrations were only available to her through her family's printing business, not an apprenticeship. Journeymen organizations were especially resistant seeing women and children as unpaid competitors for limited work. Guild rules also banned women from using oils, so Merian was only able to practice her art using watercolors.

Portrait of Maria Sibylla Merian (1647–1717).

At the time, midwifery was one of the few professions open to women and it was also a time of danger for women that spoke their minds. Frankfurt and Nuremberg, the city to which Merian moved with her husband were Lutheran. German states executed more people accused of being witches than the rest of Europe[48]. So being known as someone with an interest in raising and drawing insects, which were colloquially known as "beasts of the devil", could be looked at as a parlous endeavor. Todd argues that Merian was able to negotiate these challenges in part by her ability to form alliances with men in power.

In 1686 Merian separated from her husband and joined an obscure Christian sect called the Labadists on a farm where she would remain for five years until moving to the relative freedom of Amsterdam. In Amsterdam, she could own property, run a business, belong to certain guilds, be employed as an apprentice, and did not have to be married to be financially secure. There Merian experienced magnificent *cabinets of curiosity*, precursors to our modern day museums, and recognized the possibilities for selling insects (she had been required to give up all her property to Labadists when she joined) to make a living wage that would support her and her children. Merian wrote about her dissatisfaction with the way insects were displayed in these collect-ions. She thought it was important to include information about an insect's natural habitat (more or less), life cycle and feeding needs in her illustrations, for which she had previous experience having used detailed observations to complete three volumes of books on flowers, butterflies and caterpillars while living in Germany.

Todd notes that although Merian could never have participated in the Royal Society meetings, women were banned until 1945; she was able to read microscopist, Antoine van Leeuwenhoek's published works, which further excited her interest in understanding insects in their natural environments. In 1699 at the age of fifty-two, she funded her own scientific expedition to Suriname, a Dutch colony in northeastern South America that the Dutch had won from the English in 1667. Charles II of England had ceded Suriname in exchange for New Netherland, which included New Amsterdam, and you now know as New York City, in the Treaty of Westminster in 1674. Accompanied by Dorothea, her 21 year-old daughter, Merian planned to create her own cabinet of curiosities based on her observations of insects in a new and relatively unexplored land (for Europeans). After two years, a bout of malaria forced her to leave Suriname and return to the Netherlands where she published her most famous work, *Dissertatio de Generatione et Metamorphasibus Insectorum Surinamensium* (The Development and Metamorphosis of Insects of Suriname), in 1705. She died in 1717.

From Merian's Metamorphosis of a Butterfly.

Although the classification of insects was an open subject during her lifetime, Merian helped to popularize an interest in insects as living things with life cycles that were not based on the theory of spontaneous generation. In her writing, she differentiated between moths and butterflies, a classification that is still in use today. She could be described as one of the first entomologists and her standing as a natural philosopher was acknowledged at the time by systematist, John Ray, who was working on a thesis about insects. He wrote, "I shall not concern myself with those published by the lady Merian as neither with those by Goedartius, Hoefnagel, Hollar, Aldrovandi"[49] Merian's life history shows us some of the strategies European women used to pursue their passions in natural philosophy when professional organizations were closed to them.

Like contemporary professional organizations and associated journals, the professional organizations that emerged in the 17th century shared the goal of supporting experimental philosophy but they also developed the power to decide what counted as knowledge with respect to these 'new' knowledges. Additionally, they possessed the power to decide whether a person had the qualities they determined to be necessary to be acknowledged as worthy of admittance. Recall Newton's comment that only a person that had tried to replicate his experiments should feel that they were in a position to critique the claims he was making about light. Also, for all his accomplishments, Thomas Hobbes was never admitted to the Royal Society because according to the Society, he did not 'do' experiments and women were not admitted until the 20th century was almost half over.

IMPLICATIONS OF SCIENTISTIC BELIEFS ABOUT OBSERVATIONS, REALITY AND MATTERS OF FACT

I think belief that human observations provide a direct and undistorted view of reality still echoes in the exhortations of teachers emphasizing the dominant role of observations to science understanding. In some science classes, observations are believed to form the basis of scientific understanding. A consequence of this can be students directed to draw exactly what they observe under the microscope while at the same time, their diagrams are expected to be readily identifiable as diagrams of cells. There is an assumption that, without any theoretical background understanding of the structure of cells, students will observe reality when they look down the microscope, they will convert this observation into an accurate diagrammatic record of reality, and what they record in their workbooks will be a replica of other diagrams of cells such as those presented in the textbook. The teacher will force students to make a distinction between observation and inference as though these exist as a dichotomy. Unfortunately, when pressed this distinction becomes less and less sustainable. Hopefully, you will have noted from reading this chapter that the notion of a direct relationship between reality, observation, and representation is based on the Baconian myth of the primacy of observations to human understanding.

Observations and the Open Mind

Acceptance of the open mind can result in other ideologies that influence also the cultural practices of some science classrooms. The first of these ideologies is that everybody who observes a particular object or process, especially if they have an "open mind", will make identical observations. In this school science classroom, the belief that observations are independent of theory and that students are 'seeing the same thing' as does the teacher leads to the assumption on the teacher's part that he/she does not need to address explicitly the theoretical framework of a practical activity or even check to learn how and what students have observed. The assumption being that because everyone was present, they will have observed identically. Philosopher of science, Nicholas Hanson[50], described passive seeing as 'seeing what', but teachers often require students to apply the more active concept of 'seeing as', which requires prior knowledge. If we accept the need for students to be knowledgeable before they observe, then would it not be more appropriate for the teacher to acknowledge the exigency for students to learn the theory of the content first? For example, making sure that students know something about cell structure before observing, Hanson's 'seeing as,' so they have a better chance of recognizing cells under the microscope? And so they can adequately draw the cells they observe?

Acceptance of the primacy of observations can lead the teacher to involve students in activities designed to reveal matters of fact through the application of careful 'theory-free' observations of Nature so, not surprisingly, practical activities have a very high status. Clive Sutton, a science educator, talks of an "idolatry of the bench[51]" that has emerged in science classrooms and cautions against a tendency of these teachers to mythologize practical activities and equate them with science education to the extent that practical activities come to be thought of as 'the source' of knowledge in science. A consequence of this can be that a 'big picture' of the relationships between facts and theories is not generated; instead there is an emphasis on learning 'factoids', that is, unrelated scientific facts. A further possibility in a science classroom structured by a belief in value-free and theory-free observations is the perception that students are passive observers rather than active creators of knowledge. What might this classroom be like if, instead, practical activities were presented within a network of prior understandings and students were encouraged to be active observers, making sense of what they observed by explicitly relating together understandings and observations?

I would like you to think about your understanding of the nature of observations. Is there value in science classrooms to create situations where students make collective observations because the alternative is a focus on learning facts that are removed from any shared observations of the natural world? Nicole's comment at the beginning of this chapter, about the need to learn facts can support the development of classrooms where students sit in rows facing a teacher who has the knowledge they need to pass the exam at the end of the year. There is little focus on anything apart from learning a mass of facts and a few algorithms that are needed to pass the exam. In New York City, the situation was so dire that the state is forced to mandate laboratory activities, which must be completed by each student, for the course called living environment.

Although students might benefit from first-hand experience of the methods used by scientists to legitimate scientific knowledge, should they also be made aware of the conceptual frameworks in which both they and scientists operate? Robert Boyle and Isaac Newton did not blithely conduct a mass of unrelated experiments and then look for order. Their experimentation was based on, and informed by, underlying conceptual frameworks.

Implications of a Mechanical Cosmology

A hypothetical classroom sited within a mechanical cosmology would be dominated by a mathematical approach to learning science in which objects and ideas are connected in an orderly way. Consequently, this classroom would be dominated by the use of algorithms to apply the scientific laws of Nature to observations of reality that students have made. In this classroom, the 'scientific method' also is presented as an algorithm. Thus, the class is dominated by the myth[52] that there is only one correct way, called 'the scientific method', of conducting scientific investigations. Scientific laws are believed to work regardless of whether or not humans exist.

In a mechanistic and deterministic classroom only rational and logical approaches to solving problems are acceptable. In this classroom, science is thought of as a completely rational activity. Acceptance of such a focus raises questions about the role of creativity and discovery in the classroom. Discovery is either described as the result of logical and rational thought obtained by following methodological rules or it is presented as a happy accident and, therefore, not really part of 'true' science. Instead, in this classroom, justification or verification are viewed as 'true' science. In this class, science is presented as an approach for logically and rationally revealing the secrets of Nature.

Students are directed to observe scientific laws in Nature and practical activities are directed towards revealing these scientific laws. In this environment, application of scientific laws, usually in the form of algorithms, is expected to produce the 'right answer', that is, to reveal the appropriate scientific law. The expectation of a single right answer is acceptable in an environment where only successful experiments are reported, as happened once mechanism came to dominate the cosmology of science. Thus, in this classroom there would be an emphasis on doing activities that reinforce the importance of scientific laws.

This approach to learning science tells students that science knowledge evolves from problem to experiment to theory so that science is viewed as linearly progressive. Thomas Kuhn[53], a philosopher of science, proposed that theory development on science progresses as a series of paradigm revolutions rather than linearly. However, my criticism is different. If a teacher ignores discovery, he/she will not address the issue of the interaction between intuition, creativity and imagination and scientists' understandings of their field of study in the discovery of new scientific knowledge. If a teacher becomes fixated with a particular methodology for science then he/she is at risk of presenting to the students a very static notion of science. An emphasis on a particular scientific method can lead to scientism, an ideology presented earlier.

Implications of Baconian Experimental Activities and Experimental Reports

If there is an undue emphasis on experimental reports as records of experimental activity then students may come to equate the method of experimentation with the report. They are encouraged to accept that an experimental report represents an exact record of an experiment rather than being encouraged to evaluate critically the experimental report as a sanitized argument for the acceptance of new knowledge. In this context, experimental activities have a specific structure that has its antecedents in the writings of Francis Bacon and in the demands of the Royal Society. If the structure of an experimental report is set as consisting of aim, method, results and conclusion or discussion, a fixed and unwavering emphasis on this structure, and on a descriptive genre can lead to the use of 'recipe-type' practical activities. This approach does not inspire wonder, imagination or interest in science. Instead, it implies that science is formulaic and predictable. In this context, students are required to write their reports entirely in the passive voice, a strategy that completely removes the student as the active agent and emphasizes the object, the practical activity, as the basis of knowledge. The message implicit within this practice is that the student is less important than the activity and that student observations are universal rather than idiosyncratic because that is what happens in science.

Question. What sense are you making of my argument? How do you respond?

I do not want you to think from reading the previous sections that I am very critical of Bacon and Galileo's arguments for how one might make new knowledge. I think their contributions to Eurocentric science were very significant. If anything, I think it is difficult for us in the 21st century to imagine how writers such as these helped people, mostly men at this point, to think of new ways for constructing knowledge and how exciting that was for the people who were involved. The difficulty emerges if we forget that their recommendations were constructions and not the truth.

Perhaps you might want to end this chapter by thinking what school science might be like if its referents are construction, dynamism, and tentativeness rather than correspondence, passivity and stasis? According to the epistemology underpinning these referents, all observers are active. Collectively, observers construct multiple realities based on their observations, and the way they reconstruct these observations is influenced by the interaction between their observations and their prior understandings and beliefs, that is, their theories and values. It is possible for observers to develop a collaborative or shared notion of the implications of their observations by discussing collectively and explicitly the theory that underpins their observations. In this science, the discourses of science are made explicit so that all users are encouraged to develop the skills to use these discourses effectively. In this science, scientific discourse, which we will explore more thoroughly in Chapter 7, is accepted as a rhetoric, which scientists use to actively construct their notions of the universe and to convince their peers of the veracity of their work.

In a classroom modeled on this philosophy of science, students might be encouraged to be active observers. They might be encouraged to place their observations 'on the table' so that, as a collaborative group, they can examine each other's claims.

In this class, the teacher might demonstrate her/his awareness of the network of prior understandings that each student brings to a science classroom by encouraging students to present their ideas to their peers and by using these ideas as a basis for constructing meaningful activities for the class. In this classroom there would be a balance of discourse, discussion and practical activities!

NOTES

[1] Bacon, F. (1620/1968). Paraceve/Novum Organum. In J. Spedding, R. L. Ellis & D. D. Heath (Eds.), *The works of Francis Bacon*. New York: Garrett Press. (Original publication 1620, facsimile reprint of 1870 publication). p. 40.

[2] Bacon, F. (1620). p. 49.

[3] Bacon, F. (1620). p. iv.

[4] Bacon, F. (1620). p. 93.

[5] This is certainly Stephen Shapin's argument as applied to Robert Boyle's writings. See: Shapin, S. (1984). Pump and circumstance: Robert Boyle's literary technology. *Social Studies of Science, 14*, 481–520.

[6] Shapiro, B. J. (2000). *A culture of fact: England, 1550–1700*. Ithaca, NY: Cornell University Press.

[7] Oxford English Dictionary. (1989).

[8] If you want to try another one try: tp://www.michaelbach.de/ot/fcs_face_in_beans/index.html and http://www.michaelbach.de/ot/cog_dalmatian/index.html although the author's interest is different from mine!

[9] Shapin, S. (1984).

[10] See Guba, E. G., & Lincoln, Y. S. (1989). *Fourth generation evaluation*. Newbury, CA: Sage.

[11] Boyle, R. (1660/1965). New experiments physico-mechanical touching the spring of the air; Made for the most part, in a new pneumatical engine. In T. Birch (Ed.), *Robert Boyle: The works Vol. 1–6* (pp. 1–117). Hildesheim: Georg Olms Verlagsbuchhandlung. (Original publication 1660, facsimile reprint of 1744 publication). p. 105.

[12] Sprat, T. (1667/1959). *History of the royal society*. St. Louis, MO: Washington University Studies. (Facsimile of original publication 1667)

[13] Latour, B. (1987). *Science in action: How to follow scientists and engineers through society*. Milton Keynes, England: Open University Press.

[14] Bacon, F. (1620). p. 252.

[15] Bacon, F. (1620). p. 261.

[16] Hooke, R. (1665). The Preface.

[17] Bacon, F. (1620). p. 261.

[18] Boyle, R. (1660). p. 2.

[19] Bacon, F. (1620). p. 260.

[20] Boyle, R. (1660). p. 19.

[21] Hooke, R. (1665). The preface.

[22] Bacon, F. (1620). p. 260.

[23] Boyle, R. (1660). p. 11.

[24] Bacon, F. (1620). p. 260.

[25] Boyle. R. (1660.) p. 34.

[26] For example, see Latour, B., & Woolgar, S. (1979). *Laboratory life: The social construction of scientific facts*. Beverley Hills, CA: SAGE Publications.

[27] Ziman, J. M. (1968). *Public knowledge: An essay concerning the social dimension of science* (p. 105). Cambridge: Cambridge University Press.

[28] Riley, K. (1991). Passive voice and rhetorical role in scientific writing. *Journal of Technical Writing and Communication, 21*, 239–257. p. 248.

[29] Gross, A. G. (1985). The form of the experimental paper: A realization of the myth of induction. *Journal of Technical Writing and Communication, 15*, 15–26.

[30] For example, see Duschl, R. A. (1988). Abandoning the scientistic legacy of science education. *Science Education, 71*, 51–62 and Nadeau, R., & Désautels, J. (1984). *Epistemology and the teaching of science*. Ottawa: The Publications Office, Science Council of Canada.

[31] See Nadeau, R., & Désautels, J. (1984). p. 13.

[32] Newton, I. (1672). A serie's of quere's propounded by Mr. Isaac Newton, to be determin'd by experiments, positively and directly concluding his new theory of light and colours; and here recommended to the industry of the lovers of experimental philosophy, as they were generously imparted to the publisher in a letter of the said Mr. Newtons of July 8.1672. *Philosophical Transactions, 7*, 4004–5007. p. 4004.

[33] Gilbert, G. N., & Mulkay, M. (1984). *Opening Pandora's box: A sociological analysis of scientists' discourse*. Cambridge: Cambridge University Press.

[34] Galilei, G. (1632/2001). *Dialogue concerning two chief world systems, Ptolemaic and Copernican* (S. Drake, Trans.). New York: Random House by arrangement with the University of Chicago Press. p. 3–4.

[35] Obtained from University of Michigan online collection. Retrieved January 1, 2010, from http://www.lib.umich.edu/exhibit/galileo-galilei-1564-1642

[36] Redi, F. (1688/1909). *Experiments on the generation of insects* (M. Bigelow, Trans.). Chicago: The Open Court Publishing Company.

[37] William Harvey in *Anatomical exercises on the generation of animals* (1651), published seventeen years before Redi's book, mentions spontaneous generation but does not give much attention to it because Harvey's focus was on what he could observe of the development of the fetus mainly in birds and mammals.

[38] Brush, S. (1965). *Kinetic theory Vol. 1 The nature of gases and of heat*. Oxford: Pergamon Press.

[39] Brush, S. (1965). p. 17.

[40] Waterston, J. J., & Rayleigh, L. (1892). On the physics of media that are composed of free and perfectly elastic molecules in a state of motion. *Philosophical Transactions of the Royal Society of London A, 183*, 1–79.

[41] Wagner, E. (2009). Peer review in science journals: Past, present and future. In R. Holliman, J. Thomas, S. Smidt, E. Scanlon, & E. Whitelegg (Eds.), *Practicing science communication in the information age: Theorizing professional practices* (pp. 115–130). Oxford: Oxford University Press.

[42] O'Neill, E. (2001). Introduction. To Margaret Cavendish. In *Observations upon experimental philosophy*. Cambridge: Cambridge University Press.

[43] Cavendish, M. (2001). *Observations upon experimental philosophy* (p. 11). Cambridge: Cambridge University Press.

[44] Whitaker, K. (2002). *Mad Madge: The extraordinary life of Margaret Cavendish, Duchess of Newcastle, the first woman to live by her pen*. New York: Basic Books.

[45] Cavendish, M. (2001). p. 11.

[46] Cavendish, M. (2001). p. 125.

[47] Todd, K. (2007). *Chrysalis: Maria Sibylla Merian and the secrets of metamorphosis*. Orlando, FL: Harcourt Books.

[48] Todd, K. (2007). p. 40.

[49] Quoted in Todd, K. (2007). p. 221.

[50] Hanson, N. (1958). *Patterns of discovery*. Cambridge: Cambridge University Press.

[51] Sutton, C. (1992). *Science, words and learning* (p. 3). Buckingham: Open University Press.

[52] Following Roland Barthes, I define myths as beliefs that are accepted as truths because the history of their creation is lost and because they possess an ideological function.

[53] Kuhn, T. (1970). *The structure of scientific revolutions* (2nd ed.). Chicago: University of Chicago Press.

CHAPTER 6

UNDERSTANDING AND EXPLANATION

A ROLE for Connected and Separate Knowing

In 2004 I began collaborating on a research project with a developmental psycho-logist, multimedia design expert and cognitive scientist, and a content expert. Our goal was to explore and evaluate design principles for multimedia simulations in chemistry education; especially ideas associated with kinetic molecular theory and associated concepts of diffusion, Gas Laws, and phase change. As a feature of exploring high school chemistry students' understanding of the chemistry concepts, which we hoped our simulations assisted them to learn, we developed assessment questions that asked students to apply their learning to a different context, a process often called transfer. An example of one of these questions is presented below.

> Many of you enjoy sugar in your coffee or tea. When you first add sugar, it falls to the bottom of the cup. But if you wait for a while, even without stirring, the entire cup will taste of sugar.

> What is your explanation of this effect? Relate your explanation to the simulation you just used.

Example of a transfer question from diffusion simulation study

I am not making any claims for the quality of this question but if you read this question carefully note we are asking the students participating in our study to explain the relationship between sugar finding its way throughout the tea or coffee and kinetic molecular theory associated with the concept of diffusion. We are asking the students to make an explanation, which is an action associated with explaining. In the question, our understanding of explanation, associated with the practice of science, was implicit. Considering that the students with whom we were working are in Grade 10 and 11, we expected that they would be comfortable presenting an explanation and would be knowledgeable about the structure of an explanation expected within this context.

In everyday life, the need to explain seems to be part of the human condition. After all, how often do people you ask refuse to give you directions? I think humans feel the need to explain all sorts of experiences to each other in order to make that experience understandable and also perhaps memorable. Jon Ogborn and his colleagues[1] argue that when an explanation is being offered, this interaction is unequal, usually in the direction of the person to whom the explanation is being given. But I wonder if it is that straightforward? Explaining is interactive. If we examine one explanation, we can think if it consisting of an explainer, in the coffee/tea and sugar example that is the student, and someone to whom that explanation is being made, an explainee. So, in the case of a teaching and learning context where students are asked to provide an explanation you might argue that power is shifted to the explainee who has responsibility for deciding the quality of the proffered explanation. However, in other contexts the explainer might have more power by taking the initiative to provide an explanation. Also, there is a level of *intersubjectivity* in our request because we assume that the students who read that question also share our understanding of the question and task we have presented them and I think this expectation of a shared understanding might be the case in all explanatory situations. What do you think?

EXPLORING SCIENTIFIC EXPLANATIONS

We, the researchers using the coffee/tea question, also assumed that the students would recognize that we were asking them for a *causal explanation*, the types of explanations that are a cornerstone of a mechanistic worldview and of much of Eurocentric science.

Components of a causal explanation	*Meaning*
Effect	An observation of a phenomenon that needs to be explained *e.g., sugar can be detected throughout tea/coffee even though it was put in as a solid and there was no stirring*
Cause	A theory, model, or law that can be evoked to provide the explanation *e.g., at the particle level of liquids, particles are in constant random motion*
Casual Explanation	Combines an effect, an observation of phenomenon, with a cause which uses a theory, model or law as the basis *e.g. Over time, sugar can be detected throughout the tea because of the random motion of particles of sugar and water*

Of course, one of the challenges of these causal explanations is that the more context you incorporate into the explanation, the more complex the explanation seems to need to be. Our experience of asking questions, which required an explanation as the answer, showed us just how challenging students find this type of request, especially when there are no boundaries provided for the answer. My experiences with them encouraged me to explore further the nature of explanations especially as they relate to science and science education. I also came to this issue through the history of science as experimental philosophers, even those staunch defenders of Baconian inductive reasoning like Boyle and Hooke, found the need to try and explain the behavior of the materials they were investigating, feeling compelled to explore theories and hypotheses that helped to explain the *how* or *why* of their observations. Consider Boyle's comment about an ingredient in atmospheric air that is needed to support combustion:

> The difficulty we find of keeping flame and fire alive, though but for a little time, without air, makes me sometimes prone to suspect, that there may be dispersed through the rest of the atmosphere some odd substance, either of a solar, or astral, or some other exotic nature, on whose account the air is so necessary to the subsistence of the flame[.][2]

What is Boyle speculating about, trying to explain, in this statement? He is addressing the question of why a flame goes out when placed in a container in which the air has been pumped out by the air pump. He noted that a flame did not continue to burn. This was contrary to the accepted theory of the time in which air and fire constituted different elements, so it was believed that one could not affect the other. A consequence of this theory was that a flame should continue to burn even when as much air as possible had been pumped out of a container. Boyle speculates about the existence of an "odd substance" dispersed throughout the air that is necessary for the flame. Note how theories, like the four element theory; accepted as a truth, which is what tends to happen to theories if they seem to have explanatory power, supported people to ask questions that they could explore with experiments? You might recognize that the substance Boyle is speculating about is what we now know as oxygen. More than a century was to pass (1772–1775) before there was an ongoing nationalistic struggle over which experimental philosopher should be recognized as the discoverer of oxygen; Carl Scheele, a Swede, Joseph Priestly, an Englishman, and Antoine Lavoisier, a Frenchman. Boyle's explanation is that there is a substance, which cannot be detected with the tools available to him, that is necessary for combustion.

There has been much philosophical debate about the nature of explanation but in this chapter I want to focus on how explanation is used in Eurocentric science and the implications this might have for science education. Historically, science or natural and experimental philosophy, adopted the general idea of an explanation and applied it to a specific set of circumstances involving experience of phenomena to develop a specific notion of the features of a 'good explanation'. Boyle's experiments with burning substances supported his identification of a pattern in the data; flames went out in air if the air was not refreshed, which supported his explanation of something in the air[3]. In Eurocentric science, explanations are human inventions, arguments involving the imposition of a scheme in the form of theories, laws, and models on phenomena to impose order. This imposed pattern is subjective, dependent on context or interest. Boyle had a question, "Why do things need air to burn?" He repeated many examples of these types of tests in which he tried to burn objects without air thereby generating data, which we also call evidence when it is used in a specific context. He sees a pattern in the data generated from the situations in which he had tried to initiate combustion and proposes that this pattern is observed because of a theory thereby providing an explanation for his observations.

Explanation and Understanding

Jon Ogborn[4] asked children what was a good explanation. They responded, "Good for what?" He then asked them, "How would you explain color?" To which they responded, "To whom?" These interactions communicate the contextual nature of explanations as well as the role of interactions in the evaluation of the quality of an explanation. The format of Boyle's question and the emerging explanation depends very much on the audience to whom he is attempting to explain this phenomenon. There are additional requirements for an explanation. We assume that Boyle was genuine in his attempt at an explanation and that he is really trying to initiate an interaction in which he contributes to the understanding of the people to whom he is explaining. Explanations are social constructions. We assume Boyle is trying to explain something to his colleagues because they do not understand and, even if they do, Boyle is expected to treat them as though they do not. We can know that a phenomenon occurs. Boyle saw that over time air that was not replenished would not support combustion but understanding why air would not support combustion over time requires understanding. Some philosophers, scientists, and psychologists make an argument for the primacy of *causal explanations* in these contexts. Peter Lipton, a philosopher of science, who has written widely about explanation and understanding describes understanding as *knowing the cause of something.* For me this is a narrow notion of what constitutes understanding. In this definition, there is no place for empathy or self-knowledge, which is one reason why I find a focus on causal explanations limiting. However, causal explanations work well with a mechanistic worldview because they provide a mechanism for explanation that is consistent with the machine metaphor. Experimental philosophers also wanted to move away from the teleology of Aristotle with its emphasis on final causes and purpose, providing further justification for functional or causal explanations. Consider the studies of William Harvey and the questions he asked as he studied the roles of blood and the heart in living organisms.

The Strengths and Weaknesses of Causal Explanations

William Harvey asked questions such as how does pressing on a vein affect the flow of blood in a body and what can this tell us about valves? William Harvey might not be as well known in science education today as he has been in the past.

A look through many current biology texts shows little history and what is there does not include any reference to William Harvey (1578–1657) born into a prominent family in England. He attended King's School and then Caius College of Cambridge where he studied Greek, Latin, Physics, and Rhetoric. In 1598 Harvey began his medical studies at the University of Padua. There he was exposed to contemporary theory associated with anatomy and physiology. He graduated in 1602 and returned to England where he completed his English equivalency. In 1604 he was admitted into the College of Physicians, which was the only organization with the right to license physicians (women, of course, were excluded) to practice in London and surrounding counties. Harvey gained a position at St. Bartholomew's Hospital in 1607 and remained there for much of the rest of his life. Harvey was very short (not sure how short he was but it was a feature of his looks that was often remarked upon by his contemporaries) with black hair and dark eyes. He was also personable and in general considered a 'good sort'.

He was appointed Lumleian lecturer in 1615, which required him to produce lectures in English and Latin to inform general knowledge about (that would be male) anatomy. His lecture in 1616 was about his theory of blood flow and the heart. In 1618, he was appointed 'Physician Extraordinary' to James I of England (James VI of Scotland. Although Elizabeth I had executed his mother Mary Queen of Scots because Mary became a rallying focus for groups seeking to overthrow her, Elizabeth I died without direct heirs and James VI, a good Protestant, was invited to become the King of England), which allowed him to garner further lucrative positions with the nobility. However, with the publication in 1628 of his treatise, *An Anatomical Exercise on The Motion of the Heart and Blood in Living Beings* (De Motu Cordis), which he had published abroad with the goal of reaching the widest possible audience, Harvey's practice suffered as his reputation slipped, based on people's negative response to his book. His arguments on circulation and the heart, published in this book, were considered 'mad'. Interestingly, although his reputation with his patients was negatively affected by the publication, his professional reputation in England continued to expand with his election to more and more significant positions within the College of Physicians. In 1634, he became physician to Charles I who had succeeded James I. Charles I made animals obtained from hunts available for Harvey to use for his studies.

However, not everything was rosy in England at the time. Over a dispute concerning money, Charles I disbanded Parliament and tried to rule England without one. A revolutionary war between the Royalists (loyal to Charles) and the Parliamentary forces was enacted in 1641. The victory of parliamentary forces in 1651 opened the way for the removal of Charles I who was executed. It was during this year that Harvey's other groundbreaking book, *Essays on the Generation of Animals*, was published. Over the next nine years England functioned as a Commonwealth under the control of Oliver Cromwell, a Puritan. During this time Harvey, a Royalist, moved to the relative safety of Oxford. With Cromwell's death, Charles II was invited back with the understanding that he would agree to the policy that a monarch could not govern without the consent of Parliament. Over time, all members of parliament that had signed the death warrant for Charles I, and who were still alive, were executed and Cromwell's body was dug up and beheaded and his head put on public display. This was a period of religious instability in England with Catholics, Anglicans, and Puritans jostling for power. By the end of Charles II reign neither Puritans nor Catholics were allowed to serve in Parliament.

Prevailing accepted theories. At the time of publication of Harvey's *On the Motion of the Heart,* the accepted theory about the role of the heart and of blood came from Galen[5] (remember him from Chapter 3) and looked something like this diagram.

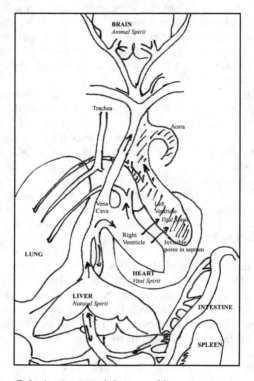

Galen's anatomical theory and human anatomy.

Galen argued that food was digested in the intestines to a liquid and transferred to the liver where it became imbued *natural spirits* to become blood. We can represent this idea as:

$$liquid\ food + natural\ spirits = blood$$

This blood was distributed to all organs of the body through the veins. The pulmonary artery was called an artery-like vein. This system also included the right side of the heart. Within the venous system, the blood was thought to ebb and flow as organs used up portions of blood and was replaced by blood from the liver.

According to Galen, the arterial system provided *vital spirits.* A special part of air called *pneuma* passed through the lungs into the pulmonary vein to the left side of the heart. The pulmonary vein was called a vein-like artery. Vital spirits were distributed to the rest of the body via the aorta and arterial system. The blood arrived at the left side of the heart by squeezing through invisible pores that existed in the septum between the right and left ventricles of the heart. Waste left by the vein-like artery. I am not sure if you feel capable of imagining the body according to Galen's theory, so refer back to the diagram.

There is evidence that prior to the publication of Harvey's work, philosophers had identified the role of valves in veins. Harvey acknowledged the study of Hieronymus Fabricus (1537–1619), his teacher at the University of Padua, and Amatus Lusitanus (1511–1568), of a Portuguese Jewish family that had been forcibly converted to Christianity. Also, Ibn al-Nafis (1213–1288), an Islamic polymath, who completed his medical studies at the Medical College Hospital in Damascus, conducted studies providing evidence of pulmonary circulation and of the role of heart contractions in the movement of blood in the arteries. However, Harvey's studies and arguments are the most complete available to us. He began his book on the heart and the blood with a systematic examination of Galen's claims. Through the use of dissections he was able to explore the nature of blood in veins and arteries. Galen had written that the blood in veins was different from the blood in arteries. Harvey was to write[6]:

If we find the same blood in the arteries that we find in the veins as I myself have repeatedly ascertained, both in the dead body and in living animals, we may fairly conclude that the arteries contain the same blood as the veins.

Harvey makes the further argument that the similar structure of both sides of the heart suggest that both have similar functions. Harvey's observations supported his thinking of the blood moving in a circle using the term *circulation* to describe the motion of the blood in a body. Harvey wrote of arteries and circulation[7]:

Precisely as in the water that is forced aloft, through a leaden pipe, by working the piston of a forcing- pump, each stroke of which, though the jet be many feet distant, is nevertheless distinctly perceptible, the beginning, increasing strength, and end of the impulse, as well as its amount, and the regularity or irregularity with which it is given, being indicated, the same precisely is the case from the orifice of a divided artery; whence, as in the instance of the forcing engine quoted, you will perceive that the efflux is uninterrupted, although the jet is alternately greater and less. In the arteries, therefore, besides the concussion or impulse of the blood, the pulse or beat of the artery, which is not equally exhibited in all, there is a perpetual flow and motion of the blood, which returns in an unbroken stream to the point from whence it commenced the right auricle of the heart.

This statement comes from an English translation of Harvey's *Motion of the Heart and Blood.* Note how Harvey uses the metaphor of a pump to explain the movement of blood in the arteries accounting for the facts; the pulse-like movement in the arteries and also a continuous stream of blood circulating through the body.

By conducting experiments in which he controlled specific variables, such as blood flow using ligatures and pressure, Harvey was able to argue for circulation as a mechanism for the movement of blood and the role of the heart in promoting circulation.

Frontispiece of William Harvey's An Anatomical Exercise on The Motion of the Heart and Blood in Living Beings (De Motu Cordis).

Harvey challenged Galen's argument that blood came from digested food. He was able to demonstrate through compression of the vena cava and aorta that the heart rapidly emptied and filled with blood. Such activity would not been possible if all blood came from digested blood via the liver as Galen had argued. He also applied mathematics to the calculation of the rate of blood flow and was able to show that circulation was the best way to explain how the quantity of blood in a body could be maintained at the levels needed for bodily function. Harvey had addressed *how* blood moved in the body. In seeking to explain *why* blood moved in the body, he proposed that circulation served to warm the extremities[8]:

> Yet can the extremities be warmed in no way, save by circulation; the chilled blood, which has lost its spirit and heat, being driven out, and fresh, warm, and vivified blood flowing in by the arteries in its stead, which fresh blood cherishes and warms the parts, and restores to them sense and motion; nor could the extremities be restored by the warmth of a fire or other external heat, any more than those of a dead body could be so recovered; they are only brought to life again, as it were, by an influx of internal warmth. And this indeed is the principal use and end of the circulation; it is that for which the blood is sent on its ceaseless course, and to exert its influence continually in its circuit,

to wit, that all parts dependent on the primary innate heat may be retained alive, in their state of vital and vegetative being, and apt to perform their functions[.]

Harvey speculated that circulation provided a mechanism to explain how diseases, like syphilis, and toxins, like the bites of serpents, which gain entry to the body at one site, could manifest symptoms in another. Additionally, the mechanism of circulation could be used to explain how medicines, applied externally, exerted an influence similar to those taken internally. Thus, in these cases, circulation provided a causal explanation. Although Harvey was not able to observe the capillaries that demonstrated the connectivity between arteries and veins, circulation of blood and the operation of the heart could be presented mechanistically and could be used to propose causal explanations of other phenomena. However, Elizabeth Gasking[9] argues that when Harvey turned his observations and experiments to fertilization and embryonic development he could not apply the same type of causal reasoning, which he acknowledges in his book, *Essays on the Generation of Animals.*

We examined spontaneous generation in Chapter 5. Recall that the accepted theory was that the fetus of animals could be engendered in three ways: from an ovum, from seminal fluid, and from putrefaction (spontaneous generation). Although Harvey did not have much to say about spontaneous generation, his observations convinced him that development of a fetus commenced with an ovum but he was unable to observe the process and materials needed for fertilization. He was to argue that at that time, the 17th century, the nature and order of generation was not open to understanding. Harvey's studies of 'generation' supported his critique of some of Aristotle's claims, such as Aristotle's claim that formation of the embryo was initiated as coagulation after mating. Through an experiment in which female deer were sequestered after mating, Harvey was able to show that the embryo did not appear until days after mating, evidence in direct critique of Aristotle's claims. Harvey also dismissed the notion of spirits but admitted that he was unable to propose an alternative. You might argue that if Harvey had better tools, like the microscope, which was used within fifteen years of the publication of Harvey's studies on fertilization and development, he would have been able to propose causal explanations for this field just as he had been able to do for circulation. If anything, I think the microscope muddied the waters as 'little animals' were observed in semen allowing men to attribute the active principle for fertilization and fetus development solely to the male. Instead, Harvey applied analogical reasoning, using contagion as a metaphor for conception, to suggest an explanation for generation.

SCIENCE AS EXPLANATION

The National Science Education Standards differentiate between two common but flawed metaphors for thinking about science: *science as getting an answer* and *science as experiment* and suggest that a more appropriate strategy for learning science requires an emphasis on *science as argument and explanation.* A metaphor, such as *science as getting an answer*, is more than amusing play on words. It communicates a connection between two objects or processes. For example, science as getting an answer is a metaphor in which an unknown, science, is associated with an object that people are thought to know better, the process of getting an answer. We can interpret this metaphor as being used to communicate that science is really about finding answers, and by implication *correct* answers. Thus, the practice of science is about finding answers with the understanding that once we have found the correct answers we will have the truth about the world. Generally, with this focus on correct answers, facts take the form of correct answers and, as we have examined in Chapter 5, this espoused vision of facts as fundamental to knowing science can be linked back to the ideas of Francis Bacon.

As we examined in Chapter 5, Bacon promoted a form of experimental philosophy based on the belief that scientific observations were mirrors of reality and were theory-free. According to him, if one's mind was cleared of preconceived notions before conducting observations then observations would yield an exact record of Nature's reality and constitute matters of fact. And because matters of fact were deemed to constitute an exact record of God's creation, Nature, they had moral as well as cognitive power. Thus, collecting facts was perceived as the true focus of scientific endeavor. Over time, beliefs about the relationship between observations and reality and matters of fact became accepted as secure truths as the process of their creation was forgotten. What remained was the understanding that a method based on observation provided the path to true scientific knowledge as creatively perceived patterns in the data provided the basis for a generalization. This generalization became a hypothesis that could be tested through further study. With this understanding, science facts had much higher status than did theories. Like other metaphors, the metaphor of science as getting an answer can be so powerful that it can lock us into thinking only one way. It can become an ideology so we find it difficult to think of science in any other way than getting an answer. The power of metaphors to limit the expansiveness of our thinking is illustrated in our previous examination of how the machine metaphor can lock people into thinking that mechanistic approaches to explanations are the only acceptable structure for an explanation.

Once the metaphor of science as getting an answer becomes incorporated into science education, it can become a strategy for learning science. Often, teachers, students, and administrators who think of getting an answer as the basis of science, use this perspective to justify an emphasis on learning facts of science as Nicolee's troubled comment in Chapter 5 illustrates. Another example comes from some chemistry teachers with whom I worked. Their claim was that students needed to have "conceptual" knowledge, by this they meant students needed to know chemistry facts before they could participate in any sort of inquiry. Remember Nicolee said that, "A fact is something which is usually observed and is proven beyond all measure of doubt."

You might recognize three problems with this definition of a fact. First, by attaching importance to the role of observation to develop facts, Nicolee could justify the use of just two teaching strategies rather than a variety, either using teacher lecture in which facts were presented to learners, or doing activities whereby learners made observations that constitute facts. Second, as I have noted previously, the issue

of 'proven beyond all measure of doubt' is not defensible scientifically or philosophically. For some scientists it is the exercise of doubt towards claims of discovery
and validation that is a fundamental feature of Eurocentric science leading one to
be skeptical always of claims that any fact can be proven beyond any measure of
doubt. Third, this statement does not help anyone including a beginning teacher
decide the facts that are important for learners to know. For that we need theories
and models. For example, atomic theory is based on an understanding that all matter
is composed of tiny discrete particles. If we accept this definition then we might
want to know how to define materials made of the same types of atoms and called
an element. For example, we could accept the fact that an element is a substance that
cannot be chemically broken down further into simpler substances as an important
fact for understanding atomic theory. But without theory how would a person
identify whether a fact is important or not? In science classrooms it is usually the
teacher, the exam, or the curriculum that informs students of the facts they need
to know, raising the question of on what basis educational decisions are made. In
situations where students sit for a final exam that is designed to assess their understanding of a specific subject discipline, teachers express concerns about the tension
between trying to infuse more science inquiry into the curriculum while preparing
students for the exam[10]. As an example, there are 110 major understandings in New
York State's Chemistry Core Curriculum and teachers are expected to teach these
understandings in fewer than 180 days. A situation such as this places teachers in
the difficult role of having to decide the facts or content that needs to be 'covered'
before students sit for a state-wide exam and, at the same time, trying to decide the
role of inquiry in the course they teach. This tension between 'content coverage'
and infusing inquiry into the curriculum was a tension articulated by pre-service
teachers with whom I worked when they were required to develop an inquiry-based
urban science unit. Under these conditions where class time becomes a valuable
resource, teachers struggle to decide what should be emphasized in the teaching
and learning of science suggesting the importance of making explicit the links
between theories and facts in the development of science curriculum and moving
beyond the metaphor of science as getting an answer.

Science as Experiment

In a science classroom informed by the metaphor of science as experiment, the
classroom is usually busy with activity. The emphasis is on 'doing' science as
students are involved in completing activities that seem to be scientific but rarely
is the science the focus of examination in these contexts. Science as experiment
is very similar to what Deanna Kuhn[11] presented as *science as exploration*. Kuhn,
a developmental psychologist, sees scientific thinking as a complex process of
intellectual development. She claims that metaphors such as science as exploration
or experiment are too limited to use when trying to understand scientific thinking.
In both metaphors, the emphasis is on process but the National Science Education
Standards ask for more than this of teachers by challenging them to emphasize
minds on as well as *hands on*. Minds on requires a focus on inquiry that involves

students identifying their assumptions, using critical and logical thinking, and having opportunities to consider alternative explanations. For some beginning teachers, 'doing' is the most important aspect of school science because it serves to distinguish science from other school subjects. It makes science "fun". I agree that learning science should be emotionally fulfilling, challenging, and enjoyable but one beginning teacher, Gavin, noted from his intern experience:

> Well that was probably most of the downfall of my lessons not enough pre-talking about what might happen and not enough conjecture about what happened (especially if the lab activity did not work out the way that was expected). But I felt as though I didn't have enough time.

In Gavin's classroom practice, there was almost no discussion, so students had little understanding of the purpose of the activity; and a lack of discussion afterwards did not provide them with an opportunity to contextualize the activity. Also, the only writing that students in this middle school classroom were asked to do was to 'fill in the blanks' in a worksheet. They were never asked to write full sentences about their discoveries and thinking as it related to understanding aspects of science. This meant that in the doing of science in his classroom students were never asked to make connections between ideas or to communicate these ideas in writing or verbally to peers, to him, or to other members of the community. Gavin's comment also illustrates a tension that all science teachers with whom I have worked have voiced at one time or another associated with time being a limited resource. His comment also indicates that his schemas for how the teaching and learning of science should be structured were based on his belief that activities were the most important aspect of science and, if students were to do science and time was a valuable resource, then activities needed to be completed and discussion and writing about the science could be ignored. It was only through being asked to reflect on his practices that he was able to recognize and acknowledge the likely limitations of his current teaching practices for the science learning of the students he taught.

Students should have opportunities to develop understanding of science. This assumes that if students are involved in activities such as growing plants or building a better box that are presented as part of their science curriculum, they also need to be involved in examination of how science can help them to *explain* why plants grow and why they grow differently under different conditions or why their box construction is better. In the construction of a better box they could be investigating questions such as how materials science can help them to use materials thoughtfully and how concepts such as tension, compression, and material characteristics can help them to explain why their box is better. Activities are seductive in science and I have observed middle school students making helicopters, making solar ovens, and extracting chlorophyll from leaves, but if there is no discussion of how objects work or why one might care, why one would want to extract chlorophyll and why chlorophyll is important, then an opportunity for students to develop some science understandings of parts of their world is lost. If there is no examination of the science implications of what students are doing, if students are just involved in doing, it is likely that there is little science being learned. Such activities imply the need for developing an understanding of explanation and argument, as students are involved in explaining how plants grow or why a specific design is the best. Have you ever found yourself thinking about this very tension? Perhaps I am making an argument here for the relationship between understanding and explanation!

Science as Argument and Explanation

Rather than science as experiment or exploration, psychologist, Deanna Kuhn, argued for the metaphor of science as argument. In the National Science Education Standards the preferred metaphor for promoting inquiry is science as argument and explanation. Why has this become such a dominating metaphor for science education? A common model of argumentation applied in science education research uses data (support) and warrants (the criteria that are applied) to justify a specific claim, a causal mechanistic form of argument. But it could also be argued that argument is a dialogue between opposing assertions and evidence is used to generate a resolution. Based on your reading of this book, what type of argument would that be? I would like to see this form of argument used more and more because it not only challenges students to use evidence as a tool, but because it also involves them in looking at the context in which these assertions are generated. Arguments are important cognitively and philo- sophically. There have been proposals to align scientific literacy in its fundamental sense with developing a capacity for argument[12]. Proponents of argumentation present this strategy for learning science as a way of moving away from the presentation of science knowledge as unequivocal, uncontested, and justified, which is often how science is portrayed in schools. However, as you have hopefully come to realize through your reading of this book, there are a number of different forms of reasoning that find their place in Eurocentric science.

Kuhn argues, and I would not disagree, that in social interactions and in individual thought, argument is important to the development of scientific thinking as scientists are involved in analyzing evidence to decide its bearing on different theories. Argu- ments based on evidence are needed to support specific explanations or theories. She differentiates between problem solving and argumentation and sees a place for argumentation in the way people make judgments about their lives. In her discussion of argument, Kuhn recognizes that in order to evaluate beliefs and develop good arguments people need to be able to make themselves a focus of study, to reflect on their values and beliefs. We can call this action distancing or objectifying.

As a strategy for generating knowledge, argument especially causal argument, can be associated with a broader structure of knowledge generation called *separate know- ing*. Proposed by, Mary Belenky, Blythe Clinchy, Jill Tarule and Nancy Goldberger,[13] who were examining the thinking of women, separate knowing was identified as the type of knowing associated with (Euro) scientific argumentation. In the process of interviewing many women about knowing and knowledge, Belenky, Clinchy, Tarule, and Goldberger also identified another strategy for generating knowledge, which they called *connected knowing*. Both these ways of knowing have salience to learning Eurocentric science but when most science teachers and researchers think of coming to know in science they think of *separate knowing*, the type of knowing that is associated with causal scientific argumentation. As examples of separate knowing, argumentation and explanation constitute powerful sets of actions but connected knowing is an equally powerful form of knowing that should also be included in our educational actions associated with learning science.

SCIENCE AS CONNECTED AND SEPARATE KNOWING

Two ways of knowing, connected knowing and separate knowing, comprise different procedures for generating knowledge. Together they constitute *procedural knowing*. Unlike separate knowing where the knower is separated from what is known so that both can be treated as objects, connected knowing begins with the knower trying to understand another's position, seeking to understand what they are saying and refraining from argument. This means that each knower seeks actively to understand another's position without necessarily agreeing with that position. Unlike separate knowing where language is organized into argument and explanation, with connected knowing, language is organized into narrative or story. For learning, we need both connected and separate knowing because each has different characteristics and when used together support the development of a richer set of resources for learning. For example, the goals of connecting knowing are understanding and discovery and the goals of separate knowing are validation and evaluation, to be convincing or convinced. Learners need tools that allow them to be both separate and connected knowers. Would you agree that a major role of education should be to provide learners with access to both these sets of tools?

In connected knowing, emotions are understood to assist thinking because they support learners to make connections between themselves and the material or process they are learning. Conversely, emotions are understood to obscure the thinking necessary for making arguments and explanations in separate knowing. Connected knowing is used in classrooms when students are encouraged to try to understand the position of another student or of an author they are reading before being critical of what they have read. Connected and separate knowing can help us to understand two areas of human endeavor: 1) what it means to understand beyond the causal understanding so valued in a mechanistic modernist worldview, and 2) how students can understand discovery in science as an aspect of scientific inquiry. Connected knowing can lead teachers and students to value stories of experience and to provide space for people to present their narratives.

You might be thinking that there does not seem to be much of a place for connected knowing in Eurocentric science but there are stories of experience associated with discovery in science that suggest there is a need for both. Evelyn Fox Keller[14] in her biography of Barbara McClintock reported that one of the reasons McClintock could see changes in strands of DNA that would escape most people was because she knew very well her field of study and would "listen to the material" developing a "feeling for the organism[15]". The same has also been said of Alexander Fleming, the microbiologist, who had an intimate knowledge of the bacterial organisms with which he was working. According to historian of science Robert Root-Bernstein[16], Fleming used his knowledge to create bacterial colony 'art work' which required him

Contrasting Features of Connected and Separate Knowing

Aspect	Connected knowing	Separate knowing
Goal	Understanding/ Meaning and discovery	Validation and evaluation, to be convinced or convincing
Relationships between knowers	Supportive	Adversarial and persuasive
Relationship between knowers and what is known	Relational	Detached and objectifying
Emotions	Illuminate thought	Obscure thought
Ontology	Reality is personal	There is an external reality even if we do not know what it is.
Authority (Epistemology)	Personal experience	Mastery of knowledge
Genre	Narrative	Argument and explanation

to know both the colors produced by specific bacterial colonies and how long specific bacteria types took to produce separate colonies. As I have noted previously[17], Fleming may not have been as intellectually gifted as Howard Florey and Ernst Chain, the scientists that worked out an initial biochemical mechanism of how lysozyme acted on bacteria and who produced the first practicable penicillin, both initially observed by Fleming. He said that he "just played with microbes[18]" but his knowledge of them was deep and personal. As Keller indicates, Barbara McClintock's scientifically unfashionable approach to genetics marginalized her position in the science community (being a woman probably did not help either). However, there was still enough support from her peers to allow her to remain part of the scientific community and ultimately to gain the respect of her colleagues and the award of the 1983 Nobel Prize for Medicine or Physiology for her discovery of "mobile genetic elements". I argue that discovery in science requires both connected and separate knowing.

Valuing Stories of Experience

Connected knowing is not just a lack of bias, but a bias in favor of what each reader or listener is examining. Connected knowing is uncritical but not unthinking. Blythe Clinchy describes connected knowing as *imaginative attachment*, trying to look at something from another's perspective and valuing the stories they have to tell[19]. Emotion and thinking are linked in connected knowing, a linkage that can be reinforced by asking questions seeking understanding of another, such as what does it mean, and what in your experience led you to that? Connected knowing also means valuing stories of experience. I am reminded of an African American student's comment that his mother made black soap during a lesson on making soap. Coming from Australia this was not a type of soap with which I was familiar, so I asked him if he knew how black soap was made but he told me did not. He was in a class studying chemistry, more specifically at that moment, the textbook representation of the chemistry of soap making. We, the educators in the classroom, could have used that student's story of experience to examine the chemistry of soap making by investigating how black soap is made through personal and public stories of experience, whether this type of soap making is regional, and how the chemical reactions involved in the making of black soap are similar or different to the traditional chemistry recipe for making soap. Although this was a quiet side conversation with this student, when I think back to that conversation I feel guilty that I did not make greater educational use of his comment because I lost an opportunity to connect with that student's knowledge and use that knowledge to expand the options for understanding for all students in that class.

Activity – the Making of Black Soap

A search of websites[20] tells us that black soap, also called Anago or Alata soap originated in West Africa and has been made for centuries. I thought its name came from the color of the soap but possibly its name also comes from its use by 'black' Africans as claimed by some websites. Using roasted plantain (*Musa paradisiacal*) skins as an ingredient, procedures for making black soap are proprietary and passed down from generation to generation. Indonesian travelers are thought to have introduced the plantain to Africa about 500 BCE[21]. The other main ingredient is either shea butter from the nuts of the shea tree (*Vitelleria paradoxa*), a vulnerable tree from the dry savanna areas of Africa that has not responded well to attempts at domestication, or palm oil (*Elaeis guineensis*), which has been grown in plantations in parts of Ghana, such as the Ashanti Confederacy (1670–1902), for centuries. Perhaps you could try to make black soap with a class if you ever need to make soap as part of a chemistry/science class.

Like all soaps, black soap is formed through a chemical reaction called saponification, which is the hydrolysis of an ester under basic conditions to form the salt of a carboxylic acid and an alcohol. The French chemist Eugene-Michel Chevreul (1786–1889) was able to show that soap was not a mixture of fats and alkali but a true salt and by 1823 he was able to show that soap was formed by a reaction between a natural fatty acid and a base[22]. What does this mean and what roles do shea butter and roasted plantain have in the making of soap? Try to write down the overall chemical equation for saponification showing where roasted plantain skins, shea butter, and palm oil could be used in the process.

Making Use of Stories

One of the cornerstones of constructivist models of teaching is the valuing of students' prior knowledge, which in these models, can take the form of a pre-test or the completion of some sort of advanced organizer. However, connected knowing helps us to recognize the value of narrative as a structure for representing prior knowledge and the importance of listening to the stories people tell so that such stories can be used to structure learning in the classroom and become part of the collective knowledge of that classroom.

Supporting space for narratives. In a science classroom connected knowing can be emphasized when listening to a student explaining how they solved a specific problem. As beginning science teacher in our program commented:

> Blythe Clinchy's chapter on separate and connected ways of knowing probably had the most impact on me because it caused me to question how I had been taught to critically think as an undergraduate student. Often being a critical thinker is prized above sympathizing with the author and their intent. This article resonated with me because it suggested the benefits of both crucially analyzing a body of work and accepting the body of work by examining it from the author's point of view. Both strategies result in increased understanding, and they do not have to be mutually exclusive.

With her statement, Sonya, was supporting Clinchy's claim that often educational practice is founded on an adversarial discourse with which many students do not feel comfortable leading them to opt for silence in the classroom[23]. Connected knowing provides a space for students to communicate in a different voice. Her comment reinforces the value of emphasizing both separate and connected knowing in the science classroom.

Encouraging students to allow other members of the class to present their views and to listen to those views as they are presented, with the goal that other members of the class will understand another student's meaning, is a further strategy for providing a space for connected knowing to be enacted. Both teachers and students are involved in listening for understanding and providing space for the author to present their stories. Teachers can assist by representing their understanding of what a student said, asking the student if they captured the student's meaning, and providing space for the student to respond. *Active listening* might be thought of as an element of connected knowing but connected knowing is much more than a practice applied in verbal contexts. It is a theory of knowledge. As Sonya recognized, central to connected knowing is the believing game and to separate knowing, the doubting game[24]. Doubting and believing are contrasting and complementary and form a dialectical relationship the outcome of which is meaning and ultimately understanding. But what does it mean to understand? In education there is often a sense that everyone has a shared knowledge of what it means to understand but as I have argued at the beginning of this chapter, a shared understanding is at best ephemeral if there is little discussion of how a culture understands understanding. For example, when I asked a group of beginning teachers what they understood by the term, *understanding*, there were varied responses leading us all to accept that there was value in examining the meaning we ascribe to understanding in order to develop a richer awareness of what it means to understand.

What it Means to Understand

Acknowledging that understanding can be an ambiguous and slippery term, Grant Wiggins and Jay McTighe ask what does it mean to understand in their book, *Understanding by Design*[25]. They argued for six overlapping and integrated facets of understanding: can explain, can interpret, can apply, have perspective, can empathize, and having self-knowledge. Of these facets, *can interpret*, by which the learner should, in their own words, be able to tell meaningful stories of what they have read or heard; can *empathize*, by which a learner can find value in the positions of others; and have *self-knowledge*, by which a learner understands how their own habits of mind, biases, and values affect how they understand others; contain elements of connected knowing. Each of these facets requires a learner to connect in some way with ideas or people and use narrative to communicate these connections. Also, in these facets, feelings are important for illuminating a learner's cognition just as Clinchy described.

The other facets, which require learners to distance themselves from phenomena and from others and to examine positions critically, contain elements of separate knowing. As I have noted already in this chapter, can *explain* is commonly related to the ability to propose theory or law-based accounts of phenomena that are justified or warranted through the use of evidence associated with finding patterns in the phenomena. This sounds a lot like *making a (causal) argument* and I think you would agree that this form of argument and causal explanations have a lot in common. Perhaps a major difference between argument and explanation lies in the goals that one has for each: explanation aims to impart culturally accepted knowledge and argument aims to convince another about a claim. The National Science Education Standards[26] assert that an understanding of science contributes to skills of being able to learn, reason, think critically, make decisions, and solve problems; skills central to inquiry. According to the Standards[27]:

> Understanding science requires that an individual integrate a complex structure of many types of knowledge, including the ideas of science, relationships between ideas, reasons for these relationships and ways to use the ideas to explain and predict other natural phenomena, and ways to apply them to many events. p. 2.

In this sentence an aspect of separate knowing, the ability to use ideas for explaining phenomena, is acknowledged as important for being recognized as understanding science. However, in *Inquiry and the National Science Education Standards*[28] the role of prior knowledge in the form of narrative is acknowledged as important to the generation of testable questions in science. Acknowledgement of the role of connected knowing provides a way of thinking about the nature of prior experience so that it can be shared amongst learners and become a basis for asking testable questions. As I discuss in the next section this strategy forms the basis of science discovery.

Facets of Understanding and Curriculum Design

The six facets of understanding proposed by Wiggins and McTighe provided an introduction to their model for curriculum development called *backwards design*[29]. The curriculum design is backwards because the teacher or curriculum developer begins planning by first identifying the learning outcomes that are used to develop the assessment tasks. The initial question might be: what understandings are essential to know, important to know, and useful to know for this unit of study? These understandings can be identified by stakeholders, including teachers, students, communities, and institutions. Once the understandings have been identified, the synchrony between desired understandings, as described in learning goals, and achieved understandings, based on assessment of student learning, provides the basis for evaluating the proposed curriculum. Both outcomes and assessment are developed before the text or content is developed. A positive feature of this approach to curriculum design is that, by valuing connected and separate knowing Wiggins and McTighe expanded the facets of understanding to be valued. Their approach served to broaden acceptable representations of understanding thereby providing students with access to a broader range of opportunities for demonstrating their learning.

Research on connected knowing provides teachers, students, and researchers with access to language that supports conversations about knowing. Connected knowing has wide applicability in classrooms because it provides learners with access to tools they can use to try to make sense of an author or presenter before imposing their own constructs on the text. Also, through connected knowing learners can be supported to make connections with phenomena as well as people. It is in this context that connected knowing can help us to understand science discovery, a component of scientific inquiry often neglected in science classrooms.

INQUIRY, DISCOVERY AND CONNECTED KNOWING

Accepted scientific knowledge has developed through the components of scientific inquiry: discovery, validation, and evaluation. However, for most students their experience in science is in the validation component of knowledge generation. Most of the laboratory and practical activities students complete have the goal of validating a specific scientific fact, concept, or theory. For example, chemistry students are asked to confirm that reactions between acids and carbonates produce carbon dioxide. Using baking soda (sodium hydrogen carbonate), sodium carbonate, hydrochloric acid, vinegar, and citric acid, an activity is designed to provide a structure for students to identify the types of reagents that produce carbon dioxide. This activity is structured to confirm a pattern that carbon dioxide is produced when carbonates and acids react. In another example, in biology, students use tools, such as clothespins, chopsticks, and tongs, as analogies for beaks of Galapagos finches to model natural selection. These are validation activities designed to confirm a scientific fact or model. Consistent with the metaphor of science as getting the answer, there is an expectation amongst students that there is a 'correct' answer for these activities. The following vignette of a presentation by students, illustrates how this norm of the correct answer constrains student science inquiry.

At a science education conference I am excited listening to a group of three Grade 11 and 12 students describe how they used readily available materials from the hardware store to make a vacuum or at least a container that could produce an air pressure much lower than the outside atmospheric air pressure. The main vessel that they have constructed reminds me of von Guericke's apparatus, which allowed him to demonstrate the strength of air pressure by using a pneumatic pump to create a vacuum within two well fitting metal hemispheres. In order to pull apart the hemispheres the efforts of a team of sixteen horses were required, clearly demonstrating to the audience that gathered, the strength of the Earth's atmospheric pressure. This group of students also used a pneumatic pump to remove air from their container, which was spherical and about two-thirds of a meter in diameter. I was excited by the creativity they demonstrated in working out how they might construct a vacuum, excited thinking about the inquiry possibilities of such an instrument anticipating the questions they were going to investigate. Imagine my surprise when I discovered they used this apparatus to confirm gravitational acceleration on earth. They presented a graph of their measurements showing that all the data points they had generated fell exactly on a line confirming 9.8 meters per second per second as the rate of acceleration. Both their calculated and graphical results were perfect. This intrigued me, so I asked them how they had collected their results. They told me that they had dropped objects inside the spherical container and measured the rate of fall using a stopwatch!

Question. Why was I surprised? Do you also find their results surprising? Why or why not?

Here is my response. Considering that in order to be able to measure gravitational acceleration in this way and get reasonable results, you need to drop something from the height of at least a five-story building and that their results were perfect, I felt as though their teacher had sold these learners short. I wondered why he had not challenged their strategy for measuring the rate of fall and had not queried the precision of the data. He could have encouraged them to a rich analysis of phenomena rather than the confirming theory activity in which they engaged, the validation component of scientific inquiry. I wondered why their teacher had not encouraged them to focus on questions their instrument would allow them to investigate rather than supporting them to conduct a flawed study designed to establish a law that they already knew and accepted as true. I felt as though this activity provided an example of an opportunity missed by the teacher to involve students in discovery, encouraging them to use the instrument to understand better the phenomena that they were creating through the equipment they had built, to explore the phenomena and develop a feeling for it, and then see what sort of questions came to them.

There is a place for validation activities in science education because such activities model an aspect of scientific inquiry and can assist students to build their knowledge of science but an emphasis on these types of activities provides a skewed vision of science. Rarely do students have opportunities to explore and develop questions that they investigate so that the discovery component of science often is missing from science studied at school. In their description of how a geologist uses scientific inquiry, the authors from the National Research Council[30] acknowledge the role of prior experience in the geologist's ability to ask answerable questions about a forest of dead cedar trees that he observed as he was mapping coastal depositions in Washington State. The authors note that:

> Using his knowledge of geology and what he learned about trees and their habitats, the geologist made *connections* (my emphasis) between the dead trees and other features of the environment, such as the coastal location[31].

In this segment the authors have described an example of connected knowing. The geologist, the focus of the narrative, had observed stands of dead cedar trees in a number of locations along the coast of Oregon and Washington. His observations led him to ask if the trees had died at the same time and to investigate that question using carbon-14 dating and studies of sediment layers. The geologist's relationship with the environment can be understood as similar to Barbara McClintock's *feeling for the organism* described earlier.

Discovery in science is associated with connected knowing because discovery requires prior knowledge of the objects or organisms that are being experienced and observed. This requires scientists to listen to the material much like Alexander Fleming did when he was studying lysozyme[32] and Cecilia Payne-Gaposchkin did in her study of stellar atmospheres described in Chapter 2.

For science learners also, connected knowing involves them in developing a level of familiarity with phenomena as a prelude to generating questions that can be investigated further. For students to travel on their own journey of discovery in the science classroom they need to become familiar with the theory/conceptual framework as they interact with phenomena. For example, students do not observe cells the first time they look down a microscope. Rather, as described in Chapter 5, they need to know about the operation of the microscope and the structure of cells before their 'seeing' becomes 'observing'.

As teachers, we need to emphasize that scientific discoveries do not occur by accident but because scientists know very well the phenomenon, process or material with which they are working. Discoverers seem to have empathy for the organisms, material, or processes with which they are working and often are excited by the work that engages them. While we do not expect that students will reinvent special relativity or plate tectonics in the classroom, there is a place in the science classroom for activities that support students developing a familiarity with materials that supports them to ask questions. From these questions they can select those that can be developed further to be investigated through scientific inquiry. Separate and connected knowing provide a basis for understanding discovery and validation in science and, with that understanding, developing a richer understanding of the nature of science.

EXPLANATION AND UNDERSTANDING

In a connected sense, in this book I have tried to take you through a range of ideas that will support teachers to develop a richer understanding of the nature of science and to begin to make varied connections between understanding and explanation. Inquiry is a story in which an inquirer subjects Nature as an information source to a series of questions. As I have argued in this chapter, we need both connected and separate knowing for scientific inquiry and for building our understanding of science. I think you might agree that understanding and explanation exist in a dialectical relationship. We need understanding to make an explanation but we also need explanations for understanding, especially in Eurocentric science. Of course, if you are going to work on connected and separate knowing then you also need to have a sense of the history of language associated with the development of Eurocentric science and this will be the focus of the next chapter.

NOTES

[1] Ogborn, J., Kress, G., Martins, I., & McGillicuddy, K. (1996). *Explaining science in the classroom.* Buckingham, England: Open University Press.

[2] Boyle, R. (1660). *Works* Vol. IV. p. 90.

[3] Development of this definition for explanation was informed by the work of philosopher of science, Peter Achinstein. E.g. Achinstein, P. (1971). *Law and explanation: An essay in the philosophy of science.* London: Clarendon Press.

[4] Ogborn, J., Kress, G., Martins, I., & McGillicuddy. (1996).

[5] Gasking, E. (1970). *The rise of experimental biology.* New York: Random House. See Chapter 1.

[6] Harvey, W. (1847). *The works of William Harvey* R. Willis (Trans.). London: The Sydenham Society. p. 11–12.

[7] Harvey, W. (1847). p. 135.

[8] Harvey, W. (1847). p. 98.

[9] Gasking, E. B. (1970).

[10] Peter, V., & Van Voorst, C. (2000). Science teacher beliefs: Toward an understanding of state science exams and their influence on teacher beliefs. In P. A. Rubba, J. A. Rye, P. F. Keig & W. J. Di Biase (Eds.), *Proceedings of the 2000 annual international conference of the Association for the Education of Teachers in Science* (pp. 405–437). University Park, PA: Pennsylvania State University.

[11] Kuhn, D. (1993). Science as argument: Implications for teaching and learning scientific thinking. *Science Education, 77*, 319–337.

[12] Simon, S., Erduran, S., & Osborne, J. (2006). Learning to teach argumentation: Research and development in the science classroom. *International Journal of Science Education, 28*, 235–260.

[13] Belenky, M. F., Clinchy, B. M., Goldberger, N. R., & Tarule, J. M. (1986). *Women's ways of knowing—The development of self, body, and mind.* New York: Basic Books.

[14] See Keller, E. F. (1983). *A feeling for the organism: The life and work of Barbara McClintock.* New York: W. H. Freeman.

[15] Pinch, T. (1992). Opening black boxes: Science, technology and society. *Social Studies of Science, 22*, 487–510.

[16] Root-Bernstein, R. S. (1988). Setting the stage for discovery. *The Sciences, 28*(3), 26–34.

[17] Milne, C. (2010). Captives of the text? How analysing science stories set me free. In K. Scantlebury, J. B. Kahle & S. Martin (Eds.), *Re-visioning science education from feminist perspectives: Challenges, choices and careers* (pp. 135–150). Rotterdam, The Netherlands: Sense Publishers.

[18] Macfarlane, G. (1984). *Alexander Fleming: The man and the myth.* London: Chatto & Windus.

[19] Clinchy, B. (1989). The development of thoughtfulness in college women: Integrating reason and care. *American Behavioral Scientists, 32*, 647–657.

[20] For example, http://www.sheabutterr.com/nasabbnew/blacksoap.htm a commercial site for the sale of black soap and other items or http://www.agbangakarite.com/ a fair trade site.

[21] Gibson, A. C. (1999). *Economically important plants. Banana and plantain.* Retrieved from http://www.botgard.ucla.edu/botanytextbooks/economicbotany/index.html

[22] Aftalion, F. (2001). *A history of the international chemical industry: From the early days to 2000.* Philadelphia, PA: Chemical Heritage Foundation.

[23] Clinchy, B. M. (1994). On critical thinking and connected knowing. In K. S. Walters (Ed.), *Rethinking reason: New perspectives on critical thinking* (pp. 33–42). Albany, NY: State University of New York Press.

[24] Phelan, A. M., & Garrison, J. W. (1994). Toward a gender-sensitive ideal of critical thinking: A feminist poetic. In K. S. Walters (Ed.), *Re-thinking reason: New perspectives on critical thinking* (pp. 81–97). Albany, NY: State University of New York Press.

[25] Wiggins, G., & McTighe, J. (1998). *Understanding by design.* Alexandra, VA: Association for Supervision and Curriculum Development.

[26] National Research Council. (1996). *National science education standards: Observe, interact, change, learn.* Washington, DC: National Academy Press.

[27] National Research Council. (1996). p. 2.

[28] National Research Council. (2000). *Inquiry and the National Science Education Standards.* Washington, DC: National Academy Press.

[29] Wiggins, G., & McTighe, J. (1998).

[30] National Research Council. (2000).

[31] National Research Council. (2000). p. 2.

[32] Root-Bernstein, R. (1988).

UNDERSTANDING DISCOURSES IN SCIENCE
AND SCIENCE EDUCATION

Language begins with words but how humans create and use words depends on lots of others factors. For example, language also contains linguistic resources; including *grammar*, which includes rules about how we combine words to form phrases, clauses, and sentences; *semantic structure*, which can be described as conventions about how we use words to identify objects and processes; and *phonology*, which is about speech sounds and rules about pronunciation. Such variety allows flexibility so that we can produce different texts in different contexts to make use of different linguistic features. However, this flexibility is limited by cultural rules about texts that are acceptable in a specific context. But language is not static. Experience with popular culture serves to highlight its dynamic nature as BFF (best friend forever), F2F (face to face), and TMI (too much information) become readily recognized and, in some contexts, valued ways of communicating. Of course, one implication of such development is that there can be a disconnect between the language children bring to science and the language of the Eurocentric science that often forms the basis of science education.

In this chapter, you will have the chance to explore how Eurocentric scientific language and discourse evolved. How experimental philosophers and scientists used language to communicate their new knowledge to their peers and to the public. And how experimental philosophers began the practice, which continues to this day, of talking facts into reality. The job of language in Eurocentric science is to construct an alternative notion of our world to that brought into reality by common sense. My approach in this chapter is to present my examination of the development and use of a small set of language tools based on an idiosyncratic cultural historical examination of some functions of language for Eurocentric science. Hopefully, this chapter will help you to begin to appreciate the central role of grammatical and rhetorical structures in this process.

SCIENTIFIC DISCOURSES

A scientist addressing a group of her colleagues uses a form of discourse, or specific genre, which follows particular rules of presentation, syntax, and vocabulary that are recognized by other members of the scientific community to whom she is making her presentation. The rules of discourse, including who speaks, the order in which they speak and the structure of the language used, lead listeners to expect a specific type of discourse that they can interpret. In a classroom, students who are not familiar with scientific discourse may miss the intended message and, instead, recognize aspects of other genres that are unintended by the teacher. Students might make assumptions about which parts of the speech are important and which are not, assumptions that lead them to misconstrue the intended meaning. If students are not fully conversant with the nature of syntax and grammar in the language of science and the rules of scientific discourse, then their understanding of scientific knowledge and processes can be unduly restricted. Remember in Chapter 4 you explored a little of the history of the introduction of the vernacular in the discourses of science. In this chapter we will explore the further development of Eurocentric English scientific discourses.

Science and Scientific Discourse in the Seventeenth Century

In the early 17th century, Francis Bacon laid out the type of language that he believed experimental philosophers should use to describe their discoveries. When Bacon presented his thesis on experimental science, he was concerned that language be re-formed so that observations and experiments of the natural world could be presented accurately. Bacon believed that words were prone to misunderstanding and, in proposing a new way of making knowledge he criticized Aristotelianism, the philosophy in which knowledge growth depended on ancient authority that was located in authoritative texts.

Experimental philosophers such as Robert Boyle, Robert Hooke and Christian Huygens who emerged in the seventeenth century, endorsed Bacon's proposal about the type of language that should be used to describe new discoveries about Nature obtained by using experimental philosophy. Bacon distinguished between prose used to present scientific observations and experiments and prose that excited the imagination. He believed that science should report on direct examinations of the reality of the natural world and not be misled by the vagaries of verbal science. For him, and for his proponents who followed the experimental method, language used to present observations had higher status than language used to provide verbal commentary. In his treatise, *Parasceve*, Bacon used an analogy of a person collecting materials to construct a ship to describe scientists' use of language for constructing new knowledge[1]:

> And for all that concerns ornaments of speech, similitudes, treasury of eloquence, and such like emptiness, let it be utterly dismissed. Also let all those things which are admitted be themselves set down briefly and concisely, so that they may be nothing less than words. For no man who is collecting and storing up materials for shipbuilding or the like, thinks of arranging them elegantly, as in a shop, and displaying them so as to please the eye; all his care is that they be sound and good, and that they be so arranged as to take up as little room as possible in the warehouse.

The explicit message of Bacon's statement is that figures of speech are eloquent but inappropriate for describing the new knowledge resulting from the conduct and outcome of experimental philosophy. Instead, Bacon argues for the use of plain, concise language, free of figures of speech to describe observations and experimentation.

In support of Bacon's distrust of certain words that would cloud our understanding of the generation of new knowledge, Robert Hooke in *Micrographia* expresses the need for plain and simple language to describe facts in the following statement[2]:

> [I]n the physical enquires we must first endeavour to follow Nature in the more *plain* and *easie* ways she treads in the most *simple* and *uncompounded bodies*, to trace her steps and be acquainted with her manner of walking there, before we venture our selves into the multitude of *meanders* she has in *bodies of more complicated* nature; lest, being unable to distinguish and judge our way we quickly lose both *Nature* our Guide and *our selves* too, and are left to wander in the *labyrinth* of groundless opinions.

Hooke's argument seems to be that complex language does not allow the observer and experimenter to interact directly with Nature but leads them to form unfounded opinions. However, note also that Hooke uses a metaphor to make his argument. Both Bacon and Hooke are arguing that simple language should be used so that the language does not hinder interpretation of Nature by observation. Using complex language to describe observations of Nature introduces the potential for human opinion to influence any interpretations made. Hence simple language, and observations and experimentation where you interact directly with Nature, were to be much more valued than theorizing and argument. Experimental philosophers moved to use simple, plain language to describe their observations of Nature and their experimental procedures, but just how plain was their language?

THE LANGUAGE AND GRAMMAR OF SCIENCE

The move to national vernacular languages described in Chapter 4, suited experimental philosophers because it allowed them to present their new knowledge to a wider audience. Descartes and other French experimental philosophers believed that all literate people, most of whom could read and write only in their national language and not Latin, should have access to the reports of experimental philosophy. The move toward the use of a national language was characteristic of scientific discourse at this time. However, the development of national languages as the medium for communication of scientific knowledge was hampered to some extent by the lack of technical terms in these languages. Remember that as early as the 14th century Chaucer felt compelled to anglicize Latin and Arabic terms and incorporate them into the English language as he described how to use an astrolabe. In his publications in *Philosophical Transactions*, Isaac Newton overcame some of the limitations of the English language by using *nominal groups* and *nominalization*, a process, which allowed him to generate new words and meanings from existing verbs and adjectives[3]. But as I hope to convince you in this chapter, nominalization is more than just a convenient way of reducing the length of a sentence and creating new technical language.

Isaac Newton (1643–1727) is probably one of the most influential experimental philosophers in human history. In his *Philosophiae Naturalis Principia Mathematica*, usually called the *Principia*, he brought together Kepler's Laws of planetary motion and Galileo's theories of terrestrial gravity serving to demonstrate the physical unity between the heavens and the earth, just as Descartes had claimed. This was a momentous achievement. Newton argued that the motion of an apple to the earth was similar to the motion of planets around the sun. He was able to make his claim compelling by developing a mathematical model that allowed gravity in all these contexts to be calculated using the same mathematical formula. In the *Principia*, he also developed the three laws of motion that serve as the basis for any contemporary high school examination of force and moving objects, also called *motion*, a nominalization. His classical mechanics was the dominant physical theory until the emergence of twentieth century theories of relativity associated with Albert Einstein. Newton also extended the study of optics, making the first reflective telescope and exploring the physics of color. As far as we know, he was the first person to demonstrate that white light was composed of many colors. Imagine what a revelation that must have been! He engaged in a somewhat acrimonious debate with Gottfried Leibniz over who invented differential calculus. He also explored the chemistry of acids and bases. He tried to develop a theory of everything (TOE) associated with the forces of attraction and repulsion.

From an upper middle class family, Newton was born prematurely three months after his father died. His mother married again when Newton was three and he was left in the care of his grandmother. He did not care for his stepfather, which was the cause of some friction. After his stepfather's death, his mother tried to make Newton into a farmer, which did not go down well with Newton. She was convinced to allow him to complete his schooling at The King's School in Grantham and by 1661 Newton was studying at Trinity College, Cambridge. Soon after Newton graduated the college was closed because of the plague in 1665. Although he did not stand out at university, he read contemporary experimental philosophers such as Kepler, Descartes, and Galileo and extended their ideas to develop binomial theorem and differential and integral calculus by the time he graduated. For the next two years, as the plague raged across the country, Newton studied optics and gravity at his farm.

In 1669, Newton was elected Lucasian Professor of Mathematics, which required him not to be active in the church. Newton used this to appeal to Charles II against the requirement at that time that all University Fellows had to be Anglican priests. Newton held non-traditional religious views, the nature of which are still being examined, although it seems that he did not accept the idea of the Holy Trinity, one of the fundamental principles of Catholic and Anglican Christianity. In 1696, he was appointed warden to the Royal Mint. He became Master of the Mint in 1699 and held this position until his death during the reign of Queen Anne. He worked hard to stabilize the currency and deter practices such as counterfeiting and clipping. Do you have a sense of what *clippers* might have done to the currency? In 1705, Queen Anne knighted Newton making him the first experimental philosopher to be so honored even though his science was likely not the reason for his knighthood! Apart from his achievements in science, Newton also influenced the language of science.

The Language of Science

According to linguists Michael Halliday and James Martin[4], Newton helped to develop a discourse of experimentation in which he developed grammatical metaphors by applying nominalization to active or descriptive terms allowing him to theorize his experience by abstracting from practice. The term, *nominalization*, is based on an adjective, *nominal*, (from the Latin) that has been changed: nominalize + action gives us nominalization. Nominalization requires the conversion of an adjective or a verb into a noun. Perhaps in our everyday conversations we do not use nominalizations as much as Newton did, but we all use them. The question is why do we use them? What purpose do they serve? And why are they used so much in Eurocentric science language?

A Deeper Look at Nominalizations

Why do people use nominalizations? According to David Banks[5] the function of a *noun* is to "express an entity[6]" of either abstract or concrete nature, that of a *verb* is to express process, and that of an *adjective* is to express quality. Whenever different forms: that is, verb and/or adjective, and a noun, are used to express the same idea, we have a grammatical metaphor. Such metaphors indicate theoretical or abstract thinking and form the basis of nominalization. For example, *refract*, a verb, and *refraction*, a noun and a nominalization, are grammatical metaphors, expressing the same process. However, each tends to be used differently when a person is making a claim about experience. *Refract* is used to describe a process where a moving object is deflected from a straight path. Using nominalization, Newton was able to talk about *refraction*, rather than *things refract*, creating a noun that turned a process (refract) into an object or participant (refraction). Another example, commonly used by Newton was turning participants like sunlight, for example *sunlight reflects* into *reflection*.

We can talk about *purification of the scrapie* (a disease of sheep) *agent to homogeneity*[7] rather than *separating out the agent causing scrapie into a pure form.* The clause, *purification of the scrapie agent to homogeneity*, includes a nominalization and two phrases. Can you identify them all? Nominalizations, and phrases and clauses associated with nominalizations, condense prior knowledge so it can be treated as a given rather than being available for comment and criticism[8]. Once you have constructed a nominalization you can then use the term without specifying the actor, the time, situation or process. In science textbooks you can find nominal groups. For example, here is a section of text from *Prentice Hall Biology*[9]:

The process *by which two species evolve in response to changes in each other over time* is called coevolution.

The pattern of coevolution involving flowers and insects is so common that biologists in the field often discover additional examples.

Note in this example, how the authors presented coevolution as a process in the first sentence but by the second sentence it had become an object? This action turning a verb into a noun is a very common linguistic strategy in English, not just science textbooks. Why do you think this might be? According to scholar, Len Unsworth[10], one of the reasons for doing this is because there are many more resources available for modifying a nominal group and nominalizations than there are for modifying a verbal group. These resources allow us to transform expository writing[11], the type of writing typically found in science textbooks, into an argument by helping us to construct generalizations and abstractions from experiences. Such a strategy can make reading and understanding the text of textbooks even more of a challenge for youth and children more familiar with narrative.

Nominalizations allow us to organize expository writing rhetorically rather than having to use language that would force us to present our experiences in a real-world time and location sequence. As you might have already noted, nominalizations allow process, such as *refract* or *soluble* or *coevolve*, to be construed as physical stable phenomena that are available for further study and can be measured just as we can measure and study *refraction* and *solubility* and *coevolution*. Perhaps you are starting to get a sense of the power and nominalizations but also how much they can obscure understanding of phenomena.

The path from experience to theorizing experience using nominalization

Experience	I have an experience
Describe the experience	I was walking in the park. I looked down at water that had formed a pool from an evening shower. I saw my face clearly reflected in the pool of water.
Nominalization	Good reflections are produced from still water.

Note how I was able to turn my specific experience of seeing *my face clearly reflected* into a generalization/abstraction (I cannot help myself!) through the nominalization, good reflections? Now all still water has the potential to produce good reflections, a generalization that can be tested by experimentation. Are you beginning to get a sense of the importance of nominalizations to the practice of Eurocentric science?

Activity – Can You Make a Nominalization?

Consider the experience: *Sarah plays the violin* and is very smart.

This statement can be theorized and turned into a generalization through nominalization: *Violin playing* (nominalization) requires smart people.

Can you turn the following experience into a generalization by creating your own nominalization?
Experience: *I did not read all the papers she posted and I still got an A!*
Generalization with nominalization:

How did you go? It can be pretty easy to create your own nominalization and your own generalization but, like all generalizations, it is partial and I think this feature of nominalizations adds an extra layer of complexity for students trying to understand science.

Activity – Identifying Nominalizations in Scientific Papers

Do you remember back to Chapter 4 and the text taken from Hai Cheng and his colleagues? Go back a read it again. How many nominalizations or extended nominal groups can you identify?

One that stands out for me is, "the 100 thousand-year (ky) – recurrence period of ice ages." What assumptions do the authors make by using this nominalization? First, the authors assume the reader is familiar with ice ages as phenomena that over 100,00 year cycles expand out over land and oceans and then recede again, in the process affecting the livelihood of living things. Second, the studies about this field of science that preceded this one support this understanding of ice ages. Third, these recurring ice ages are facts or givens and provide a stepping off point for the authors to argue that they have found a mechanism, which can explain these phenomena. As you read this section again note how the authors used nominalizations to make an argument about the state of knowledge of the field in which their study is situated and how their study adds to this knowledge by proposing a mechanism for ice age expansion (I can't help myself) and retreat that is consistent with all the available data.

Based on what you have read so far, you can probably understand why scientists use nominalizations. A journal like *Science* in which Cheng et al. published their report has a limit of 4500 words for a research report. Materials and Methods used in the study are not published in the report but in an online repository. You might be able to understand the lure of using nominalizations that allow an author to reduce the words they use in sections of a report such as the introduction, where authors introduce the argument that they have constructed new knowledge, and the conclusion where they establish the quality of their new knowledge as it conforms to what is known and accepted as knowledge? The authors also most likely assume that if you are reading their paper, you are familiar with these ideas and are able to interpret their text. However, using nominalizations in science education can be especially problematic because these nouns or collection of nouns and adjectives mask the processes that are central to how they were created. Carol Reeves[12] argues that for youth and children nominalizations sound both learned and scary and rarely in the science classroom is the process of turning a verb into a noun examined critically by students and teachers. Perhaps as educators we should do this more often?

Activity

As you read through the text below ask yourself, "What are the nominalizations I can identify?" And, "What are some of the questions or processes that are obscured by the nominalizations I identify?" The following segment of text is taken from Holt Biology, a high school biology textbook[13]:

> During his experiments, Griffith unwittingly manipulated genes. Today, the manipulation of genes is known as genetic engineering or recombinant DNA technology. Transformation, in particular, is a common modern-day genetic engineering technique. For example, bacteria can be used to introduce foreign

genes into plant cells. Whole plants can then be grown from the altered genetic material, producing plants with desirable traits such as long shelf life or resistance to crop pests.

The first nominalization I notice is in the first two sentences:

In the first sentence we have the experience, "Griffith ... manipulated genes" and in the second sentence this experience is turned into theory, "the manipulation of genes." When Griffith's act is written this way it becomes theorized into a more general idea with the implication that any reader should understand what this means. But what if you do not? Where are you left as a reader and a learner? There are many more nominalizations or nominal groups in this paragraph. Can you identify at least five?

Newton Takes Nominalization Further

Although some nominalizations like "The Laws of Refraction" were in common use before Newton published his early work on Optics in *Philosophical Transactions*, Newton took nominalization further. He used nominalization to bring into existence new words which he could then use to develop theoretical concepts and which led to the expansion of the vocabulary of science. According to Halliday and Martin, words that Newton created by using nominalization he then presented as accepted concepts in subsequent segments of the same paper also suggesting the rhetorical nature of nominalizations. As we have examined in this chapter, scientists continue this practice today. Such an approach to the construction of language and knowledge also assisted Newton to create word pictures about his experiments as these segments taken from his paper in *Philosophical Transactions* of February 19, 1671/1672[14] demonstrate:

Then I began to suspect, whether the Rays, after their trajection through the Prisme, did not move in <u>curve</u> lines, and according to their more or less <u>curvidity</u> tend to divers parts of the wall.

And so the true cause of the length of that image was detected to be no other, then that *Light* consists of *Rays differently <u>refrangible</u>*, which, without any respect to a difference in their incidence, were, according to their degrees of <u>refrangibility</u>, transmitted towards divers parts of the wall.

These statements come from the report Newton wrote that included his *Expermentum Crucis* (Crucial Experiment) in which he was able to show that the colored lights from the spectrum, which he obtained by refracting white light from the sun through a prism, could not be further broken down into other colors indicating that these lights were pure unlike white light which was "a Heterogeneous mixture of differently refrangible rays."[15] According to the Oxford English Dictionary, Newton was the first person to use the terms refrangible and refrangibility. Today we would use the term, *refraction* instead. I wonder why?

The development of scientific grammar by nominalization also allowed a process to be constructed as an object, so that 'refractive' became 'refraction', 'incident' became 'incidence' and 'attract' became 'attraction', as Newton demonstrates in his theorizing about the nature of acids[16]:

> For whatever doth strongly <u>attract</u>, and is strongly <u>attracted</u> may be called an acid: And such things as are dissolved in Water, we see, become so easily, without any Effervescence: But where the <u>Attraction</u> is strong, and the particles of the Menstruum [liquid agent] are every way <u>attracted</u> by those of the Metal or rather where the Particles of the Metal are every way <u>attracted</u> by those of the Menstruum; then the Particles of the Menstruum environ those of the Metal, tear them to pieces and dissolve it.

Through the process of changing verbs and adjectives into nouns, Newton was able to reconstruct his experience for his audience and at the same time move his thinking and that of his audience towards the theoretical.

As we have noted, nominalizations serve to transform expository writing, like that found in science textbooks, into argument, hence their use in science textbooks! Have a look at some of the textbooks you commonly use and see where nominalizations are being used. Think whether the section of the textbook you are examining looks like an argument or an explanation.

Nominalizations became an accepted grammatical feature of scientific discourse and evolved concurrently with the development of technical terminology. Nominalizations helped experimental scientists, like Newton, to relate the processes of experimentation with theorizing based on reflection, allowing Newton and other inductive experimental philosophers to introduce theory without seeming to introduce theory. In English, the introduction of Latin and Greek terms combined with the use of nominalization allowed experimental philosophers to generalize and abstract experience. At the same time these words allowed the experimenter to be removed from the data, so the data could became the central focus of the text. However, this was not the only language tool available to early experimental philosophers. Another was to introduce words into the language, if the precise word was not available for use in the vernacular.

THE TECHNOLOGY OF WORDS AND SCIENCE

In 1787 chemist, Antoine Lavoisier, and his colleagues, Antoine Fourcroy, Claude-Louis Berthollet, and Guyton de Morveau, began a project to create terminology for the New French Chemistry.[17] In this year, Lavoisier argued to the Academy that the word ought to bring about the birth of the idea; that the idea should represent the fact; that idea, fact, and word were different representations of the same entity[18]. Lavoisier saw the reformation of the language of chemistry as central to developing chemistry as an analytical discipline. In his textbook, *Traité élémentaire de chimie* (Treatise on the Elements of Chemistry), Lavoisier argued:

> We must trust to nothing but facts: These are presented to us by Nature and cannot deceive. We ought, in every instance, to submit our reasoning to the test of the experiment, and never to search for truth but by the natural road of experiment and observation[19].

In this short text, Lavoisier's argument is clear; experimental evidence provided the basis for the development of facts and we should not be seduced by claims passed down from previous generations that were based on claims lacking the veracity of experiment. Like Galileo, Lavoisier saw mathematics as the highest form of reasoning and therefore the reasoning that should be used by chemists as a basis for reforming their discipline. Lavoisier proposed the use of chemical equations to represent chemical reactions. The method for symbolically representing chemical reactions used in chemistry education and communication today, can be linked directly back to this argument of Lavoisier and his colleagues. Lavoisier proposed the label, *oxygen*, for the now well-known gaseous element. He constructed the name from the Greek *oxys* for acid and *genes* for producer with the purpose of using the name to communicate a defining analytical characteristic of the element and of emphasizing the experimental nature of the discipline. The work of Lavoisier and his colleagues on the language of chemistry had, over time, a profound influence on the discipline of chemistry. However, Lavoisier was not the first, nor would he be the last person to propose new terminology. But his argument that the name should not just express an idea but have some connection to analytical methods that would allow scientists to move the unknown to the known has not always been followed in science.

Theodore Savory[20], scientist and linguist, in his book, *The Language of Science*, argues that all humans have a desire to label and categorize objects and processes. Often, unlike Lavoisier's proposal for a formal constructed language in chemistry, the connection between the word used and the object is not obvious. Taking the word, *dog*, as an example, Savory argues that often the only link between a word and the object to which it refers, is tradition and long-standing custom. When you read the word, dog, did you think of a hairy quadruped that likes humans and going for walks? If you belong to the culture that uses that label for that object or process, your cultural experiences allow you to connect the label, dog, to the animal to which that label has been given but there is no way that you can reason out the connection. Through the 17th and 18th centuries, the glory days for experimental philosophy, experimental philosophers were faced with having to label and categorize a range of phenomena and so they *borrowed* words from everyday language, *imported* words from other languages such as Greek and Latin, and *invented* words.

One of the issues with borrowed words such as the word *life*, for example, is that the meaning of a word in everyday life (see what I mean?) and in science is obscure or uncertain or both[21]. The word, life, can be understood variously as the length of time a person is active, that is between birth and death; the condition that distinguishes animate from inanimate; a record of living, my life; and even the in-animate can be described as life when created by an artist. 'Life' can even be used to refer to imprisonment. As a word, *life* comes to us from Old Frisian and Old Saxon and meant sustenance or body. The Latin equivalent is *vita*, which you might have read in contexts associated with life. Usually, we need a context to try and work out which meaning of life is appropriate for the instance with which we are engaged. There are other issues experienced with burrowed words. For example, words such as *salt* or *acid* have a more limited meaning in science than they do in everyday discourse, which has implications for how youth come to learn these more restricted Eurocentric science meanings. Other words such as *force* and *work* have a very different meaning in Eurocentric science to their use in everyday contexts making the understanding of such terms one of the challenges of learning science.

Some words that have been invented by scientists to label scientific terms have subsequently entered the English language where the meaning has become less defined. An example of this is the term *enzyme*. In science it can mean a protein or a specific form of RNA, which catalyses a chemical reaction, but in everyday life it is a substance present in washing powders that helps remove grease and dirt in order to clean clothes. Even in science, meanings are not fixed. For example, teachers use the word *meniscus* to mean the curve at the top of a column of water, particularly in a glass column, but meniscus as a concavo-convex lens predates this common classroom usage by at least 100 years. Other words invented by scientists to label and categorize include *vitamin* (Casimir Funk 1911), *hydrogen peroxide* (Louis Thénard 1818), *hormone* (Ernest Henry Starling 1905), *allergy* (Clemens von Pirquet 1906), *catalysis* (Jöns Jacob Berzelius 1836), *nuclear fission* (Lise Meitner 1939), and *prion* (Stanley Prusiner 1982). For me, one of the interesting features of words originally introduced into science that then become accepted more broadly into everyday language is how these words, and the ideas they represent, then become part of our reality. So much so, that their creation is often lost and the words and associated ideas become timeless and stable, as though they had always existed.

One feature of development of technical vocabulary in science is that as it helped to establish specialized disciplines, which were dependent on an understanding of the terminology, concurrently it served to reinforce a distancing aspect of science language for those, like students, at the margins of the discipline. Historically, the increasing technicality of science language meant that the general public was gradually removed from an understanding of science as it became accessible to only a few people who studied the disciplines that were emerging with the evolution of technical grammar.

Activity- Finding the Words

Robert Hooke is often presented as the first person to use the word *cells* to describe something, which he observed as a structural feature of particular bodies including cork, the bark of the cork oak, *Quercus suber*. Previously the word, cell, had been used in English to describe a monastery, or a small apartment in a building, and then later one of the structures into which something was divided, such as a pigeon-hole or a wax comb of bees[22]. Hooke records his musings on both the structure and an appropriate word to describe his observations of this structure when he writes in Observation XVIII of his book, *Micrographia*[23]:

> I could exceeding plainly perceive it to be all perforated and porous, much like a Honey-comb, but that the pores of it were not regular; yet it was not unlike a Honey-comb in these particulars.
>
> First, in that it had very little solid substance, in comparison of the empty cavity that was contain'd between, as does more manifestly appear by Figure A and B of the XI *Scheme* [see Hook's Figures on the following page], for the

Insterstitia, or walls (as I may so call them) or partitions of those pores were neer as thin in proportion to their pores, as those thin films of wax in a Honey-comb (which enclose and constitute the *sexangular cells*) are to theirs.

Next, in that these pores, or cells, were not very deep, but consisted of a great many little Boxes, separated out of one continued long pore, by certain *Diaphragms,* as is visible by the Figure B, which represents a sight of those pores split in the long ways.

1. How many different words does Robert Hooke use to describe the porous structures he sees under his microscope? What are these words?
2. How many words does he use to identify the wall-like structures?
3. How important are metaphors to Hooke as he tries to help his readers develop their own image of what he observed when he looked at some cork under a microscope?

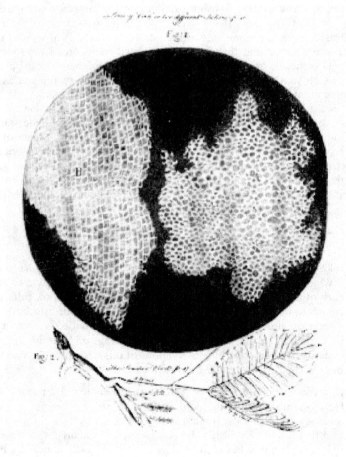

Hooke's diagrams of his observations of cork under his microscope.

In his description of his observations, Hooke seems to be searching for a word in English, which provides a meaning that he thought would communicate to his readers some thought images for the porous structures he observed. How many words did you find in the segment of Hooke's text? Did you note that he used the words 'cells', 'pores', 'boxes' and 'empty cavity' to describe the major structures that he observed in cork, and 'interstitia', 'wall', 'partitions' and 'diaphragms' to describe the separating structure? Hooke's reflections supported a new set of terms and the words, 'cell' and 'wall', were adopted as appropriate labels for these microscopic plant structures in preference to the other options that he presented. However, the adoption of the terms, 'cell' and 'cell wall', for the structures that Hooke observed was not as immediate as might be imagined from reading school science text books on the topic:

Senior Biology:1665 The term 'cell' was used for the first time by Robert Hooke, curator of experiments for the Royal Society of London. In examining a thin slice of cork, using a microscope, which he had built, he noted that cork (and other plant materials) was made up of tiny box-like compartments. These he called cells, though it was more than 200 years later before the term was used to include the contents or living material[24].

Biology Two: Since Robert Hooke's first observation of cells, using a primitive microscope in 1665, microscopy has advanced dramatically[25].

The Living Environment – Biology: Leeuwenhoek described his discoveries in letters to the Royal Society of England, a group that included the most important scientists and thinkers in the world at that time. They were so surprised they sent one of their leaders, Robert Hooke, to investigate. Robert Hooke also made a most interesting discovery with a simple microscope of his own design in 1665. Looking at very thin slices of cork - the outer bark of a species of oak that is used to plug bottles - Hooke observed rows of tiny spaces. Under the microscope, the thin slice of cork looked like a honeycomb constructed by bees. Hooke called the spaces he observed "cells"[26].

Concepts in Modern Biology: Robert Hooke, an English physicist, combined two sets of lens and produced a *compound microscope*. In 1665, while examining a thin piece of cork with his microscope, Hooke discovered that it was not solid as had been believed, but was made up of walled compartments. These looked like the honeycomb of a beehive. Hooke called these hollow boxes "cells." We know now that Hooke saw the walls of empty dead plant cells. He concluded the cell was an empty box[27].

Note all of these historical narratives excerpted from high school Biology textbooks mention Robert Hooke and cells but the sub-text or message is somewhat different in each. We might assume that the authors of each of these textbooks had access to the same facts so a question you might ask is: why are the texts different? An answer to this question is that each group of textbook authors has selected specific elements or facts on which to focus and by that process has imbued their narrative with specific values. Robert King and Frank Sullivan in their text *Senior Biology* provide their student readers with some historical background on the constructed nature of the term 'cell' for the 'box-like compartments' that Hooke had observed. However, they present the term as though it was developed and accepted readily by society as soon as it had been used by Hooke to label what he was observing.

In their text *Biology Two*, Evans, Ladiges and McKenzie present cells as eternal objects that happened to be observed by Robert Hooke. There is no indication that Robert Hooke proposed the name 'cells' for the structures that he observed under the microscope. Reading this section of *Biology Two*, a student might imagine that the term 'cell' had always existed and as a consequence was timeless and secure. In both of these texts, the selection of specific facts or events for the telling imbues each text with values as well as content. In the first two texts presented above, labeling of experimental concepts is not presented as creative constructive activity that it undoubtedly is. In the section of *Micrographia* you read, Hooke demonstrates both creativity and construction as he tries to communicate to his readers, what he was observing. He uses the metaphors of boxes, cells, honeycomb, and pore to try to support his readers to imagine what these structures look like because they do not have access to the images he has as he looks through his microscope. His musings also communicate the creative component as he struggles to label the structures he has observed using words that will have some meaning for his readers.

Question.   Read carefully the last two text segments (shown previously) from the textbooks, *The Living Environment – Biology* and *Concepts in Modern Biology*, and see if you can identify values about discovery and labeling that are embedded in those texts about Robert Hooke and 'cells'.

Discovery and Challenge in Science

In the previous section, I made the argument that often in science textbooks the history of a concept is lost or ignored as textbook writers present concepts and their labels as timeless and stable, as having always existed. However, there is status in being acknowledged as the discoverer of a concept, so for scientists there is profe-ssional and personal value in arguing your concept or a concept into reality. Social scientist, Bruno Latour[28] shows how Louis Pasteur, one of the founders of micro-biology as a scientific discipline, used a range of rhetorical strategies; including making yeast the hero of a narrative, to talk into reality the role of yeast in lactic acid fermentation. This is not the first time you have read of Pasteur in this book. Louis Pasteur (1822–1895), a chemist and microbiologist, worked closely with industry and is probably best known as the developer of the process that bears his name, pasteurization. Look at a container of milk from your refrigerator or dairy cabinet at a supermarket and see if you can find *pasteurized* written on a milk container. What is the meaning of this term? How was it constructed? Pasteur also built on the work of experimental philosophers such as Anton van Leeuwenhoek, Francisco Redi, and Lazzaro Spallanzani to try and resolve questions about the theory of spontaneous generation. In so doing, he generated evidence for the *germ theory of disease*, that is, the notion that many diseases were caused by living things called microorganisms.

Another example of using a word to create a hero is Stanley Prusiner's paper[29] in *Science* in which he proposes the existence of a new infectious agent, different from viruses and bacteria. He called this agent a *prion*, which stood for *proteinaceous infectious particle*. Some members of the science community criticized Prusiner for what they saw as his unseemly haste at rushing to publication before the infective mechanisms had been clarified but many more argued that he had assisted the field to move forward because then researchers could focus on an entity, a prion, for study even if members of the community were divided on what mechanism of infection prions used. In 1997, Prusiner was awarded the Nobel Prize in physiology and medicine for this discovery.

The history of the label, *cell*, for the structures Hooke observed had a slower transition into the reality of a fact than did the prion. In 1682, almost twenty years after Hooke published *Micrographia* in which he mused about an appropriate word for the microscopic objects he observed, Nehemiah Grew, in *Anatomy of Plants*[30], was still struggling with an acceptable name for such structures, describing them as 'pores', 'cells' and 'bladders'. It was not until the nineteenth century that *cells* became the accepted label for these structures as scientists associated cells with both animals and plants (1838) and then associated cells with life[31]. By 1888, William Carpenter could write that in living things the cell was, "the elementary form of all organized structures."[32] Note how the label, *cells*, is being talked into reality? Even though people had never "seen" cells until Hooke looked at some cork under his microscope, within one hundred and fifty years, cells had become a fact that could then be taught in schools as a concept that was true and eternal.

Clearly, as the concept of the cell developed in science and it became part of the reality of science, the meaning of the word became more structured. One characteristic of science language is that there is an attempt to ensure that words in science undergo less change than do words in everyday language, perhaps because these words are so tied up with notions of reality. The stability of science language is assisted by its literary nature in contrast to the oral nature of everyday language. But humans tend to use language creatively and find uses for words beyond their initial label and meaning. Since Robert Hooke proposed the term 'cell' for regular structures that he observed under the microscope, it has been applied in everyday language to 'prison cells', to the 'electric cell' and to 'political cells', amongst others.

Sometimes a word that is created by a scientist to name a phenomenon or structure is then adopted into everyday speech and with usage undergoes change so that the word does not necessarily, in the minds of learners who communicate in everyday language, have the same meaning as is associated with the word in science. For example, the word *inertia* was originally introduced into the English language via the work of experimental philosophers who wrote in Latin. *Inertia* was first used in physics by Joannes Kepler and then by Newton in his three Laws of Motion in *Principia* (1687) where he used the term to refer to the 'force of inactivity'[33]. Inertia then entered everyday English usage and came to mean laziness or apathy. So, even though the language of science, which constitutes a literary discourse, might not undergo the rapid changes of oral discourse, meanings for words used in science are not fixed and do change with the generation of new knowledge and changes in thinking. There have been attempts to fix the meanings of scientific terms. Theodore Savory cites Dr Whewell as saying[34]:

> When our knowledge becomes perfectly exact and purely intellectual; we shall exclude alike vagueness and fancy, imperfection and superfluity, in which each term shall convey meaning steadily fixed and vigorously limited. Such is the language of science.

But Whewell was writing at the height of modernism when science was seen as the path to true knowledge enlightenment. I am sure that you all recognize the futility of trying to get the toothpaste back in the tube once it is out. Labels or terminology in science experience the same phenomenon. Once they grab public attention and are available to everyday uses of language, there is no taking them back.

Implications for Teaching Science

Hopefully, this discussion of some of the language tools used in Eurocentric science has helped you to understand how these tools aided theorizing and supported the construction of a form of systematic knowledge, Eurocentric science. At the same time, these tools could be used to restrict access to the knowledge that was being constructed. I think it is important that educators give some thought to presenting the language of science as a vibrant, evolving aspect of scientific endeavor, and not something that is fixed and unchanging. The application of one meaning for each word tends to be emphasized in science teaching. As a consequence, the meanings of words are presented as unchanging. If teachers believe that meanings are fixed then words become identified with a specific object or idea. If the classroom is imbued with the concept of one word-one meaning, then the pedagogical emphasis of the classroom can be on writing the correct definitions rather than understanding the constructed nature of science language and how students can also be participants in that construction. The ability of students to write 'correct' definitions in science is perceived commonly in science teaching as a fundamental step towards student understanding in science. In many science texts, definitions comprise a significant proportion of the science knowledge presented to students and constitute an aspect of scientific language. However, if definitions are presented as historical constructs then students might develop a greater awareness of the constructed nature of scientific understandings and begin to appreciate the human nature of science.

SCIENCE STORIES

Earlier in this Chapter, you examined the narratives used by various biology textbooks to tell about cells. I called these segments, *narratives*, but I could also have called them *science stories*. Features important to the development of narrative include an understanding that, while in any context there are many events *available* for the telling, the construction of a narrative involves *selecting* specific ones[35]. We had the chance to examine this first hand with the various cell narratives. All the authors of these texts had numerous events about Robert Hooke and cells from which they could select to tell their narrative. As we noted in the analysis of the textbook 'cell' narratives, the process of selecting specific events for the telling of a narrative imbues the narrative not only with meaning, but also values and temporality. Sasha Barab and colleagues[36] describe this aspect of a narrative as the *plot* that takes place in a *setting* where *characters* participate. The power of the plot is that it contextualizes content so that facts can be transformed from things to be memorized into useful tools for addressing specific issues or questions and for imbuing specific values. Even for scientific knowledge, which is typically presented through arguments and explanations in which embedded empirical evidence supports specific models and theories, humans seem to want to tell stories in the construction of knowledge[37].

Three of the four stories in the cell activity have the obvious structural features of a narrative. They have a beginning, in which Robert Hooke is introduced, a middle, which is used to progress the story, and an end, which usually finishes with the use of the label, 'cell' for microscopic structures Hooke observed. Hooke is the hero in all of these stories, unlike the foreigner, Leeuwenhoek.

You might wonder about the place of stories in science since Eurocentric science prides itself in its attachment to facts and theories. There are lots of different types of stories told in school science and with each are embedded implicit notions of the nature of science. I have categorized and analyzed a number of different types of stories I identified in science textbooks[38]. These categories are illustrative rather than comprehensive. I called them: heroic science stories, discovery science stories, declarative science stories, and politically correct science stories. Heroic science stories focus on a hero of science who single-handedly contributed to the development of science. This fits with the Great Men theory of history, which attributes the development of science to a few 'great men'. Of course, there is generally no place for a woman in these stories unless she is Marie Curie.

In discovery science stories[39], scientific knowledge is presented as having occurred as the result of an accident rather than insight based on a deep knowledge of the field. In declarative science stories, processes or scientific concepts become objects and are represented as open to observation in nature by anyone. These particular stories present concepts such as cells, acid, gravity, genes and temperature as secure and timeless, and as a consequence, any sense of the construction of these concepts is lost. Some of the stories you read in the 'cell' activity fit this category. Which ones? Politically correct science stories are a relatively recent development in school science as some teachers and texts attempt to represent more fairly the contribution of people from different cultures, genders, religions, and countries to the development of modern Eurocentric science and to examine critically the interaction between science and society as they mutually construct each other. However, very often when stories attempt to 'balance the books' in representing different groups of people in a story, the authors can represent other facets poorly. Often the role of narratives in school science is to assist the construction and transmission of a particular notion of the culture of science. However, as I discussed in Chapter 6, I believe also that narratives can be used to be transformative.

Activity – Representing and Analyzing Stories

Read the following role-play, which was a slightly modified version of a narrative taken from a science textbook for middle school science.

Great Moments in the History of Heat

In the 1770's there was a brilliant scientist living and working in France. His name was ANTOINE LAVOISIER. Lavoisier is famous today for the work he did in chemistry. However, he also studied **PHYSICS**. (Lavoisier is shown writing at his desk with chemical apparatus in the background) Lavoisier's wife often helped him in his studies. She would translate papers from English to French for him.

Antoine: Marie Anne. Could you bring me another candle, please? Mine is nearly out.

(*Marie Anne picks up one of the candles out of the candle holder on her desk*). Sometimes she would discuss his studies with him … as she is about to do now. (*Some wax from the candle drips on to Marie Anne's hand*)

Marie Anne: OUCH!
Antoine: **What Happened?**
Marie Anne: Nothing really. I burned my hand slightly as I changed the candle.
Antoine: Now that's interesting! I was just working out a theory on how heat moves…
Marie Anne: May I see? (*Marie Anne reads the paper Antoine is writing*)
             So, your hypothesis is that heat is a substance that has mass.
Antoine: Yes… Let me draw you a diagram to explain. I'll use what happened to you as an example.

Lavoisier has written on his notebook, 'How heat moves from object to object. Caloric – a fluid with heat in it.'

Antoine: Which was hotter Marie, the candle wax or your hand?
Marie Anne: My burned finger proves that the candle wax was hotter!
Antoine: When an object touches a warmer object, the caloric fluid flows from the warmer object into the cooler object. It was the **caloric** that burned your hand.
Marie Anne: Antoine, I have one question about your hypothesis… What is the mass of caloric?
Antoine: (*Yawning*) I must design an experiment to test my hypothesis. However! Since it is late and since we are tired, I'll leave it till later.

DESIGN AN EXPERIMENT TO TEST LAVOISIER'S HYPOTHESIS. (In Activity 4–9) Do you think he is right?[40]

---

1. What was the content of this story? What did Mary Anne and Antoine Lavoisier observe? What question about the natural world is being explored in this role-play?
2. What 'politically correct' aspect is being addressed and how is this issue addressed in the story? How could this aspect of the narrative/role play be represented more strongly?
3. How are scientific processes misrepresented in this story?
4. Can you suggest some ways to edit the story so that it more accurately represents to students the accepted practices of Eurocentric science?

What does this Story Imply About the Relationship Between Marie Anne and Antoine?

I believe that this story represents a move to find a place for women in science stories but this particular story does not grant Marie Anne Lavoisier (1758–1836) the significant role history indicates she deserves. *Great Moments in the History of Heat* tells us Marie Anne translated papers for Antoine, but not why this activity was important. There is historical evidence to support the notion that she learnt English so that she could read the work of researchers such as Joseph Priestly, an English chemist, with whom Antoine Lavoisier engaged in discussions about the existence and role of phlogiston and the nature of a gas Priestly called *dephlogistated air* and Lavoisier called *oxygen*. Antoine never learnt to read English so he was dependent on her interpretations[41]. Marie Anne kept all the notes on "his" experimental work and drew all the diagrams for the published scientific papers.

Mary Anne Lavoisier's drawing of experiments in human respiration. Can you identify Mary Anne in the drawing? What about Antoine?

In the *Great Moments* narrative, Antoine is the initiator of all scientific discussion and explains to Marie Anne the implication of the observation about heat. Yet, this story ignores the possibility of an intellectual environment where Marie Anne and Antoine worked together to develop new scientific ideas. The notion that Marie Anne was scientifically astute is further supported by her continued organization of science meetings attended by the foremost experimental philosophers of the day after Antoine's untimely death by guillotine during the French Revolution in 1794. He was fifty years old (her father also was executed on the same day as Antoine). Perhaps her dissatisfaction with her second marriage to Count Rumford, which lasted less than four years, can be attributed to the lack of such a collaborative environment. At least that is my version of the story!

As you read to the end of this story did you note the closing question, "Design an experiment to test Lavoisier's hypothesis. Do you think he is right?" What does this sentence imply? What might this question suggest to students about the relationship between theory and experiments in Eurocentric science? I read the instruction to design an experiment and the question that followed as implying that one piece of evidence from experimentation would be enough to lead scientists to relinquish or change their theories about an aspect of science. What do you think?

If we look briefly at the of the theory of 'matter of heat' or 'caloric', mentioned in this story, we would learn that long before Lavoisier's time, at least as far back as ancient Greece and possibly much further back in time, people had asked questions about hot and cold. The caloric theory was more useful for explaining known thermal phenomena in the 17th and 18th centuries than was the alternative and, at that time, underdeveloped notion, that heat was associated with the motion of particles[42].

As I previously mentioned, in 1787 Antoine began working with other French scientists to revise chemical terminology and introduced the term 'caloric' to replace 'matter of heat'[43]. According to the caloric theory, heat was a material substance so Antoine and Marie Anne may have conducted experiments to examine the material nature of heat. However, what does this story with Mary Anne and Antoine imply about the longevity of the caloric theory in Eurocentric science? Is the implication that one experiment showing that heat does not have weight has enough explanatory and emotive power to convince other scientists to overturn the caloric theory, and adopt the theory that heat is the result of particle motion?

An historical examination of the development of the caloric theory suggests a different story. One of the most trenchant critics of the caloric theory, Count Rumford (Benjamin Thompson, 1753–1814), conducted a series of experiments in 1786–1799 testing aspects of the caloric theory. Benjamin Thompson was a Loyalist officer during the American Revolutionary War and at its end traveled to England where he was made a junior minister in the government and knighted in 1784. In 1785 he moved to Bavaria where he conducted some of his most memorable experiments. He was an accomplished inventor and had already influenced English society with his development of a better fireplace. Working with the Bavarian army, he improved both their uniforms and the quality of their rations. He was made a Count of the Holy Roman Empire in 1791.

In his 1798 paper to the Royal Society[44], Rumford describes how he noticed a large amount of heat was produced when boring bronze cylinders to make cannon. A question he explored was, whether the chips of metal produced as he, his workers, and horses bored out a hole in a solid mass of metal was a source of heat. If the heat came from the chips then, according to the caloric theory, the chips' capacity for heat should be changed and this change should be enough to account for all the heat produced in the process. But when he took equal quantities of chips and sections of the block of metal and put them into the same quantity of water at the same temperature, he could find no difference in the water. The water containing the chips was not heated any more or less than the water containing the metal from the block. He found that heat was given off in all directions. It was continuous and could be produced without exhaustion leading him to propose that that heat could not be a material substance and therefore not caloric.

The philosophically naive notion presented the story of Marie Anne and Antoine is that one piece of evidence that counters a theory is enough to cause the rejection of that theory. But in response to Rumford's experimental data, supporters of the caloric theory argued that the reason Rumford had not found caloric with his experiments was because heat was 'weightless' but had all the other features that characterize a material substance or that heat was too 'subtle' for its weight to be detected. The debate surrounding whether heat had weight indicates how unlikely it is for a simple experiment to settle a question about theory choice. Well into the 19th century caloric theory remained the theory of choice for studies of heat, heat transfer, and mechanical efficiency.

According to Lawrence Learner, a professor of physics, and William Bennetta, a biologist and journal editor, textbooks particularly in the life sciences undermine teachers' efforts to provide a clear introduction to theory[45]. Often these textbooks present "the message that theory is any kind of notion that happens to appeal to any-one for any reason"[46]. As we know, historically spontaneous generation was accepted as part of the theory about the origins of generation and we have Redi's experiments on spontaneous generation to assist us to make an assessment about the historical development of specific theories. The history of theories in science is partly about the tendency for researchers to hold on to their pet theories with all their might (remember interpretive repertoires in Chapter 5), especially when these theories have explanatory and predictive power like that of the caloric theory. They do not relinquish them on the basis of one set of disconfirming evidence. History is replete with other examples illustrating the fervor with which scientists hold onto theories when the data indicates support for an alternative theory, for example, the phlogiston theory of combustion, the effects of L-DOPA, phototropism, germ theory of disease, Mendelian genetics, and the heliocentric theory of the universe. But sometimes these theories are retained because they do seem to explain phenomena more usefully than poorly developed alternative theories. Caloric theory is a good example because an alternative theory was the theory that heat could be understood as the motion of particles, which had been proposed on and off by experimental philosophers, like Count Rumford, for more than a hundred years but caloric theory seemed to explain phenomena better than the concept of particles moving.

You might think from my critical review of this story that I do not think there is a place for stories but if we consider connected knowing I think we would agree that stories have a powerful place in science and that educators should make greater use of stories especially when one realizes that narrative is the genre with which we seem to be most familiar because we use it every day. I would like to see more use made of narrative to teach and learn about science and provide an example to follow.

I think stories like this, which both students and teachers can construct, can be tools for exploring the cultural and historical origins of the Eurocentric science that forms the basis of school science and of science standards in many different countries. Starting with narrative, recognizing that all narratives, like my narratives of Spallanzani and Rumford, are partial and serve a rhetorical purpose, we could also apply such awareness to other forms of text that are presented using genres such as exposition or argument. I could have used Spallanzani's work on spontaneous generation where he showed that microscopic organisms traveled through the air and were destroyed by heating to boiling point only to have his critics argue that through heating he had destroyed the 'life force' necessary for spontaneous generation. Too often the people at the margins of Eurocentric science find that they are as much excluded from the discipline as they are from the narratives. But narratives also offer the chance to include stories from students or include accounts that often are excluded from more traditional forms of texts, such as those commonly found in textbooks.

My comic about Spallanzani's experiment with frogs and competing theories of the spermists and ovists

Activity – Creating Your Own Science Story

Why not try creating your own story using using graphic stories or roleplay similar to the ones you have read to explore and outline the history of a concept and develop a creative way of making some aspect of this concept a problem for students you might teach? Here are some sites that you might find useful.

http://pixton.com/
http://pixton.com/schools/overview
http://pixton.com/comic/gw9v8s32 (This example was created by a former student)
http://www.readwritethink.org/files/resources/interactives/comic/
http://www.makebeliefscomix.com/Comix/
http://www.toondoo.com/
http://stripgenerator.com/strip/create/

IMPLICATIONS OF BELIEFS ABOUT SCIENTIFIC DISCOURSE

Scientific discourse, which was presented in the 17th century as the appropriate discourse for reporting experimentation, became a discourse of power as Boyle, Hooke, and other experimental philosophers sought to convince their readers that they were revealing facts about Nature. Scientific discourse has always had a rhetorical character with arguments based on the molding of facts into evidence. Hopefully, this chapter has provided you with enough evidence to challenge the ideology of what is scientific discourse and to understand some of the tools such as nominalization and technical words that were developed to move experimental philosophy in to the realm of generalization, abstraction, and theorizing. Students should have opportunities to use different language genres as they communicate their understandings of science. However, often students are not encouraged to use different genres or to challenge their use. This lack of critical analysis means that often discourse operates as a silent partner which influences the representation of science but which is apparently invisible to the participants in the classroom. An emphasis on the use of the passive voice can remove from students their sense of agency as active constructors or interpreters of the data of their explorations. Extensive use of the passive voice and an emphasis on plain and simple language encourages the students to use description and recount in their explication of activities. I wonder if students were encouraged to be more active and more rhetorical in their presentation of their scientific understandings would they experience an enhanced sense of involvement and gain greater enjoyment from the literary aspects of school science?

Also the ideology of the security of scientific definitions and acceptance of a belief in the direct relationship between word, meaning, and object leads to situations where 'scientific definitions' and scientific words are presented as timeless and secure. In such science learning contexts, there is an emphasis on learning the 'correct' definitions as laid down by teacher or textbook. Because words are accepted as having one true definition, and meanings are presented as fixed, there is a tendency in classrooms for scientific concepts, which have been developed by scientists working through the ages, to be presented as 'facts of Nature' with no acknowledgement of the history of their construction.. In a classroom where these facts become the starting points of the science curriculum, any sense of the constructed, dynamic, and organized nature of Eurocentric science is lost.

Students should be encouraged to be active constructors of knowledge by learning about different genres that are used in science discourse and by learning about the power of rhetoric. They should have the opportunity to use multiple forms for experimental reports that could model contemporary and historical versions of scientific reports. They should be encouraged to represent scientific knowledge in a multitude of ways. Students should be engaged also in activities in which they examine the underlying meanings and values of accounts about science so that they have the chance to develop a critical facility especially in their understanding of the relationship between theory and facts in Eurocentric science.

NOTES

[1] Bacon, F. (1620/1968). Paraceve/Novum Organum. In J. Spedding, R. L. Ellis & D. D. Heath (Eds.), *The works of Francis Bacon* (pp. 254–255). New York: Garrett Press. (Original publication 1620, facsimile reprint of 1870 publication).

[2] Hooke, R. (1665/1961). *Micrographia*. New York: Dover Publications. p. 1.

[3] Halliday, M. A. K., & Martin, J. R. (1993). *Writing science: Literacy and discursive power*. London: The Falmer Press.

[4] Halliday, M. A. K., & Martin, J. R. (1993).

[5] Banks, D. (2005). On the historical origins of nominalised process in scientific text. *English for Specific Purposes, 24*, 347–357.

[6] Banks, D. (2005). p. 348.

[7] McKinley, M. P., Masiarz, F. R., & Prusiner, S. B. (1981). Reversible chemical modification of the scrapie agent. *Science, 214*, 1259–1261.

[8] See Reeves, C. (2005). "I knew there was something wrong with that paper": Scientific rhetorical styles and scientific misunderstandings. *Technical Communication Quarterly, 14*, 267–275.

[9] Miller, K. R., & Levine, J. (2003). *Prentice Hall biology New York State* (pp. 432–433). Upper Saddle River, NJ: Prentice Hall.

[10] Unsworth, L. (2005). Some practicalities of a language-based theory of learning. In Z. Fang (Ed.), *Literacy teaching and learning: Current issues and trends* (pp. 144-152). Upper Saddle River, NJ: Pearson Merrill Prentice Hall.

[11] Expository writing is definitive, designed to present information as directions or explanations. Studies have shown that at about the Grade 4 stage children begin to experience difficulty with understanding text. The explanation for this difficulty is that this is the stage at which children are introduced to expository writing.

[12] Reeves, C. (2005).

[13] Johnson, G., & Raven, P. (2004). *Holt biology* (p. 191). Austion, TX: Holt, Rinehart, and Winston.

[14] Newton, I. (1671). A letter of Mr. Isaac Newton, Professor of the Mathematicks in the University of Cambridge; containing his new theory about light and colors: Sent by the author to the publisher from Cambridge. *Philosophical Transactions, 6*, 3075–3087. p. 3078.

[15] Newton, I. (1671).

[16] Newton, I. (1692/1978). Some thoughts about the nature of acids. In I. B. Cohen (Ed.), *Isaac Newton's papers and letters on natural philosophy and related documents*. Cambridge, MA: Harvard University Press.

[17] Bell, M. S. (2005). *Lavoisier in the year one: The birth of a new science in an age of revolution*. New York: W. W. Norton.

[18] If you are familiar with Alan Johnstone and Dorothy Gabel's argument about the role of levels of representation in learning chemistry you might note some resonances between their arguments and that of Lavoisier.

[19] Bell, M. S. (2005). pp. 140–141.

[20] Savory, T. (1967). *The language of science*. London: Andre Deutsch. p. 32.

[21] Savory, T. (1967). p. 32.

[22] See Savory, T. (1967).

[23] Hooke, R. (1665/1961). *Micrographia*. New York: Dover Publications. p. 113.

[24] King, R. J., & Sullivan, F. M. (1991). *Senior biology*. Melbourne, Australia: Longman Cheshire. p. 8.

[25] Evans, B. K., Ladiges, P. Y., & McKenzie, J. A. (1995). *Biology two* (2nd ed.). Melbourne, Australia: Heinemann Educational Australia. p. 3.

[26] Hallam, R. (2000). *The living environment – Biology*. New York: Amsco School Publications.

[27] Kraus, D. (1999). *Concepts in modern biology (Revised)* (7th ed.) New York: Globe Publishers.

[28] Latour, B. (1993). Pasteur on lactic acid yeast: A partial semiotic analysis. *Configurations, 1*, 129–146.

[29] Prusiner, S. B. (1982). Novel proteinaceous infectious particles cause scrapie. *Science, 216*, 136–144.

[30] Grew, N. (1682). *The anatomy of plants*. London: W. Rawlings. Reprinted facsimile (1965) New York: Johnson Reprint Corporation.

[31] Carpenter, W. B. (1888). *Nature and man: Essays scientific and philosophical*. London: Kegan Paul, Trench and Company.

[32] Carpenter, W. (1888). p. 51.

[33] Savory, T. (1967).

[34] Savory, T. (1967). p. 125.

[35] Milne, C. (1998). Philosophically correct science stories? Examining the implications of heroic science stories for school science. *Journal of Research in Science Teaching, 35*, 175–187.

[36] Barab, S. A., Sadler, T. D., Heiselt, C., Hickey, D., & Zuiker, S. (2007). Relating narrative, inquiry, and inscriptions: Supporting consequential play. *Journal of Science Education and Technology, 16*, 59–82.

[37] Bruner, J. (1996). *The culture of education*. Cambridge, MA: Harvard University Press.

[38] Barab, S. A., Sadler, T. D., Heiselt, C., Hickey, D., & Zuiker, S. (2007).

[39] Milne, C. (2010). Captives of the text.

[40] Modified from Clark, H. (Ed.). (1992). *Science directions*. Book 1. Melbourne: Longman Cheshire. pp. 170–171.

[41] Board, P. (1994). The aristocrat who revolutionised chemistry. *New Scientist, 142*(1924), 33–35.

[42] Roller, D. (1957). The early development of the concepts of temperature and heat: The rise and decline of the caloric theory. In J. B. Conant (Ed.), *Harvard case histories in experimental science* (Vol. 1, pp. 117–214). Cambridge, MA: Harvard University Press.

[43] Roller, D. (1957).

[44] Rumford, B. C. (1798). An inquiry concerning the source of heat which is excited by friction. *Philosophical Transactions of the Royal Society of London, 88*, 80–120.

[45] Lerner, L. S., & Bennetta, W. J. (1988). The treatment of theory in textbooks. *The Science Teacher, 54*, 37–41.

[46] Lerner, L. & Benneta, W. J. (1988). p. 38.

FINAL COMMENTS

Over the course of this book I have tried to provide you with a sense of some of the major historical developments associated with Eurocentric science while addressing features of the nature of that science. Eurocentric science is the science most national education standards, including the National Science Education Standards in the US, and international testing programs, such as the Program for International Student Assessment (PISA) and Trends in International Mathematics and Science Study (TIMSS) call *science*. But as you might have noticed as you read through this book there are many forms of systematic knowledge that share some elements with Eurocentric science but which typically are not called science. Some historians of science argue that a defining characteristic of Eurocentric science is its use of structures, especially theories and models, to explain observed phenomena. But activities such as finding patterns in dice faces and deriving models within black boxes indicate that experience and measurement of phenomena already implies a facility with theoretical concepts or constructs. As you examined in Chapter 5, observations can never be theory-free. Even as 17th experimental philosophers were trying to adhere their interpretation of the philosophy of Francis Bacon they acknowledged the value of theorizing for making sense of phenomena. If theory remains a key element of science then it surprises me when I learn that courses in chemistry or biology or physics can be offered to high school students without any reference being made to scientific theories that are central to each of these sciences. I wonder how students can be expected to learn biology without reference to the scientific theory of evolution or chemistry without reference to kinetic molecular theory (particle model).

My goal with this book was to combine aspects of the philosophy and history; not just to focus on specific scientific ideas but to provide a hint of the complex relationship between place and history, space and time, in the development of Eurocentric science. It will not have escaped your attention that most of the people I used to illustrate developments in Eurocentric science were men. As I mentioned in Chapter 6 women were pretty much excluded from the practice of Eurocentric science, especially after the development of the universities and professional societies. Although women were allowed to be witnesses (they were sensible enough for that), very rarely, as the structures and symbol systems of Eurocentric science began to coalesce, were women involved as constructors of theory. In Chapter 7 you had the chance to think about how the language of science can exclude and admit and how the text of science can lead and mislead. How the language used in textbooks can present an image of science that is difficult to challenge unless you use history to look at sources of information about the history of concepts, models, and theories.

You will have also recognized the role of values in the public face of Eurocentric science. Historically, some of these values were proposed to emphasize the difference between the secretiveness of practices associated with 'old' forms of knowledge, such as alchemy, and the open laboratories of experimental philosophy where witnesses, both men and women (if you were Robert Boyle doing the experiments) were welcome. Other values that were presented as central to science and part of the public face of Eurocentric science included self-discipline, quantification, empiricism, and objectivity. Quantification required precision based on clarity of concepts; accuracy based on developing mathematical models that were a 'fit' with the phenomenon under study; impartiality, not allowing your emotions to influence your decisions; and communication in the form of text and symbols. Empiricism, valuing sensory perceptions and the conduct of experiments as the basis of evidence for scientific claims, is a belief system. It is a fundamental tenet of empiricism that all scientific theories, models, and hypotheses must be tested by experience in the form of observations from experiments. As we examined in Chapter 5, empiricism as a method for science, depends on trusting the observational claims of those presenting such claims. In the seventeenth century, experimental philosophers used witnesses and rich descriptions to convince readers that an experiment as described had been performed and the observations collected had been generated by that experiment. Empiricism also made curiosity acceptable. Facts, which are so important to science education, became the basis of Baconian science but without theory you have to ask what value is a fact. However, a focus on facts continues to be the major emphasis of many assessment programs, like the New York State Regents Exams, for various science subjects.

Some might argue that Eurocentric science has broken away from its local roots and become a global enterprise but what does that look like in practice? Hopefully this idiosyncratic examination of the history of science has helped you to understand that there is not one Eurocentric science even though I used that term throughout the book to help us to think about the origins of the science that is typically taught in schools. Strategies that are considered acceptable for exploring the natural world and the structure of acceptable outcomes are as variable as the disciplines that exist under the banner of Eurocentric science: field ecology, radio astronomy, particle physics, materials science, physical organic chemistry, molecular biology, volcanology, paleontology, metallurgy, to name just a very few.

As Joan Fujimura has shown in her study of genomics in Japan and the United States[1] there are differences in how science is enacted in Japan and the US. She describes how the Japanese genome project of the 1990s provided an opportunity for both scientific and cultural advancement. She describes how Professor "Suhara" (a pseudonym she uses), a famous Japanese molecular biologist, was instrumental in the development of the Japanese Human Genome project. He believed one area of scientific endeavor where Japan could compete with United States and European science programs was in genomic informatics, so this could be a source of national competition and glory. He also saw the need for strong lines of communication between international networks of laboratories. He believed that computer informatics would be central to genome analysis and that wet laboratories would decline as computers became more and more important.

However, the scientist also believed that promoting informatics for understanding the human genome would also lead humans to reevaluate human's place in nature. He commented that because of Japanese scientists' association with Buddhism or Shintoism, they were more able to accept human's place in nature than US/European scientists with their Judeo-Christian beliefs of sovereignty over nature since God was said to have placed humans over all living things. The human genome project had the potential to force humans to understand how closely associated they were with other living things and therefore the responsibility they have for maintaining the Earth for all living things. He was able to use this cultural argument to gain Japanese support for funding of the genome project. His argument was that science could be used to support Japanese cultural values. What do you think?

Genomic science is at the same time, national and transnational, and I believe for other areas of scientific endeavor this is the case also. Many countries see maintaining or developing science centers in areas such as stem cell research or fundamental particle research or nanotechnology research as helping to maintain a national identity even as they develop transnational collaborations.

Hopefully, this book has encouraged you to think more deeply about the know-ledges that you and the youth you teach bring to a science classroom. Hoepfully this book has also challeneged you to find space to support both connected and separate knowing in the classes you teach and courses you develop, and to ask some challenging questions about the science that you are called upon to teach. Finally, look back over the responses you made to the questions I asked you to reflect on at the beginning of Chapter 1. Would you now respond differently to some of those questions? I hope so!

NOTES

[1] Fujimura, J. H. (2000). Transnational genomics. In R. Reid & S. Traweek (Eds.), *Doing science + culture* (pp. 71–92). New York: Routledge.

Printed in the United States
By Bookmasters